TEACHING ESL K–12:
VIEWS FROM THE CLASSROOM

Helene Becker
Norwalk, Connecticut Public Schools

WITH COMMENTARY FROM
Else Hamayan
Illinois Resource Center

A TeacherSource Book

Donald Freeman
Series Editor

HEINLE & HEINLE

THOMSON LEARNING

Australia • Canada • Mexico • Singapore • Spain • United Kingdom • United States

HEINLE & HEINLE

™

THOMSON LEARNING

Teaching ESL K–12: Views from the Classroom
Helene Becker with commentary from Else Hamayan

Vice President, Editorial Director ESL: Nancy Leonhardt
Acquisitions Editor: Sherrise Roehr
Associate Developmental Editor: Sarah Barnicle
Marketing Manager: Charlotte Sturdy
Production Editor: Jeffrey M. Freeland

Sr. Manufacturing Coordinator: Mary Beth Hennebury
Compositor: Ethos Marketing and Design
Cover Designer: Ha Nguyen
Printer: Webcom

Printed in Canada
5 6 7 8   08 07

For more information contact Heinle & Heinle, 25 Thomson Place, Boston, Massachusetts 02210 USA, or you can visit our Internet site at http://www.heinle.com

Text Credit:
The excerpt on p.35 from *The Sign of the Beaver* was reprinted with permission from Dell Publishing.

For permission to use material from this text or product contact us:
Tel   1-800-730-2214
Fax   1-800-730-2215
Web   www.thomsonrights.com

Library of Congress Cataloging-in-Publication Data

Becker, Helene—
   Teaching ESL K–12: views from the classroom/ Helene Becker; with commentary from Else Hamayan.
      p. cm.—(A teachersource book)
   Includes bibliographical references.
   ISBN-13: 978-0-8384-7901-8
   ISBN-10: 0-8384-7901-4
   1. English language—Study and teaching— Foreign speakers. 2. English language—Study and teaching (Primary)—Foreign speakers. 3. English language—Study and teaching (Secondary)— Foreign speakers. 4. English language—Study and teaching (Elementary)—Foreign speakers. I. Hamayan, Else V. II. Title. III. TeacherSource

PE1128. A2 B33 2001
428'.0071—dc21

                                          2001024560

ASIA (excluding India)
Thomson Learning
60 Albert Street #15-01
Albert Complex
Singapore 189969

AUSTRALIA/NEW ZEALAND
Nelson/Thomson Learning
102 Dodds Street
South Melbourne
Victoria 3205 Australia

CANADA
Nelson/Thomson Learning
1120 Birchmount Road
Scarborough, Ontario
Canada M1K 5G4

LATIN AMERICA
Thomson Learning
Seneca, 53
Colonia Polanco
11560 México D.F. México

SPAIN
Thomson Learning
Calle Magallanes, 25
28015-Madrid
España

UK/EUROPE/MIDDLE EAST
Thomson Learning
Berkshire House
168–173 High Holborn
London, WC1V 7AA, United Kingdom

To my husband,
Jonathan Shankman.

HELENE BECKER

To my ESL teachers, who taught me
that I would eventually get there,
and to Vladimir who kept Ludmila happy
while I worked on this book.

ELSE HAMAYAN

Thank You

The series editor, authors, and publisher would like to thank the following individuals who offered many helpful insights throughout the development of the **TeacherSource** series.

David Barker — Maine Township High School, Illinois
Linda Lonon Blanton — University of New Orleans
Tommie Brasel — New Mexico School for the Deaf
Jill Burton — University of South Australia
Margaret B. Cassidy — Brattleboro Union High School, Vermont
Louise Damen — Independent Consultant
Florence Decker — University of Texas at El Paso
Silvia G. Diaz — Dade County Public Schools, Florida
Margo Downey — Boston University
Alvino Fantini — School for International Training
Sandra Fradd — University of Miami
Jerry Gebhard — Indiana University of Pennsylvania
Fred Genesee — McGill University
Stacy Gildenston — Colorado State University
Jeannette Gordon — Illinois Resource Center
Else Hamayan — Illinois Resource Center
Sarah Hudelson — Arizona State University
Joan Jamieson — Northern Arizona University
Elliot L. Judd — University of Illinois at Chicago
Donald N. Larson — Bethel College, Minnesota (Emeritus)
Patsy Lightbaum — Concordia University, Canada
Numa Markee — University of Illinois at Urbana Champaign
Michael McCarthy — University of Nottingham
Denise E. Murray — NCELTR Macquarie University
Gayle Nelson — Georgia State University
Meredith Pike-Baky — University of California at Berkeley
Sara L. Sanders — Coastal Carolina University
Lilia Savova — Indiana University of Pennsylvania
Donna Sievers — Garden Grove Unified School District, California
Ruth Spack — Tufts University
Leo van Lier — Monterey Institute of International Studies

TABLE OF CONTENTS

ACKNOWLEDGMENTS

What I thought would be a relatively straightforward four-month project back in the fall of 1996 turned into an extensive four-year journey, complete with detours, stalls, restarts, and thankfully, a conclusion. I was able to persevere only because of the support and contributions of numerous colleagues, friends, and family members for whom I have deep gratitude. I would especially like to thank the following people:

My former ESL colleagues in the West Hartford (Connecticut) Public Schools with whom I taught for 14 years, for contributing ideas, videotapes of lessons, and allowing me to observe their classes;

My former colleagues in the Hawaii Public Schools (especially at Kanoelani Elementary School, Waipahu) for welcoming me with "aloha" and teaching me about elementary school children;

My former colleagues in the Sewanhaka Central High School District (Floral Park, New York) for continuing to educate me about secondary students;

My current colleagues in the Norwalk (Connecticut) Public Schools for their support and encouragement;

The many ESL teachers and administrators across the United States who contributed their "voices." Their contributions would not all fit into this book, but I am grateful to everyone who took the time to offer their perspectives on various topics regarding K–12 ESL teaching;

The supportive and insightful staff at Heinle & Heinle and at Ethos Marketing and Design, as well as the anonymous reviewers for their much appreciated suggestions;

Donald Freeman, the series editor, for inviting me to join the project and offering invaluable insights, faith, and support;

Else Hamayan, my co-author, for elevating the project to a new level;

Melissa Reeve, my research assistant in Hawaii, for her hard work;

My parents, family, and friends for putting up with me during "crunch" times;

My husband, Jonathan, for his patience, love, support, and ability to solve any and all computer problems;

My many, many students for teaching me most of what I know about ESL education.

—Helene Becker

SERIES EDITOR'S PREFACE

As I was driving just south of White River Junction, the snow had started falling in earnest. The light was flat, although it was midmorning, making it almost impossible to distinguish the highway in the gray-white swirling snow. I turned on the radio, partly as a distraction and partly to help me concentrate on the road ahead; the announcer was talking about the snow. "The state highway department advises motorists to use extreme caution and to drive with their headlights on to ensure maximum visibility." He went on, his tone shifting slightly, "Ray Burke, the state highway supervisor, just called to say that one of the plows almost hit a car just south of Exit 6 because the person driving hadn't turned on his lights. He really wants people to put their headlights on because it is very tough to see in this stuff." I checked, almost reflexively, to be sure that my headlights were on, as I drove into the churning snow.

How can information serve those who hear or read it in making sense of their own worlds? How can it enable them to reason about what they do and to take appropriate actions based on that reasoning? My experience with the radio in the snowstorm illustrates two different ways of providing the same message: the need to use your headlights when you drive in heavy snow. The first offers dispassionate information; the second tells the same content in a personal, compelling story. The first disguises its point of view; the second explicitly grounds the general information in a particular time and place. Each means of giving information has its role, but I believe the second is ultimately more useful in helping people make sense of what they are doing. When I heard Ray Burke's story about the plow, I made sure my headlights were on.

In what is written about teaching, it is rare to find accounts in which the author's experience and point of view are central. A point of view is not simply an opinion; neither is it a whimsical or impressionistic claim. Rather, a point of view lays out what the author thinks and why; to borrow the phrase from writing teacher Natalie Goldberg, "it sets down the bones." The problem is that much of what is available in professional development in language-teacher education concentrates on telling rather than on point of view. The telling is prescriptive, like the radio announcer's first statement. It emphasizes what is important to know and do, what is current in theory and research, and therefore what you—as a practicing teacher—should do. But this telling disguises the teller; it hides the point of view that can enable you to make sense of what is told.

The **TeacherSource** series offers you a point of view on second/foreign language teaching. Each author in this series has had to lay out what she or he believes is central to the topic, and how she or he has come to this understanding. So as a reader, you will find this book has a personality; it is not anonymous. It comes as a story, not as a directive, and it is meant to create a relationship with you rather than assume your attention. As a practitioner, its point of view can help you in your own work by providing a sounding board for your ideas and a metric for your own thinking. It can suggest courses of action and explain why these make sense to the author. You in turn can take from it what you will, and do with it what you can. This book will not tell you what to think; it is meant to help you make sense of what you do.

The point of view in **TeacherSource** is built out of three strands: **Teachers' Voices**, **Frameworks**, and **Investigations**. Each author draws together these strands uniquely, as suits his or her topic and—more crucially—his or her point of view. All materials in **TeacherSource** have these three strands. The **Teachers' Voices** are practicing language teachers from various settings who tell about their experience of the topic. The **Frameworks** lay out what the author believes is important to know about his or her topic and its key concepts and issues. These fundamentals define the area of language teaching and learning about which she or he is writing. The **Investigations** are meant to engage you, the reader, in relating the topic to your own teaching, students, and classroom. They are activities which you can do alone or with colleagues, to reflect on teaching and learning and/or try out ideas in practice.

Each strand offers a point of view on the book's topic. The **Teachers' Voices** relate the points of view of various practitioners; the **Frameworks** establish the point of view of the professional community; and the **Investigations** invite you to develop your own point of view, through experience with reference to your setting. Together these strands should serve in making sense of the topic.

Teaching ESL K–12 addresses the central question in English-medium education: How to prepare English language learners so that they can enter successfully into the structures and demands of new classrooms, curricula, and schools. While other books may speak to the topic, this book is unique in weaving together the voices, insights, and expertise of two thoughtful teachers—one a practitioner and the other an observer and supporter of this complex undertaking. Helene Becker brings her varied classroom and school-based experience to provide the foundation and substance of the discussion, while Else Hamayan offers a rich commentary that links the day-to day work of classroom teaching to larger frames of research and policy. In this interplay of voice and expertise, we hear practice and theory talking to each other. There are finely grained discussions about classroom strategy and technique alongside more general conversations about larger curricular and pedagogical issues, all of which are conducted through this dialogue between practitioner and commentator. In a very real way, *Teaching ESL K–12* shows the kind of meaningful professional conversation that teachers deserve to have as they relate what has been called their "wisdom of practice" to the social discourse of research and policy-making. Thus this book embodies in an essential way the original impetus of the **TeacherSource** series that teachers' voices and their experiences can serve as useful and compelling vehicles for understanding teaching with the aim of doing a better and perhaps more fulfilling job of it.

—*Donald Freeman, Series Editor*

1

THE CONTEXT OF THIS BOOK

This is how it all began for me, Helene Becker.

I started my language teaching career in 1974, as a Spanish teacher in a parochial school in the Bronx, New York. Spanish was the only foreign language offered in this small middle school/high school, so there were just two of us in the "language department." Our responsibilities included, well, teaching Spanish. That was pretty much it. We did not overly concern ourselves with how the students were doing in their other subjects, such as social studies or science; we just concentrated on teaching Spanish. Three years later, I was still teaching Spanish (in a different secondary school) when I was also given the opportunity to teach English to a small group of newly arrived foreign students. I loved the experience so much that I decided to return to school to earn a master's degree in teaching English as a second language (ESL).

When I entered the field of ESL, I thought that I was simply switching subject matter—from Spanish to ESL. However, I came to realize early on in my career that teaching ESL in an elementary or secondary school setting involved much more than teaching the subject matter—that is, the English language. It soon became clear that, besides concerning myself with the issues of my actual teaching (such as teaching techniques, classroom management strategies, and English grammar rules), I needed to understand and make decisions about many other issues that surround and permeate ESL classroom instruction. This book is an attempt to express my beliefs about the many issues and decisions that ESL teachers face daily in the real world of ESL teaching in elementary and secondary schools.

Why must ESL teachers deal with so many issues in addition to classroom instruction? This is best explained by considering that "The major objective of ESL programs at the elementary and secondary levels in the United States is *to prepare students to function successfully in classrooms where English is the medium of instruction for all subject areas*" (Chamot and O'Malley, 1987, p. 227; italics added). Therefore, besides teaching English, ESL teachers need to have an understanding of how to prepare ESL students for success in the subject areas they encounter in school, and for functioning in a culture that may be quite different from their own. ESL teachers cannot simply close the classroom doors and teach English in isolation. Decisions about issues such as curriculum (that is, what to teach) must be geared toward helping students develop the necessary tools to learn their school subjects, and adjust to American society; consequently, these decisions are infinitely more complex for teachers of ESL than for teachers of other subject areas.

My own teaching experiences have been instrumental in shaping my beliefs about the myriad of issues involved in teaching ESL; most of these experiences took place in the public schools of Connecticut, Hawaii, and New York. But within my own beliefs are embedded the collective experiences and beliefs of the many ESL colleagues with whom I have interacted over the years. For four years as an ESL Program Coordinator, I had the opportunity to design and revise ESL programs, work on committees, train teachers, work with parents, observe classes, and learn from ESL, grade-level, and content-area teachers who teach kindergarten through twelfth grade. I also networked with other ESL administrators to learn about their K–12 programs. By being active in professional organizations, I have had the opportunity to talk to and learn from ESL and EFL teachers from many countries. This interaction has had a tremendous influence on my own teaching. I decided to interview teachers from different parts of the United States in order to present a somewhat wider perspective of K–12 teaching. Their remarks are included in the Teachers' Voices sections in this book. When my own remarks describe my personal teaching experiences, they are also included in the Teachers' Voices sections. (While the Teachers' Voices sections describe actual classroom experiences, all student names have, of course, been changed.)

You may disagree with some of the practices described in this book. I disagree with some of them, as well! However, as an ESL teacher working in a public school setting, one does not always have the authority to dictate policies. Large school districts, especially, have several levels of administrators, each making decisions regarding such issues as curriculum, budget, scheduling, and student assessment, all of which affect teachers. Even in my role as a program coordinator, I had no control over for example, the budget allotted to each school to pay for materials and ESL teachers' salaries.

You may also find that the situations described here do not resemble the teaching situation in which you find yourself. You may say, "These students do not sound like my students." When I started working on this book, I quickly came to realize that I could not possibly write a book that applied to all elementary and secondary ESL programs or even to most of them—they are all so different from one another. What is feasible and works well in West Hartford, Connecticut—where there are approximately 400 ESL students from 25 different language groups spread out among a total of 15 elementary, middle, and high schools—may not work well in Los Angeles, California, where there are approximately 300,000 ESL students in about 900 schools, the majority of whom speak Spanish (Los Angeles Unified School District, 1998). Therefore, this book is not an attempt to dictate policies for specific school districts, but rather an effort to share experiences that I and others have had, and to express the beliefs that have emerged as a result of these experiences.

In reading this book I hope that novice teachers will be able to consider the ESL teaching theories they have studied in school in terms of the day-to-day realities and issues of teaching ESL in K–12 environments. It is my hope that an ESL teacher starting a first job in a K–12 setting will be able to realistically address the daily challenges, being familiar with some of the decisions and dilemmas that he or she will inevitably encounter.

I hope that experienced teachers will be able to make comparisons with their own teaching experiences and extract helpful insights and suggestions. In addition, I hope that experienced teachers will be able to use the many personal accounts presented here to make sense of their own teaching, as I have been able to do from talking and listening to colleagues over the years. All readers will be able to do further inquiry and exploration by doing the suggested Investigations.

When my non-teacher friends and relatives talk about their jobs, some of them express regret about not having careers that are highly meaningful and important. Teachers of English as a second language to elementary- or secondary-school children will never have this regret. I hope that this book will contribute to the efforts of ESL teachers as they strive to do the best possible job to help their students attain the necessary tools they need to lead productive and successful lives.

Now you will hear from Else Hamayan who will explain who she is and how she became involved in writing this book. As you will see, because of the collaboration between Else and me, this book differs significantly from other professional texts in that it is written from two very different perspectives on the field of teaching ESL.

 I STARTED MY CAREER IN ESL EDUCATION as a teacher of English as a foreign language (EFL) in Lebanon, as I was learning English myself! Later, I became interested in questions regarding second-language acquisition and teaching, and conducted some research studies in that area. The bulk of my work, however, has been to act as a resource to teachers, in a sense, as a translator of research and theory into practice. I was fortunate to be asked to provide commentary in this book, and the way that I'd like to think of my commentary is as the musical score that accompanies Helene's rich text.

This commentary has two goals. The first goal is to consider the theoretical basis for the pedagogical decisions and the teaching strategies that Helene describes. The second goal is to provide the larger social and political context in which ESL teaching takes place. So, in a sense, I will take a step back from the classroom and attempt to describe the larger picture.

In the last few years, I have been away from the classroom and have had the opportunity to work with teachers and researchers who have taught me to ask questions such as the following:

- How do students become proficient in a second language to the extent that they are able to learn new concepts through that language?

- How can teachers help students achieve in an academic setting when they are not completely fluent in the language of instruction?

- What is the best setup for schools so that linguistically and culturally diverse students attain proficiency in English, learn the academic content required in the mainstream curriculum, and continue to develop in their own language?

Questions such as these should guide the ways in which we teach students who are learning English as a second language. The insights that can be gained from asking these large-scale questions—and, consequently, seeing the big picture—are essential in the making of a good teacher. Unfortunately, however, many teachers do not have the luxury of stepping back from the classroom to observe what a colleague is doing or to get a clear sense of the whole long-term learning environment of their students. In many schools, important pedagogical decisions have been taken away from teachers. Helene bemoans the fact that, as a program coordinator, she had no control over the amount of money allotted to the ESL program. Many teachers do not have much say in other equally important issues that affect the day-to-day operation of a classroom, such as what materials to use, or even the use of specific teaching strategies. These decisions, as well as the lack of power to make them, have a strong impact on how effective a teacher is. At a later point in the book, we will discuss the advocacy role that ESL teachers play and the power they hold within the larger school environment.

Regardless of the status or position of an ESL teacher within the school, the larger pedagogical, social, and political issues regarding second-language learning and teaching must frame what we do as ESL teachers. It is important for ESL teachers to take these issues into account as they make everyday decisions in their classrooms. We hope that a dialogue similar to the one that Helene and I have throughout this book, between what goes on in the daily life of a classroom and the issues reigning in the larger field of teaching English as a second language, will also take place for you and your colleagues.

2

ESL Curriculum

ESL students enter elementary and secondary schools every day at all ages and grade levels. They have a daunting task ahead of them: They must learn English, and at the same time, they must learn their school subjects such as science, math, literature and social studies. Since learning a language is a process that takes a considerable amount of time, it will be argued in this chapter that ESL students cannot post-pone learning their academic subjects until they have developed the same level of academic language skills as their native English-speaking peers (Cummins, 1994). The ESL teacher in an elementary or sec-ondary school faces the challenge of determining how to help students accomplish most expediently the dual task of learning a language and learning their school subjects. A central aspect of this challenge is choosing exactly what to teach students—that is, the curriculum.

This chapter deals with designing ESL curricula that help students not only learn English, but also acquire the skills and knowledge necessary for success in their content-area subjects. The first section addresses the limitations of ESL curricula traditionally used in many elementary and secondary ESL programs. The second section presents an argument for using a **content-based curriculum** and illustrates ways that ESL teachers have implemented this type of curriculum.

WHAT ARE THE LIMITATIONS OF TRADITIONAL ESL CURRICULA?

It would seem that a practical way to design a curriculum for teaching English as a second language would be to make a list of grammar and vocabulary top-ics that are essential for communication and put them in a logical sequence. The teacher could design lessons around each topic, thus exposing students step by step to the structure and vocabulary of English. In fact, most approaches to lan-guage teaching do employ—implicitly or explicitly—a curriculum based on grammar points (Celce-Murcia, 1991). A few other approaches have de-emphasized the teaching of grammar and have instead used curricula based on communication. For example, one type of communicative curriculum revolves around "functions," which are social interactions such as agreeing, disagreeing, and asking for information. These curricula do usually include grammar topics, but only in conjunction with the function being taught.

ESL teachers report that using grammar-based, function-based, or any other kind of curriculum that emphasizes communication can help students become quite proficient in day-to-day oral skills (Chamot and O'Malley, 1987). This became apparent to me early on in my ESL teaching career as I taught groups

On designing
ESL curriculum,
see Graves,
*Designing
Language
Courses:
A Guide for
Teachers,*
Chapter 4
(2000).

of elementary and secondary students who seemed to develop fairly good oral skills within a year or two. However, as I became more familiar with the academic demands of the grade-level and content-area* classrooms, which seemed to go far beyond the communication skills I was teaching my students during ESL class, I began to question the appropriateness of using curricula that put such heavy emphasis on day-to-day communication. Here is my story.

Helene Becker

In 1982 I began teaching ESL in the West Hartford Public Schools, a suburban public school district in central Connecticut. The position available was a split assignment—half-time in an elementary school and half-time in a high school. In each school curriculum guides and textbooks were available, both structured around grammar points. I was comfortable using these materials because my teaching up to this point had always revolved around grammar and vocabulary. I knew that with the younger children, however, the teaching of grammar would be implicit rather than explicit, since they were too young to understand grammatical concepts. For example, at the high school level, in addition to having students do oral and written practice of the present tense, we could discuss rules about using *don't* and *doesn't* in negative sentences. With first-graders at the elementary school we would simply do the practice part and skip the discussion of the rules.

From the start I was satisfied with my beginning-level classes at both the elementary and high school levels; since these students knew very little English, anything they learned in my class seemed to be beneficial to them. I planned lots of speaking and listening activities, as well as reading activities revolving around short, vocabulary-controlled passages from the textbook. Their writing consisted mainly of copying from the board or doing grammar or vocabulary exercises.

I planned the same kinds of activities for the intermediate and advanced students, but with materials incorporating more difficult vocabulary and verb tenses. At first, I was satisfied with the job I was doing with students at these proficiency levels, as well.

As the months went on and I got to know the students better, I learned more and more about the kinds of academic demands they were facing in their grade-level/content-area classes. In the elementary school, when I entered a grade-level classroom to pick up my students, I would overhear the social studies, science, or reading lesson that was taking place. I began to wonder how much the activities in ESL class were helping my students succeed during these academic lessons in their grade-level classrooms. In other words, if they were reading a story in their ESL textbook with me, to what extent would the acquired language and skills be helpful to them when they were reading a grade-level social studies text?

In the high school, when I looked at some of my students' notebooks from their other classes, I realized that there was a large gap

---

*Grade-level and content-area classrooms refer to what are typically known as mainstream classrooms in an elementary and secondary school, respectively. These terms are preferable to "mainstream," which has connotations from special education and is inappropriate in school districts where the majority of the student population is from language minority backgrounds (O'Malley and Valdez Pierce, 1996).

between the kinds of activities they were doing in my ESL class and the kinds of activities they were attempting to do in their content-area classes. I knew that my students at both the elementary school and high school were developing good communication skills, but I was slowly realizing that communication skills were not enough.

Now let's look at Else's perspective on the issue of ESL curriculum.

 TWO ISSUES COME TO MIND when Helene talks about the inter-face between the grade-level/content-area classroom curriculum and the ESL curriculum. The first issue relates to the need for a separate ESL curriculum; the second has to do with the need to integrate the instruction of academic content and the instruction of ESL. Let's consider first the issue of why a separate ESL curriculum is necessary.

Although some people may argue that ESL students can become proficient in English simply by being immersed in it, we know that for most students coming with a linguistic background other than English, the only way to proficiency is through extensive instruction in ESL (Wong-Fillmore, 1991). The ESL student who picks up English naturally and without the help of specialized formal instruction is the rare exception (Thomas and Collier, 1995; Collier, 1995). We also know that the needs of ESL students are different from those of their native English-speaking peers because they enter school without even the basic vocabulary that their peers already possess. These needs simply stem from the fact that ESL students have not acquired the proficiency in the language of the classroom that their native English-speaking peers have by the time they enter school. These language needs are hardly ever adequately met in grade-level/content-area curricula or materials, making it essential that these students receive specialized instruction that allows them to gain shortcuts to second language proficiency (TESOL, 1997). However, rather than having a separate curriculum for ESL, we might think about having an ESL curriculum that is closely aligned with and connected to the grade-level/content-area classroom curriculum.

This brings us to the second issue, that of integrating the instruction of academic content and ESL. Research has shown that providing ESL students with second-language instruction that is connected to academic content areas is essential for those students to succeed in school. The research conducted by Thomas and Collier (1995; Collier, 1995) shows that, on standardized academic achievement tests administered in English, students receiving content-based ESL instruction perform better than their peers who receive more traditional language-focused ESL instruction. Other studies have shown that ESL students lack content-specific language that is essential for them to succeed in the grade-level/content-area classroom (Snow, Met, and Genesee, 1989; Short, 1991). Throughout this book, Helene will describe how she manages to teach her students the academic content dictated by the curriculum through ESL strategies by preparing the students linguistically for the concepts introduced in the academic subject area lessons. Without this preparation, it may be very difficult for students to learn abstract concepts in the various subject areas.

On content and language instruction in bilingual programs, see Cloud, Genesee, and Hamayan, *Dual Language Instruction*, Chapter 6 (2000).

This integration between content and language instruction must also be considered when students are in a bilingual program and are receiving instruction in at least some of the content areas through the native language. The task of the ESL teacher in that situation is not so much making sure that students know the content-area concepts but rather ensuring that they develop the language for concepts that they are learning through their primary language. In either case, whether the students are schooled entirely in English or bilingually, the ESL teacher must coordinate very closely with the teacher who is primarily responsible for content-area instruction.

Teachers' Voices

Helene Becker

HOW CAN ESL TEACHERS MEET THE BASIC LANGUAGE AND SOCIOCULTURAL NEEDS OF BEGINNING-LEVEL ESL STUDENTS?

Early on in my career I felt confident that the curriculum I was using with my beginning-level students was helping them acquire basic communication skills. I planned activities involving vocabulary and grammar associated with school, the neighborhood, sports, food, animals, colors, family members, and other topics relevant to their lives. I incorporated cultural information whenever possible so that students were learning about American culture in the context of these vocabulary topics. For example, when we discussed "places in the neighborhood," we looked at characteristics of American neighborhoods in general, and how they differed from neighborhoods in the students' respective countries. I also included survival questions such as "May I go to the bathroom?" and "Could you please repeat that?" making sure that students learned the polite way to make requests. Beginning ESL students can easily sound pushy and impolite simply because they have been taught to say the simpler "Open the window!" rather than the slightly more complex but socially correct "Could you please open the window?" It is important to help beginners learn socially appropriate language.

Investigations

2.1 SURVIVAL ENGLISH

Think about the survival vocabulary that beginning-level ESL students might need to learn when they first arrive. It may be helpful to consider the kinds of situations in which students need to communicate, such as the classroom, the cafeteria, on the bus, at a store, and so forth. Choose either elementary or secondary—or both—and, with a partner or by yourself, make a list of survival vocabulary expressions, and questions to teach beginning-level students. After you have generated your list, if possible, share it with another group, discuss your items, and modify your list if necessary. When you have finished, look at the table of contents of some beginning-level ESL textbooks to see if you want to modify your list further. (Try looking at some of the following texts: Amazing English *[Walker, 1996] and* Hello English *[Zaffran, Krulik, and Scheraga, 1990] for elementary school;* Go For It *[Nunan, 1999] and* Making Connections *[Kessler, Lee, McCloskey, Quinn, and Stack, 1996] for secondary school.)*

Else's Perspective THE INVESTIGATION SUGGESTED ABOVE is sure to help teachers figure out what students need and can be expected to learn, especially at the beginning levels. In addition to this challenge, however, ESL teachers must ensure that they are not only setting sensible expectations for their students, but that they are basing their instruction on standards set for students in general. Standards-based instruction has become an essential part of teachers' repertoires, and it is essential that ESL teachers know how to get their students on the path that leads to content-area attainment. To help teachers determine what language skills ESL students need to survive in an academic setting and how these basic skills can relate to academic standards set for other students, the professional organization Teachers of English to Speakers of Other Languages (TESOL, 1997) developed ESL standards for Pre-K–12 students. These standards list expectations for three major goals of language: the use of language (1) for everyday social interactions, (2) for academic purposes, and (3) in culturally appropriate ways. The goals and standards developed by TESOL are listed below:

GOAL 1: TO USE THE SECOND LANGUAGE TO COMMUNICATE IN SOCIAL SETTINGS

Standard 1 Students will use the second language to participate in social interactions.

Standard 2 Students will interact in, through, and with spoken and written forms of the second language for personal expression and enjoyment.

Standard 3 Students will use learning strategies to extend their communicative competence.

Sample indicators for early second-language development: to give and ask for permission, offer and respond to greetings, introductions, and farewells, and to ask information questions for personal reasons.

GOAL 2: TO USE THE SECOND LANGUAGE TO ACHIEVE ACADEMICALLY IN ALL CONTENT AREAS

Standard 1 Students will use the second language to interact in the classroom.

Standard 2 Students will use the second language to obtain, process, construct, and provide subject matter information in spoken and written form.

Standard 3 Students will use appropriate learning strategies to construct and apply academic knowledge.

Sample indicators for early second-language development: to ask for assistance with a classroom task, compare and contrast information, and define, compare, and classify objects according to their physical characteristics.

GOAL 3: TO USE THE SECOND LANGUAGE IN SOCIALLY AND CULTURALLY APPROPRIATE WAYS

Standard 1 Students will use the appropriate language variety, register, and genre according to audience, purpose, and setting.

Standard 2 Students will use nonverbal communication appropriate to audience, purpose, and setting.

Standard 3 Students will use appropriate learning strategies to extend their communicative competence.

Sample indicators for early second-language development: to make requests politely, demonstrate an understanding of ways to give and receive compliments, show gratitude, apologize, express anger or impatience, and use acceptable tone and intonation in various settings.

As you can see, these standards cover the entire range of language skills that ESL students need in order to function well in an academic setting where the language of instruction is English. As Helene discusses in the following section, Goal 2 of the ESL standards is crucial for students to develop the cognitively demanding language necessary for learning abstract concepts in science, math, and social studies. These are the aspects of language that are essential for ESL students to survive and thrive in a standards-based instructional context.

HOW CAN ESL TEACHERS PREPARE INTERMEDIATE- AND ADVANCED-LEVEL ESL STUDENTS FOR CONTENT CLASSES?

Helene Becker

I realize now that although the curriculum I was using early in my career was (and still is) useful for beginning-level students, since it helped them develop oral language and rudimentary reading and writing skills, it did not offer students with higher levels of language proficiency the opportunity to go beyond those skills in order to develop the tools needed for success in the grade-level/content-area classroom. For example, a typical social studies assignment in a fifth-grade classroom might include having students read about the different regions of the United States and make a chart comparing the weather, topography, crops, and so forth. This lesson would require students to comprehend vocabulary specific to social studies and to analyze information in order to make comparisons. A typical fifth-grade literature lesson might require students to react in writing to a chapter in a novel. This type of assignment demands that students first understand the literature, and then organize their thoughts into a cohesive paragraph. The vocabulary and grammar I was presenting and the activities I was facilitating in my ESL classes did not relate enough to the kinds of cognitively demanding tasks my ESL students needed to do in the grade-level/content-area classroom. A curriculum based on these typical academic skills, as well as the concepts and vocabulary associated with the content areas, is called a **content-based curriculum**.

CURRICULUM WITH ACADEMIC FOCUS

Research conducted by Cummins (1981a) suggests that students acquiring English as a second language in schools usually take about two years (with considerable individual variation) to develop good enough oral skills to communicate effectively with teachers and peers. ESL teachers generally report that the research holds true; that is, ESL students learn oral skills rather quickly (Brinton, Sasser, and Winningham, 1988). Cummins (1979) used the term **BICS—Basic Interpersonal Communication Skills**—to describe these oral communication skills. The more advanced academic skills that students need for success in the content areas he named **CALP—Cognitive Academic Language Proficiency**. Cummins's research suggests that the development of CALP typically lags behind the development of social communicative language (BICS), and can take from five to seven (or more) years to develop to a level comparable to that of ESL students' native English-speaking peers. Since these important academic skills take much longer for students to acquire, it makes sense to start teaching these skills as soon as possible.

BICS and CALP

Students tend to be successful at developing BICS with a traditional ESL curriculum because that is precisely what the curriculum teaches—communication skills. Communication skills are essential to address, especially in a beginning-level class, but they comprise only a part of the skills needed for success in school. ESL teachers may need to increase the emphasis put on CALP by conducting lessons with more academic focus, since the academic skills acquired may help students succeed in the content areas.

Else adds some helpful insights about BICS and CALP and discusses important implications in the ESL classroom.

> *Else's Perspective*
>
> THE DISTINCTION THAT HELENE TALKS ABOUT between cognitively complex language and everyday social language initially conceived and presented as such by Cummins (1979), is a simple way of conceptualizing the complex array of language skills that constitute proficiency. The dichotomy, as Helene presents it, is easy to understand, and is easy to explain, especially to those who are not aware of the complexity of language proficiency. However, it is important for ESL teachers to understand the complexity of language proficiency in order to develop it in their students, to be able to assess it, and to evaluate whether students are ready to learn abstract concepts through that language.
>
> As Helene explains below, language tasks lie along two continua; one continuum is characterized by how clear the context of language is, and the second continuum relates to the abstractness of the concepts represented by language. Figure 2.1 on p. 14 shows the two continua. Everyday social interactions are most likely to fall in Quadrant I. Discourse in academic subject areas tends to fall in Quadrant IV. However, some social interactions are extremely sophisticated and require higher-order thinking and linguistic skills. The teasing banter among adolescents can revolve around some rather abstract social relationships and can have only vague shared social norms as their context. In contrast, an explanation of an abstract concept in science or math can be made clear by showing concrete examples. A good ESL teacher takes a classroom activity that lies somewhere in Quadrant IV and presents it in such a way as to make it concrete and clear. That is, ESL

teachers who are integrating the instruction of content into the development of secondlanguage skills must attempt to push the language task toward Quadrant III. Ways to do this are discussed later in the chapter.

Thus, it is important for ESL teachers to be aware of the dimensions of language proficiency, especially if they are teaching academic subject-area concepts at the same time that they are developing the language that represents those concepts.

Thomas and Collier (1995) have found in their studies that a curriculum with an academic focus can help improve ESL students' performance in school. "Students achieve significantly better in programs that teach language through cognitively complex academic content in math, science, social studies, and literature…"(p. 2). This makes perfect sense; using academic content to teach English to ESL students exposes them to skills, concepts, and specialized vocabulary that they need in order to be successful in school. As Genesee (1994) states, "It is now widely believed that language varies even across academic domains so that different language skills are needed in a mathematics classroom in comparison to a science or history classroom. The differences include not only specialized vocabulary but also special forms of expression related to specific academic domains, such as describing technical procedures or articulating hypotheses in science. This means that knowing how to use language in one context does not necessarily mean knowing how to use it effectively in another" (p. 9).

2.2 *SELECTING TEXT*

The selections below come from an ESL textbook (Walker, 1992) designed for elementary school students. Take a look at the selections and think about the following: What does each selection attempt to teach (content, grammar, vocabulary)? How are the selections different from each other? Is one more beneficial to students? Why or why not?

Selection I:

Kim got up early. She took a shower and got dressed. She ate some cereal and drank some milk.

She got on her bike. She went to the corner. She put twenty newspapers in her basket. She rode through the neighborhood. She delivered all the papers. Then she caught the bus for school (p. 109).

Selection II:

Christopher Columbus lived in Genoa, Italy. He was a sailor. He sailed on many ships to many places. He wanted to sail to Asia. In those days, people called Asia "The Indies." They traveled east to get there. They went across land and water. The trip was long and very dangerous.

Columbus had a different idea. He wanted to sail *west*! Many people said, "That's crazy. The world is flat. You'll sail off the edge of the world. You'll never come back." Columbus didn't listen. He was sure the world was round (p. 19–20).

ACADEMIC FOCUS IN THE CLASSROOM

The ESL teacher can help students acquire this specialized language for each subject area by using it as a basis for ESL lessons. "To learn only communicative language skills in a traditional ESL classroom is insufficient preparation for the more demanding and specialized academic language which all ELL* students in public schools must eventually be able to use" (O'Malley and Valdez Pierce, 1996, p. 165). The situation is exacerbated in the upper elementary grades and at the secondary level where the academic material is more complex, more abstract, and less related to everyday conversation. In fact, at the secondary level, even when ESL students are released from (traditionally taught) ESL programs and are supposedly prepared for content-area classes, they can encounter serious difficulties with the academic program (Chamot and O'Malley, 1987). A content-based curriculum attempts to do a better job of preparing students for academic challenges.

Using a model developed by Cummins (1982), Chamot and O'Malley (1987) have contrasted the kinds of activities that take place in an ESL class when a grammar-based or communicative-based ESL curriculum is used (Figure 2.1: Quadrants I and II) and when a curriculum with an academic focus is used (Figure 2.1: Quadrants III and IV). Activities in Quadrant I are the easiest because they are nonacademic and context-embedded (that is, a context such as pictures, actions, or gestures is provided). ESL students can rely on the context to derive meaning even if they do not fully understand the language. Activities in Quadrant IV are the most difficult because they are academically demanding and context-reduced (that is, few if any context cues are provided).

ESL curricula for beginning students need to include the activities in Quadrants I and II, but as soon as possible, the ESL teacher should consider using curricula that give students the opportunity to do the kinds of activities found in Quadrant III and even in Quadrant IV. Since the typical demands in an upper elementary grade-level classroom and in a secondary content-area classroom include using the skills listed in Quadrant III and Quadrant IV, ESL students should be working toward developing those skills in ESL class. If not, they master Quadrant I and II skills in their ESL class and then are thrown into Quadrant IV activities in the "mainstream" without adequate preparation.

By offering ESL students the opportunity to engage in classroom activities that have an academic focus, the ESL teacher is recognizing that linguistic limitations are not the same as cognitive limitations. ESL students may not as yet be proficient in English, but their lack of language proficiency is not related to their ability to think and do complex tasks (Brinton, Sasser, and Winningham, 1988). By recognizing the cognitive abilities of ESL students and exposing them to more complex academic work, ESL teachers are preparing ESL students to enroll in content-area classes sooner, and thus, possibly, allowing them to squeeze in more content-area classes in their programs before graduating from high school. In this way, capable ESL students are more prepared for the demands of post-secondary education.

LEARNING STRATEGIES INSTRUCTION

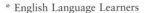

Along with incorporating into the curriculum the kinds of academic activities that will help ESL students acquire the language and skills needed for success in content areas, research suggests that ESL teachers can facilitate students' learning even more

* English Language Learners

Figure 2.1: Classification of Language and Content Activities Within Cummins's Framework

Nonacademic or cognitively undemanding activities	Academic and cognitively demanding activities
Quadrant I (context-embedded) • Developing survival vocabulary • Following demonstrated directions • Playing simple games • Engaging in face-to face interaction • Practicing oral language exercises and communicative language functions	**Quadrant III (context-embedded)** • Developing academic vocabulary • Understanding academic presentations accompanied by visuals, demonstrations of a process, etc. • Participating in hands-on science activities • Making models, maps, charts, and graphs in social studies • Solving math computation problems • Solving math word problems assisted by manipulatives and/or illustrations • Participating in academic discussions • Making brief oral presentations • Using higher-level comprehension skills in listening to oral texts • Understanding written texts through discussion, illustrations, and visuals • Writing simple science and social studies reports with format provided • Answering higher-level questions
Quadrant II (context-reduced) • Developing initial reading skills: decoding and literal comprehension • Reading and writing for personal purposes: notes, lists, recipes, etc. • Reading and writing for operational purposes: directions, forms, etc. • Writing answers to lower-level questions	**Quadrant IV (context-reduced)** • Understanding academic presentations without visuals or demonstrations • Making formal oral presentations • Using higher-level reading comprehension skills: inferential and critical reading • Reading for information in content subjects • Writing compositions, essays, and research reports in content subjects • Solving math word problems without illustrations • Writing answers to higher-level questions • Taking standardized achievement tests

(Adapted from Chamot and O'Malley, 1987, p. 238)

by including **learning strategies** in the curriculum (Chamot and O'Malley, 1987). Learning strategies are techniques used by effective learners to help them learn more expediently. For example, efficient learners will monitor their reading to see if they understand the material. If they do not understand it, they will take steps to accomplish the task—they will reread the passage or ask questions for clarification. Self-monitoring and asking questions for clarification are examples of learning strategies that ESL students need to learn and practice often in the ESL classroom so that they will be able to transfer these skills to learning in the grade-level/content-area classes. Here are some important learning strategies students need to learn and practice.

Figure 2.2: Learning Strategies

METACOGNITIVE STRATEGIES

Advance organization—looking at chapter/section headings to preview what they are going to read

Organizational planning—planning how to present ideas orally and in writing

Selective attention—deciding what information to look for in spoken or written language

Self-monitoring—checking one's comprehension; checking one's oral and written production as it is taking place

Self-evaluation—judging how well one did a task

COGNITIVE STRATEGIES

Using resources—consulting dictionaries, encyclopedias, etc.

Grouping—classifying words, concepts, etc. according to given criteria

Note-taking—taking notes during a listening or reading activity

Summarizing—extracting main ideas from spoken or written language

Deduction—applying rules to understand or produce language

Induction—formulating rules based on language examples

Imagery—using images (mental or actual) to aid in comprehension or memory

Connecting—taking new information and relating it to prior knowledge or to personal experience

Transferring—taking skills already learned and using them to learn new skills

Inferencing—using information to predict outcomes or make assumptions

SOCIAL-AFFECTIVE STRATEGIES

Questioning—using questions to get clarification, rephrasing, more information, etc.

Cooperation—working with peers to solve problems, pool information, get feedback, etc.

Self-talk—using mental techniques to reduce anxiety about doing a learning task

(Adapted from Chamot and O'Malley, 1987, p. 248–249)

There is some overlap between learning strategies and academic skills. For example, making a chart or graph to compare the heights of mountain peaks is a typical academic skill required in a social studies class. But making a chart or graph is also a learning strategy students can use to aid in understanding and remembering new information.

Else adds some important points about learning strategies.

Else's Perspective

HELENE IS RIGHT TO PAY ATTENTION to the issue of learning strategies, an often-ignored area of second-language instruction. Teaching these learning strategies is especially important for ESL students who have limited formal schooling. For the most part, these students are not accustomed to doing things like self-talk, note-taking, summarizing, and self-monitoring as a way of learning. In fact, even ESL students with a strong academic background in their native language may need practice in using learning strategies in English; as they focus on using the new language, they may neglect to use these learning strategies. Learning strategies are also especially important in the grade-level/content-area classroom, where new concepts are introduced in the academic subject areas and where even native English-speaking students can have difficulty learning if they have not mastered the strategies. The importance of learning strategies is acknowledged in the ESL standards developed by TESOL (TESOL, 1997): The third standard of each ESL goal addresses learning strategies. The following is a partial list of descriptors of the learning strategies standard for each of the three goals of language.

LEARNING STRATEGIES IN THE ESL STANDARDS

GOAL 1, STANDARD 3

To use English to communicate in social settings: Students will use learning strategies to extend their communicative competence.

- Testing hypotheses about language
- Listening to and imitating how others use English
- Comparing nonverbal and verbal cues
- Practicing new language

GOAL 2, STANDARD 3

To use English to achieve academically in all content areas: Students will use appropriate learning strategies to construct and apply academic knowledge.

- Applying basic reading comprehension skills such as skimming, scanning, previewing, and reviewing text
- Using context to construct meaning
- Taking notes to record important information and aid one's own learning
- Determining and establishing the conditions that help one become an effective learner (e.g., when, where, how to study)

GOAL 3, STANDARD 3

To use English in socially and culturally appropriate ways: Students will use appropriate learning strategies to extend their communicative competence.

- Observing and modeling how others speak and behave in a particular situation or setting
- Experimenting with variations of language in social and academic settings
- Seeking information about appropriate language use and behavior
- Analyzing the social context to determine appropriate language use

CURRICULUM ALIGNMENT

An issue related to academic focus is that of **curriculum alignment**; that is, attempting to align the ESL curriculum with the grade-level or content-area curriculum. Curriculum alignment entails working closely with the grade-level/content-area teachers so that ESL students are learning the same or similar content as their native English-speaking peers. This is somewhat different from the issue of academic focus in that the ESL teacher could use a curriculum that has academic focus and is cognitively demanding, but is not necessarily aligned with the grade-level or content-area curriculum. For example, if the grade-level teacher is presenting a unit on the explorers and the ESL teacher is presenting a unit on the same general topic (possibly with different kinds of activities, materials, and assignments), the curricula are aligned. However, if the grade-level class is studying explorers but the ESL students are studying U.S. presidents, the curricula are not aligned, even though the lessons in both units could have academic focus.

Because of logistical differences between the elementary and secondary educational programs, the issue of curriculum alignment will be discussed separately for elementary schools and secondary schools.

In the Elementary School Program

Using an ESL curriculum that closely matches what students are learning in their grade-level class allows the ESL teacher to help students accomplish their dual goal in school—learning English, and learning their school subjects along with their native English-speaking peers. In other words, ESL teachers can use the content to develop language while simultaneously helping students master the content material (Met, 1994).

I asked an ESL teacher who has worked for many years with elementary school ESL students to talk about the benefits to her students of aligning the ESL curriculum with the grade-level curriculum. Here is what she had to say.

> In our town we first determine ESL students' oral proficiency levels (1 through 5, 5 being fluent). I use our ESL curriculum (and ESL textbooks) mainly with my Level 1 and Level 2 students; they need to build their vocabulary and become more comfortable listening to and speaking English before they can tackle the work in the classroom. However, for students at Levels 3–5, I use the classroom cur-

For a description of oral proficiency levels (1–5), see Appendix A p. 207.

Lillian Rausch, Charter Oak Elementary School, West Hartford, Connecticut

riculum as the basis for my ESL lessons, and I integrate the ESL curriculum into it. The grade-level teacher decides what unit to work on or cover next, and I adapt that unit to the level of the ESL students.

Using the classroom curriculum as a basis for my ESL lessons helps to build the students' knowledge in the academic areas, which benefits them now and will benefit them later on. Also, the children feel more a part of the class because they are learning the same things that the other students are learning, but at their own level.

Since working with grade-level curriculum requires coordination with grade-level teachers, I asked the ESL teacher if that posed any particular problems or challenges. She responded:

Social integration is discussed further in Chapter 3.

> A challenge that I sometimes face when using classroom curriculum is convincing classroom teachers to have different expectations for the ESL students. When I work with ESL students on classroom curriculum, some classroom teachers expect magic; they expect the ESL students to produce the same or similar results (on tests, projects, etc.) as the native English speakers. The classroom teachers need to understand that since the ESL students are still learning the language while they are learning the classroom content, they need to be assessed in a different way from the other children.

See Chapter 5 on Assessment, p. 128.

> Another challenge is finding materials that match the classroom curriculum but are at a lower linguistic level so that they are suitable for the ESL students to use.

2.3 *ALTERNATIVE EVALUATIONS*

This teacher has found that some grade-level teachers have unrealistic expectations of what ESL students are able to do considering their English proficiency levels. Suppose you were working with a group of ESL students on a social studies unit about explorers. At the end of the unit, the classroom teacher wanted the ESL students to take the same test as the rest of the class. How would you convince the grade-level teacher that using the same test and grading scale for the ESL students might be unrealistic and unfair to the ESL students? Can you think of any suggestions to offer the grade-level teacher who is concerned about evaluating the ESL students' work?

THE ISSUE THAT HELENE RAISES IN THIS SECTION—having different expectations for ESL students—is a very sensitive and delicate one (August and Hakuta, 1997). Unfortunately, many people may interpret the terms "different expectations" as "lower expectations." Perhaps we need to refer to this issue by talking about "differentiated expectations," just to draw attention away from the possible association with the idea of lowered expectations.

We have to be very careful not to suggest having lower expectations of language-minority students who are learning ESL than we do for native

English-speaking students. The research on teacher expectations points to the importance of setting the same high expectations for all students.

Even students who enter high school with very limited proficiency in English, and even those who come from limited formal school backgrounds, have the potential to learn and to attain the same academic standards as their native English-speaking counterparts. High academic achievement must be an objective for all students regardless of their language background. What needs to be different for students who are not proficient in the language of instruction is the way in which we provide instruction to them rather than what we expect them to attain.

Standards-based instruction

A discussion of this issue is particularly timely given the recent establishment in the United States of academic standards in all the major content areas at local, state, and national levels. Standards have begun to drive instruction and assessment and, in an attempt to ensure equal educational opportunity for every student, every national standards document includes a statement that standards apply to all students. Interestingly, however, most of these documents do not offer any discussion on the issues raised by Helene: What implications do these standards have for students who are not proficient in the language of instruction? For ESL students who receive content-area instruction through their primary language, how do we measure attainment of these standards? In an atmosphere that promotes standards-based instruction, it is vital to address these questions.

We must distinguish between setting different standards for ESL students (which is not appropriate) and establishing different ways of teaching and assessing these students. Different ways of teaching these students include sheltering content-area instruction for them and using the strategies that Helene describes in this book. It also means giving ESL students more time to learn. It is becoming clear that ESL students, especially those who come from atypical educational experiences (such as students with interrupted schooling or students from remote rural areas), have much more to accomplish at school than their native English-speaking peers. However, we rarely give them enough additional opportunities to reach the same goals as other students. Some school districts have begun to offer after-school and summer school programs for ESL students, but more often than not, these programs are inconsistent at best and rely too heavily on unreliable funding sources. Changing the way we assess these students entails changing assessment procedures as well as building a solid database that will eventually help in the interpretation of ESL students' scores on standardized tests.

See Chapter 5 on Assessment, pp. 114–116.

Thus, rather than changing our expectations of ESL students, we need to change the access they have to educational opportunities that bring them up to par with those who are not limited in their English proficiency. TESOL suggests that, in order to ensure that ESL students receive quality educational experiences, they need to have access to a positive learning environment, appropriate curriculum, full delivery of services, and equitable assessment. (For a listing of these access standards, see TESOL, 1997.)

The elementary school ESL teacher in the Teachers' Voices section above raises the issue of locating content materials that might be more suitable for ESL students than on-grade-level materials.

One way to locate appropriate materials is to check with school or public librarians. They may know of books that match the grade-level themes but are written in simpler English. The grade-level teachers of the grade just below the grade level of the ESL students may have useful materials. ESL textbooks for elementary school published in the last few years can also be useful since they reflect the shift in focus to grade-level content. It is possible to pick and choose units that match the grade-level curriculum in a particular school. For example, the textbook series *Into English!* (Tinajero and Schifini, 1997) is organized by grade-level content so that each book in the series (Levels A through G) covers skills and content from a particular grade level (K through 6, respectively). The unit entitled "To the Moon!" in the Level D book (designed for third-graders) may coordinate well with the third-grade science curriculum in a particular school. The unit can be used to introduce the study of landforms such as mountains, volcanoes, and valleys before the ESL students study a similar topic in their grade-level classrooms. In this way, the ESL students are familiar with the concepts and vocabulary related to the topic and are prepared to learn the new information in their grade-level classroom. The teacher's guide offers multilevel teaching strategies so that a third-grader at any English proficiency level can benefit from lessons involving the third-grade content.

Using grade-level curriculum to design ESL curriculum can take several different forms. It could mean teaching the same topics taught in the grade-level classroom, but adapting them to the proficiency levels of the ESL students (as explained by the ESL teacher above). In this way, ESL students have the opportunity to learn the same or similar content as their native English-speaking peers, but in a way that fits the ESL students' needs. It could mean teaching a lesson to ESL students to prepare them for a lesson they are about to learn in their grade-level classroom (as mentioned above regarding landforms). This type of experience can provide students with valuable background knowledge that can serve as an advance organizer for the lesson they will receive in their classroom with their native English-speaking peers (Met, 1994). It could also mean reteaching, in an adapted way, a lesson that has already been taught in the grade-level classroom, but that might not have been understood satisfactorily by the ESL students. Examples of some ways of aligning the ESL curriculum with the grade-level curriculum are explained after Else's commentary below.

HELENE'S DISCUSSION OF HOW CONTENT and language curricula can be coordinated brings up issues of power and advocacy in teaching ESL. Supporting the ESL student's content-area learning is one example of how the ESL teacher can offer a tremendous service and help to the grade-level classroom teacher and begin to draw that teacher into the role of advocating for the ESL students. By paying close attention to the grade-level curriculum, the ESL teacher is, in fact, helping the grade-level teacher's efforts to get content across to all students in the grade-level classroom. The strategies that Helene describes in this book can be quite useful to grade-level classroom teachers; these teachers might welcome some help from the ESL teacher. The ESL teacher may even offer to come into the grade-level classroom to show some of the strategies that work particularly well with ESL students and are, at the same time, helpful to all students regardless of their language backgrounds.

The knowledge that ESL teachers have gives them power. Once a positive relationship has been established between the ESL teacher and the grade-level classroom teacher, and power has been shared, the classroom teacher begins to see the ESL teacher as an ally and friend. When that happens, grade-level teachers, who do not always see themselves as primarily responsible for the education of language-minority students, are more likely to advocate on behalf of ESL students.

Teaching the Same Topic

If the ESL students' proficiency levels are not yet high enough for them to benefit from instruction in a particular academic subject or on a certain unit in the grade-level classroom, the ESL teacher can attempt to teach the same unit, but in an adapted way, to the ESL students. The advantage of choosing the same topic is that students know that they are doing "real" schoolwork and that ESL class will help them participate in activities associated with that schoolwork along with their peers in their grade-level class. The human need to belong to a peer group can be a powerful motivator (Stevick, 1976, 1998). In addition, challenging academic material used in grade-level classrooms can be inherently engaging to students (Chamot and O'Malley, 1987).

See Chapter 3 for more on social integration.

An ESL teacher in Hawaii talks about how she used the grade-level curriculum, in this case literature, to motivate a reluctant student to try his best and succeed in doing grade-level work.

Joanne Kajihiro, Kanoelani Elementary School, Waipahu, Hawaii

> Last September I started working with Daniel, a sixth-grader originally from American Samoa. Daniel was the only ESL student in this particular sixth-grade class, so I had the opportunity to give him individual attention. I was able to work with him every day for a half hour at a time.
>
> Daniel had been back and forth several times through the years between American Samoa and Hawaii and had attended school in both places. Because of his somewhat limited exposure to English, his frequent school changes, and possibly other factors, he was struggling with reading and writing in his sixth-grade class. His grade-level teacher and I decided that, during his ESL time, I would work on his reading and writing skills. I decided to experiment with stories from several ESL reading/writing textbooks until I had a sense of his current level and what would be beneficial to him. I was looking for materials that would motivate him, challenge him, and help him to become a better reader and writer. I was careful, however, not to select materials that were too difficult and potentially frustrating for him.

Although it seemed that I had selected materials at the appropriate level of difficulty, Daniel was unmotivated and, at times, uncooperative. He clearly did not want to do his ESL work. I tried different approaches and activities, in an attempt to make his learning enjoyable, but he continued to resist. When I asked him what the problem was, he responded, "This is extra work." "Apparently, Daniel viewed his ESL work as just another thing he had to do, rather than as a means to help him improve his reading and writing in order to do better in his grade-level classroom.

The classroom teacher and I met, and we decided that I would take a different approach. Instead of giving Daniel easier reading material to work on, I was going to attempt to have him read the novel that the rest of his classmates were reading, *Brian's Winter* (Paulsen, 1996). Up to now, his teacher had tried to have Daniel read the book along with the class and to do some of the assignments, but he was not able to do much.

The book was about a teenage boy who was the only survivor of a plane crash in the Canadian wilderness and was now alone, stranded, and struggling to survive. It was good literature, and many of the sixth-graders enjoyed reading it; perhaps Daniel would also enjoy the story if he could manage to read it with some form of assistance. Perhaps he would be motivated to read and write with me if there were a clear connection between his ESL lessons and the classroom work. Maybe another motivating force would be that he would be able to participate more fully during class activities involving the book. The book would be difficult for Daniel to read, but it was worth a try.

The result of this experiment was truly amazing. Although the book was hard for Daniel to read, he was motivated to try, and his attitude was excellent. We went through the book slowly doing shared reading (he would read one paragraph and I would read the next) and stopping for frequent discussions and clarifications of vocabulary and content. I had Daniel keep a vocabulary book of the words he learned. At the end of each session I asked him to summarize orally what he had read, and at the end of the week, he would write a summary of what he had read that week using some of the vocabulary words from his "dictionary." Because of the slow pace at which we worked, we skipped over some parts of the book so that he could keep up with the rest of the class. I orally summarized those parts for him so that he did not miss any of the story line. Daniel never forgot to come to ESL class; he wanted to complete the book and all his assignments. Daniel's grade-level teacher reported that during class discussions of the book, Daniel was an enthusiastic participant.

When he finished the book, he created his own "book" about *Brian's Winter* that included some of his chapter summaries, a reaction paper, a "dictionary" of words he had learned, and drawings of how he perceived some of the scenes in the book. I was proud of Daniel's hard work, and I could tell he was proud of himself.

In this example, the teacher's decision to use the same content as the grade-level class resulted in motivating the student to read. Perhaps this was due to Daniel's realizing (consciously or subconsciously) that if he did his work with the ESL teacher, he would be able to participate during reading lessons in his grade-level classroom, thus satisfying his need to belong. Another possible motivating force was the literature itself. The teacher reported that Daniel seemed to enjoy the story line and reading about the struggles of the main character. Connecting the ESL lesson to the grade-level content and using interesting literature made the ESL lessons more meaningful to Daniel and meaningful content provides motivation for learning language (Genesee, 1994).

Although, in the interest of time, the ESL teacher had to skip over certain parts of the book and summarize them, Daniel still had the opportunity to read a considerable amount of the book. This type of modification of the grade-level curriculum is often necessary in order to make it accessible to ESL students; Daniel would not have been able to keep up with his grade-level class and participate in discussions if he had read every page in ESL class.

Reading a grade-level novel (and doing other grade-level work) is not possible with every ESL student—it depends on each student's current level of English proficiency. But it is often possible to use the classroom program as a guide and decide, along with the grade-level teacher, what parts of the curriculum are both essential and "teachable," given the ESL students' current proficiency levels. The ESL teacher can then use a repertoire of strategies so that the ESL students learn as much as possible of the grade-level curriculum, acquire language associated with that curriculum, develop the skills needed for learning academic content material, and have a successful learning experience.

2.4 *DEVELOPING ACADEMIC SKILLS*

Take a look back at the Teachers' Voices section above, describing the lessons the teacher did with Daniel. What were some of the academic skills she was helping Daniel to develop? What other academic skills could be developed during these lessons (you might want to refer to Figure 2.1)? What learning strategies could also be developed (see Figure 2.2)?

Supplying Background Knowledge

In addition to teaching adapted lessons on the same topics as those taught in the grade-level classroom, when appropriate, the ESL teacher can also assist ESL students by activating and supplementing their **background knowledge** in preparation for a topic. This type of lesson is particularly useful to students with intermediate or advanced language proficiency who can benefit from unadapted lessons in the grade-level classroom as long as the students are prepared for the lessons.

Background knowledge (or "prior knowledge") is the knowledge and experience students already have when they enter a new learning situation. Schema theory suggests that comprehension is an interactive process that emerges from the relationship between the student's background knowledge and the new knowledge (Young, 1989). "Existing knowledge is used to give meaning to new knowledge, and vice-versa" (p. 4). ESL students may have difficulty understanding the grade-level curriculum because, coming into the lesson, they may not possess the same background knowledge as their native English-speaking peers. This may be due to their having had cultural and academic experiences very different from their native English-speaking peers. It may also be due to their lack of background knowledge in the form of vocabulary words needed to understand the lesson.

When I moved to Hawaii a few years ago, I encountered difficulties because of my lack of cultural and linguistic background knowledge. This was my experience:

Helene Becker

> Being new in Hawaii, I didn't know my way around at first, so I often stopped my car to ask for directions. I had difficulty understanding the directions because the local way to give directions was to refer to landmarks rather than exit names or numbers. I would be told such things as, "Get off the highway at the exit after the Big Boy Restaurant."
>
> Since I had not yet lived there very long and did not share the common background knowledge of knowing where these popular landmarks were, I could not successfully follow these directions. I was more used to watching for an exit number or name, but the people I asked could not give me that information. I often missed the exit because I didn't see the landmark, or saw it too late.
>
> I also had linguistic problems. The terms *north, south, east,* and *west* are not usually used in Hawaii to indicate which way to head. Instead, the Hawaiian words *makai,* which means "toward the ocean," and *mauka,* which means "toward the mountains," are used (see Figure 2.3). I needed to add these vocabulary words to my background knowledge before I could understand what people were telling me.

Figure 2.3: **Sign outside an apartment building in Honolulu, Hawaii**

"Use Makai entrance" tells motorists to enter through the driveway closer to the ocean.

Here is an account of a lesson I taught at Kanoelani Elementary School in Hawaii to six fifth-grade intermediate-level ESL students. In this lesson, I tried to access and supplement students' background knowledge to prepare them for work in their grade-level classroom.

The students were going to be reading a novel used in the fifth-grade classes, *Sign of the Beaver* (Speare, 1984). This historical novel depicts the lives and traditions of Native Americans of the Northeast in the 1700s. I began the lesson by accessing students' background knowledge. I asked them to think of everything they already knew about Native Americans, and then I wrote the information on the board in the form of a web. As I wrote, I explained vocabulary words, clarified ideas, and added new information and vocabulary words (see Figure 2.4). I then used a map of the United States to show the students where the story took place (in the state of Maine). In the remaining ESL time, I asked the students to start reading the novel in small groups, using a teacher-made study guide to help them interact with the text. During this lesson the students learned valuable background information to prepare them for the upcoming work in their grade-level classroom, as well as language in the form of new vocabulary words in the context of the novel.

Teachers' Voices

Helene Becker

Figure 2.4: Web from Lesson on *Sign of the Beaver*

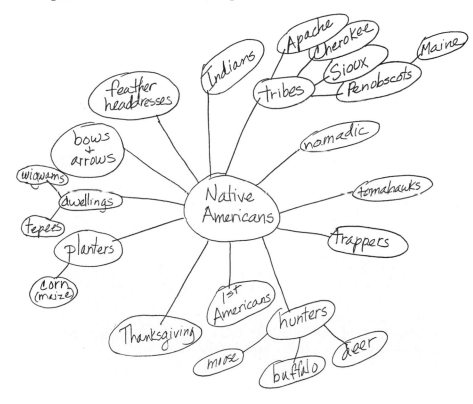

If I had been using an ESL curriculum not aligned with the grade-level curriculum, I could have conducted a similar reading/vocabulary activity and the students could probably have learned just as much English. However, because this lesson provided students with background information needed to set the stage for learning, in the form of vocabulary words, geography, and history, it would seem logical that they were more prepared to participate in and benefit from the grade-level lesson. They were also practicing two learning strategies: using an advance organizer to see relationships among words, and cooperating with each other to arrive at answers to questions about the story. They were able to work on developing academic skills by interacting with authentic grade-level literature. As in the case of Daniel in the previous account, students seemed motivated to learn, possibly because they saw the connection between instruction in their ESL class and their ability to participate and belong in the grade-level classroom.

Now, Else discusses an additional benefit of giving ESL students a preview of what is to come in their grade-level classes.

Else's Perspective JUST AS THE STATUS OF THE ESL TEACHER WITHIN THE CULTURE of the school is important in how effective the learning environment is, so is the status of ESL students. In most schools, ESL students are not held in high prestige. This is typically not in direct correlation to their being second-language learners; rather, it is a result of their minority status within the larger society (Ogbu, 1983). The fact that they cannot fully participate in the grade-level classroom because of their limited proficiency in English does not help. The ESL teacher can give students' standing a boost within the grade-level classroom by giving them access to information that their native English-speaking peers may not yet have. The students can thus embark on a given content-area lesson with bits of information about the topic that other students do not have. This strategy is particularly effective if ESL students can share something related to the content-area topic that comes from their own funds of knowledge, based on their own cultural background (Moll and Greenberg, 1990).

In order for this approach to work, several conditions that Helene discusses must be in place:

1. The ESL teacher must be able to use academic content as the base for language instruction.
2. Both ESL and grade-level teachers must have a clear understanding of the importance of sociopolitical issues, such as status, in education.
3. The grade-level teacher must understand the importance of encouraging ESL students to share their funds of knowledge with their English-speaking peers.
4. There must be close coordination between the ESL teacher and the grade-level classroom teachers.

2.5 DETERMINING AND PRESENTING BACKGROUND KNOWLEDGE

Locate a textbook used in any elementary grade for social studies, science, math, or literature. By yourself or with a partner, pick a chapter or unit and jot down the background knowledge (cultural, academic, linguistic) that would be helpful for students to know before they attempted to understand the text. What are some ways you could present this background knowledge to ESL students?

2.6 MODIFYING ASSIGNMENTS

An ESL teacher is likely to encounter some grade-level teachers who choose assignments appropriate for their ESL students' current proficiency levels, and some who do not. Suppose you were the ESL teacher who just taught the lesson described above. The next time you meet with your students they bring along a study sheet with 15 questions about the first chapter of the book. The students are very anxious because they do not understand all the questions and they are overwhelmed by the number of them. You decide to talk to the teacher about modifying the assignment. How would you explain to the teacher that the assignment should be modified for the ESL students? How would you suggest it be modified? If possible, discuss your answers with a colleague.

Since using the grade-level curriculum is generally not a suitable plan for beginning-level ESL students (except possibly for students in kindergarten and first grade where the grade-level lessons revolve around the same basic topics that ESL students need to learn when they first arrive—school life, family, animals, colors, etc.), I would not have introduced *Sign of the Beaver* to new arrivals. A beginning-level ESL student in the fifth grade has more immediate survival needs than learning the words *bow* and *arrow* and the traditions of Native Americans. Even if the beginning-level ESL students did learn the vocabulary words from *Sign of the Beaver*, the words would not have a meaningful purpose; since the story is written at a fifth-grade reading level, the students would not be able to use those few words to understand the story. The grade-level and ESL teachers need to decide together when the beginning-level ESL students have acquired enough "survival" proficiency to benefit from ESL instruction aligned with the curriculum in the grade-level classroom.

In the Secondary School Program

Using all the Content Areas

At the elementary school level, aligning ESL instruction with grade-level curriculum is feasible since, in many cases, ESL students in the same grade are grouped together for ESL instruction. On the other hand, at the secondary level, aligning the ESL curriculum with the various subject areas studied can be tricky. Since middle and high school ESL students are typically placed in ESL classes by English proficiency level rather than grade level, ESL classes are often comprised of students from mixed grades studying a wide range of subjects. Even if they are all in the same grade, they do not necessarily study the same subjects.

The ideal situation would be for the ESL teacher to meet regularly with each student's different content-area teachers to find out what concepts, vocabulary, and skills the ESL students are learning in any given week. In that way, the ESL teacher could provide the cultural, academic, and linguistic background knowledge ESL students need for the lessons in their content classes. For example, if some students were going to be studying "living things" in science class, the ESL teacher could introduce the topic in the ESL class so that students could learn key concepts (such as the similarities and differences between the animal and plant world) and important vocabulary words (such as *cell, energy,* and *matter*). Unfortunately, however, this approach is impossible in most secondary schools because of the number of different students all studying different subjects.

The solution to the problem of aligning the ESL curriculum with the content-area curriculum at the secondary level depends on how the ESL classes fit into the ESL program as a whole. For example, some programs offer ESL students **sheltered classes** in the content areas. In these classes, strategies and materials appropriate for ESL students are used to teach academic subjects to intermediate- and advanced-level ESL students (sometimes to high-beginning-level students, as well). If a sheltered biology class, for example, is offered to ESL students, it may not be necessary to address the subject of biology in the ESL classroom, since ESL students will be able to learn the subject matter in a class designed to accommodate their needs. On the other hand, if the ESL program does not include, for example, a sheltered American history class, then it may be wise to include the subject of American history in the ESL curriculum in order to prepare students for the "mainstream" American history class they will be taking in the future.

If sheltered classes are not offered within the overall ESL program, it becomes necessary to consider aligning the ESL curriculum with all the major subject areas: science, social studies, literature, and math. In this way, ESL students learn English while being exposed to the vocabulary and concepts they will encounter when they enroll in these courses in the "mainstream." In any case, whatever content is included in the ESL curriculum, it needs to be presented in a way that exposes students to the kinds of academic activities (such as those listed in Quadrant III and IV of Figure 2.1) that they will encounter in content-area classes. For example, whether the content being taught in ESL class is literature or American history, students should be given the opportunity to write essays and answer questions beyond the literal level.

Now, Else offers further detail about sheltered instruction.

◇ Else's Perspective ◇ **HELENE'S IDEA OF CURRICULUM ALIGNMENT IS USEFUL,** and it requires sheltering instruction in at least some core content areas. **Sheltering instruction** means using language in such a way as to make the concepts presented more concrete and to make the context as clear as possible—that is, to use the framework presented in Figure 2.1, to move classroom tasks from Quadrant IV to Quadrant III. Sheltered instruction strategies can be quite effective in making academic content-area lessons comprehensible. When students concentrate on understanding concepts that are presented in a meaningful way, their language proficiency also advances. Thus, "mainstream" teachers need to learn how to shelter their instruction. Short of following an extensive course of training in ESL, they may benefit from some help in doing this from the ESL teacher.

Effective sheltered instruction strategies include the following (adapted from Echeverria, Vogt, Short, and Montone, 1988):

- Use a variety of question types that promote higher-order thinking skills.
- Pace the lesson appropriately for the students' ability level.
- Speak at a rate that is appropriate for the students' proficiency level.
- Use vocabulary that is appropriate for the students' proficiency level.
- Use short, simple sentences rather than complex ones.
- Avoid pausing before the end of sentences.
- Exaggerate intonation and gestures.
- Repeat sentences without using too many different expressions and idioms.
- Emphasize key words.
- Provide frequent opportunities for interaction among students and between teacher and student.
- Provide sufficient wait time for student responses.

An ESL teacher in New York talks about how she uses content in her ESL classes to prepare students for future content-area classes.

Julia Roldan, Sewanhaka High School, Floral Park, New York

In my Level 1 ESL class, I try to get into content work as soon as possible. After the first few months we usually do some math vocabulary words and some basic social studies. One of the units I do requires students to learn the names of the 50 states and fill them in on a map (we don't learn them all at once!). This may sound like pure memorization, but I find that it familiarizes students with their new country, gives them spelling practice, and creates a point of reference for them when they read something in the newspaper, or when they hear about a specific place in one of their classes or on the radio or TV. I then have them pick a state and do research about it. They work in groups to formulate questions and we go to the library to get resources. They also try to locate some pictures of the most important landmarks in their respective states. When they are ready, they do a short oral presentation for the class.

I think this is a good experience for the ESL students because they need to know the names of the 50 states and some information about them for social studies and literature classes (they will have a better sense of where a story is taking place). This is part of the background knowledge ESL students need to help them in their academic classes, now and in the future.

2.7 *Developing Academic Skills and Learning Strategies*

What academic skills and learning strategies do students develop during this unit on the 50 states? What other academic skills and learning strategies could be taught or practiced during this unit?

2.8 *Examining Textbooks*

If an ESL department in a secondary school wants to change the core textbooks being used with students, the ESL teachers may be asked to evaluate some ESL textbooks. Try locating samples of several ESL textbooks designed for secondary ESL teaching; if you are studying in a class with others, perhaps you could each bring one textbook to the next session. Here are some textbooks currently in use in secondary schools:

> *Building Bridges* (Chamot, O'Malley, and Kupper, 1992)
> *Classmates* (Molinsky and Bliss, 1996)
> *Go For It* (Nunan, 1999)
> *Making Connections* (Kessler, Lee, McCloskey, Quinn, and Stack, 1996)

Take a look at the tables of contents and examine some of the units in each book. With what kind of curriculum is each book designed to be used (grammar-based, content-based, other)? Notice the kinds of activities students are instructed to do. Which activities in the units have an academic focus (refer to Figure 2.1, Quadrants III and IV)? Which book(s) do you think would appeal to students? Why? With which book(s) would you like to teach? If you were in charge of picking the textbook series to be used with ESL students in your school, which one would you pick, and why?

Using Literature

In programs where ESL students have the opportunity to learn social studies, science, and math through sheltered classes, literature can be used as the content of ESL classes. Students can benefit from a literature-based curriculum early on in their ESL studies if selections are chosen carefully; they should be short, with relatively easy-to-understand vocabulary and themes. A good resource for such selections and accompanying activities is the ESL series *Voices in Literature* (McCloskey and Stack, 1996).

In some ESL programs, a general content-based curriculum (using all content areas) is used for beginning and low-intermediate students to give them a foundation for their content-area and sheltered classes. Then, a literature-based curriculum is used in the intermediate and advanced ESL classes. Studying literature in ESL class provides many benefits for ESL students. It exposes them to a rich source of authentic language within the context of a story line and can promote discussions about American culture and other cultures. The activities, discussions, and assignments experienced in ESL class can help students grow academically and prepare them for other literature courses they will take in their academic careers. If students enjoy the literature, they may be motivated to read more often, which will help them improve their reading proficiency.

I asked a high school ESL teacher/coordinator experienced in using a literature-based curriculum to discuss her views on using literature with ESL students. Here is what she had to say:

> I teach a literature-based curriculum to my students, who are in ninth through twelfth grades, with intermediate to advanced ESL proficiency (in the same class). This means following, more or less, the standard state curriculum for ninth-graders (world literature).
>
> I love teaching a literature-based curriculum. Everything you need is there and it's all contextualized. For ESL students to grow, I feel that it's critical for them to be challenged academically as well as linguistically; they cannot afford to spend a year or two (or more!) marking time academically while they "work on their English." So that's one critical point for me. Secondly, so much rich language work can come out of a literature-based curriculum. There's the reading, of course. I also work a lot with writing, moving back and forth between reading and writing. By the time we finish a piece of literature, my students have a folder of written work ranging from quick-writes to lists to graphic organizers to more developed pieces, some of which can then be used as a basis for more extensive essays. And, of course, vocabulary and grammar work can be pulled directly from the text. I also do a lot of communicative and speech activities built around any piece of literature.
>
> The major objection most people seem to have to a literature-based curriculum is that the texts are "too hard" for ESL students. By that, they are usually referring to the language. I don't agree for the most part. Obviously, I judge the abilities of my class and choose accordingly. But I think people often aim too low. I've taught *The Odyssey, Cyrano de Bergerac,* and unadapted short stories and novels. It takes a lot of preparation, scaffolding, feedback, and continual comprehension checking, but it's worth it. We don't always read through the whole text (for example, when we do *The Odyssey*), and sometimes we use adapted versions.
>
> I aim for three goals: understanding the basic story line, looking closely at selected passages, especially at the language, and taking a broader look at themes, literary devices, etc. If I don't start with the first goal (story line), I've lost the students. So I get that across first in any number of ways—adaptations, dramatizations, detailed group work, and so forth. Then we are free to explore the language and deeper dimensions of the work.
>
> The only drawback I have encountered when using literature to teach ESL is that it's sometimes hard to do in a class made up of different ages and maturity levels. I have had very mature seniors and very immature freshmen in the same class, so it's hard to hit it right in terms of material selection for that wide a range of interests and maturity levels. But overall, I think it's the way to go in terms of ESL instruction. I guess I consider it a type of content-based ESL instruction, the content being literature.

Greta Vollmer,
International
Studies Academy,
San Francisco
Unified Schools

2.9 *ORIGINAL VS. ADAPTED VERSIONS OF TEXT*

When using a literature-based ESL curriculum, the ESL teacher sometimes has the opportunity to use an adapted version instead of the original version of a book, play, short story, etc. What do you see as the advantages and disadvantages of using adapted versions? Original versions? You can use a chart like the one below to record your thoughts. If possible, compare your answer with that of a colleague. Can you agree on any general guidelines in making this choice?

ORIGINAL VERSION	ADAPTED VERSION
Advantages	Advantages
Disadvantages	Disadvantages

Else adds some important points about the different types of texts ESL students must be able to read successfully.

Else's Perspective AS THE TEACHER IN THE PRECEDING TEACHERS' VOICES section points out, the advantages of literature-based ESL instruction are tremendous. However, it is also important to pay attention to expository text that students are likely to encounter in content-area classes. In addition to understanding narrative text, which comes with the study of literature, students must be able to understand writing that compares and contrasts, describes, or explains cause and effect (Meyer, 1996). Besides the more abstract nature of expository writing, cultural differences may also make comprehension harder for ESL students. The organizational patterns that characterize U.S. American expository text may, in fact, be quite different from those used in the students' native languages. Thus, students need to receive instruction in this area. The ESL standards developed by TESOL (1997) acknowledge the importance of reading and writing in the content areas and suggest student performance indicators that show proficiency in that area.

Many publishers are currently including instruction in expository text reading strategies in their ESL materials; it is common to see prereading questions and reading strategies such as the use of graphic organizers in textbooks. However, teachers still need to pay special attention to it in the ESL class. Many students do not internalize these strategies on their own even if they are able to complete the activities in the textbook. As Meyer suggests, it may be more important for students to be able to identify the relationship between concepts and the text structure used than to complete the activities representing those strategies. Completing a Venn diagram at the end of a selection is useful, but to be able to identify when a comparative relationship is being presented in a text is far more useful. Knowing how to organize the information to be better able to retain the concepts is a skill that will be applicable to many situations in the future (Meyer, 1996).

WHERE DOES GRAMMAR FIT IN?

The previous sections have dealt with the reasons for using an ESL curriculum that is content-based rather than grammar-based or communicative-based (especially for students with more than beginning-level language proficiency). However, this does not mean neglecting the teaching of grammar altogether.

Through the years popularity has shifted back and forth between teaching approaches that encourage a focus on grammar and those that claim that language use alone is necessary for students to be effective language learners (Larsen-Freeman, 1991). Although it may be true that grammar instruction is not necessary to be able to communicate, Larsen-Freeman, citing Eskey (1983) and Pienemann (1984), points out that some research suggests that focusing on the use of language without any attention to grammar does not necessarily promote accuracy, particularly not in the most efficient way possible.

Because elementary and secondary schools are academic environments, ESL teachers need to be concerned with accuracy in students' speech and writing. As students continue on through the elementary and secondary grades and beyond, they are expected to produce oral and written work that is as grammatically correct as possible. ESL teachers may be able to help students accomplish this goal by addressing grammar in the ESL classroom. Depending on their learning styles, some students probably benefit more than others from grammar instruction, especially those who think analytically. These students continually ask for grammatical explanations and appear to be aided in their self-correction by their knowledge of grammar.

Teaching grammar explicitly provides the ESL teacher and the students with a common language with which to discuss errors and suggestions for improvements. For example, if a student says "I didn't ate breakfast this morning," and the class has already studied the past tense, the teacher can ask, "What is the rule for negative sentences in the past tense?" At that point the student who made the error may be able to self-correct or another student in the class can explain that when the sentence is negative, the simple (or base) form of the verb is used, in this case *eat*.

Grammar can be addressed when using a content-based curriculum by analyzing the structure used in a particular lesson and developing a lesson enforcing that particular structure. The grammar is then taught in a meaningful context that enhances learning (Stevick, 1976). For example, in teaching a unit on solving word problems in math, the ESL teacher might start out by presenting the problem below, taken from the textbook *Building Bridges Level I* (Chamot, O'Malley, and Kupper, 1992, p.34):

> Kenji takes 25 minutes to walk to school. On Saturday, he goes to the park. This takes 15 minutes less. How many minutes does it take to walk to the park?

After making sure that students understand the meaning of *How many*, the teacher can ask students to decide what the problem is asking *(How many minutes does it take to walk to the park?)*. After that, some students will find it helpful to turn the question into a statement. In this case it would be *It takes _____ minutes to walk to the park*. After sufficient practice in solving problems, the teacher can focus students' attention on the present tense and how it is used in many word problems. Students can learn how the present tense is formed, and can then practice the formation by making up their own word problems. The teacher can extend the lesson by having students practice the present tense in different contexts.

Now, Else offers the broader context surrounding the issue of teaching grammar.

HELENE'S DISCUSSION OF THE IMPORTANCE OF TEACHING grammar reflects a much larger issue that has been the focus of large-scale debates, not only in the field of ESL, but in education in general. This issue relates to holistic/functional versus a structural approach to language teaching. This debate has been most polarized in the field of reading instruction between those who support whole language and those who support phonics. Some proponents of a more holistic approach to teaching reading have sometimes taken the extreme position of advocating that no structures or specific rules of language be taught (Goodman, 1986). At the other extreme, proponents of a phonics approach claim that mastering the specific rules of the language is primary in helping children develop reading skills (Chall, 1983). Fortunately, many educators see the polarization of these two approaches as misguided, and much of the current literature examines ways in which the two approaches can be balanced with one another (Pearson, 1996).

The key to building a rich instructional environment is to provide students with ample opportunities for natural development and use of the second language as well as explicit instruction in the specific structures of language, presented in as meaningful a way as possible. Thus, the ESL teacher needs to establish a meaningful context and to extract from that context minilessons about specific aspects of language; that is, effective instruction goes from the whole to the part. Any meaningful activity where language is used functionally can provide an opportunity for direct instruction of specific aspects of language or for highlighting special features of the language. The discourse that you use as a springboard for the language minilessons can be generated from activities that students engage in—a book they have been reading or a piece of writing they have completed. The focus on skills can happen at the sentence level, at the word level, or at the sound or letter level. The following are examples of tasks at these different levels (Gordon, 1997).

Focus on sentence-level skills

- Identify examples of sentence or clause types.
- Take two or more sentences, identify how the author used sentence reduction techniques to combine two ideas.
- Take separate sentences, use punctuation clues and logical reasoning to combine the sentences.

Focus on word-level skills

- Identify parts of speech in a familiar passage, taken either from a book or something that the students wrote.
- Categorize words from a selection according to given semantic or grammatical characteristics.
- Find connections among two or more words in a list of words selected from a text, then explain rationale.

Focus on sounds and letters

- Using comprehensible words from a selection, classify the words based on spelling patterns.
- Identify all the words in a text that share a given characteristic, such as beginning sound, number of syllables, tense.

2.10 *TEACHING ENGLISH STRUCTURE*

Here is a paragraph from the novel Sign of the Beaver *(Speare, 1984), mentioned earlier as an example of literature used in some fifth-grade classrooms. After students have read and understood the content of this paragraph, how could you use these sentences to teach one or two specific features of English? (You may want to look back at the commentary above for some suggestions.) What kinds of activities might you have students do? Compare your answers with those of a colleague, if possible. Looking at your lists of activities, which would probably be the more meaningful and/or motivating for students? Why?*

Sample Paragraph from *Sign of the Beaver,* Chapter 10, p.46

They walked some distance, Matt managing to keep pace with the Indian's swift stride, determined not to let Attean know that his ankle was aching. They seemed to be following no particular trail. Finally they came out on a part of the creek that Matt had not seen before. It was shallow here, studded with rocks and pebbles, so that the water, rippling over them, made little rapids or collected in quiet pools. Here Attean stopped, broke off a sapling, and instead of making a fish pole, drew his knife from his pouch and quickly shaved a sharp point, making a spear. Then he stepped gently into the stream. Matt stood watching.

Because grammar is no longer the main focus when using a content-based curriculum, to ensure that students do receive adequate grammar instruction, teachers can include a daily grammar challenge in the lesson plan. A sentence can be written on the board that contains one or two grammatical errors. Students can copy the sentence and try to correct it. The class can then discuss the answer and the applicable grammar rule. The grammar challenge allows students to spend some time daily working on grammatical accuracy. Good sources of sentences for the grammar challenge are the editing exercises in the *Process Writing Portfolio Program* (Skidmore, 1994), as well as unedited student sentences.

2.11 REFLECTING ON PERSONAL EXPERIENCE

Think back about your own experience learning a foreign language; if you have not had such an experience, work with a colleague who has. What role do you perceive that learning grammar had in increasing language proficiency? Do you believe that explicitly teaching grammar in the ESL classroom is useful to students? Why or why not?

CHAPTER SUMMARY

Designing an ESL curriculum is a complex task with many possibilities. Factors that influence the design are the grade and proficiency levels of the students, the program model used (discussed in Chapter 3), and, at the secondary level, the availability of sheltered classes. However, to be most effective in helping students learn English as well as their school subjects, the ESL curriculum should have an academic focus where students learn the skills needed for academic success. Whenever possible, the ESL curriculum should be closely aligned with the subject areas that students are studying or will study in the future. Considering how much ESL students need to learn in the way of language and content, ESL teachers need to make wise choices regarding curriculum in order to expedite student learning as much as possible.

2.12 OUT IN THE FIELD...

Find out what type of curriculum is being used in ESL programs in your area by interviewing an elementary or secondary ESL teacher in a nearby school. Here are some possible questions:

1. Briefly describe the curriculum you use to teach your ESL students.

2. What do you believe are the positive and negative aspects of using this curriculum?

Analyze this teacher's answers in terms of your own beliefs about curriculum. Do you agree or disagree with this teacher's assessment of his or her curriculum? Why?

Suggested Readings

For more on curriculum, three useful books are: *Sheltered Content Instruction: Teaching English-Language Learners with Diverse Abilities* by J. Echeverria and A. Graves (1998); *Whole Language for Second Language Learners* by Y. S. Freeman and D. E. Freeman (1992); and *Restructuring Schools for Linguistic Diversity: Linking Decision Making to Effective Programs* by O. B. Miramontes, A. Nadeau, and N. Commins (1997).

An excellent resource for specific content-based lesson ideas is *New Ways in Content-Based Instruction* edited by D. M. Brinton and Peter Master (1997). This book is a compilation of practical lesson plans which can be adapted for use in many ESL teaching environments, contributed by a variety of teachers.

3

ESL PROGRAM MODELS IN ELEMENTARY SCHOOLS

It would be ideal if every elementary school classroom in which ESL children were enrolled had two full-time teachers—one grade-level and one ESL—who could work together to plan and carry out instruction for the benefit of all children in the class. The specific mission of the ESL teacher would be to meet the linguistic, academic, social, and cultural needs of the ESL students. Unfortunately, the reality in public schools is quite different. More often than not, ESL teachers in elementary schools have to divide their time among many students and classes within the school and sometimes even among schools (Carrasquillo and Rodriguez, 1996). ESL teachers must figure out how to effectively help ESL students succeed in school when the instructional contact time with each group of students may be only a few hours per week.

This chapter is about three program models currently in use for delivering ESL instruction to elementary ESL students: the **pullout model**, where students are "pulled out" of their grade-level classroom for ESL instruction; the **inclusion model**, where the ESL teacher goes into the grade-level classroom to teach ESL students; and the **team-teaching model**, where the grade-level and ESL teachers plan and teach lessons together as a team. Each model is explored in terms of four aspects, explained further following Else's commentary below: **curriculum coordination**—how well the ESL curriculum is coordinated with the grade-level curriculum; **social integration/stigmatization**—how the model integrates the ESL students with their grade-level peers; **scheduling issues**—how ESL instruction is scheduled into the students' school day; and **teaching facilities**—how the physical space where ESL instruction takes place may affect students as well as teachers.

> ◇ Else's Perspective ◇ THE COMMON LANGUAGE THAT MANY PEOPLE USE to refer to the type of education that ESL students receive could be misleading. ESL instruction is but one component of ESL students' schooling, yet we often talk about students being in "an ESL program." Also, in the media, "ESL programs" are often contrasted with "bilingual programs." In reality, ESL instruction is always a part of any ESL student's schooling, regardless of whether the student also receives instruction through his or her native language, and regardless of whether bilingualism is an ultimate goal for that student. In fact, students are in "an ESL pro-

gram" whether or not they receive formal ESL instruction. Needless to say, a school that does not offer its ESL students formal instruction in ESL cannot be considered as having an effective ESL program.

Helene's discussion of ESL program models is based on schools where students are offered little or no systematic native language instruction. However, the discussion is relevant to any educational system designed for students for whom English is a second language. Some of those educational systems include native language components, others do not. Some of the most successful programs that include a native language component offer instruction in two languages for English speakers and other language speakers, for the duration of school. (These programs are referred to as *dual-language programs*.) In these programs, all students learn a second language, and the issues raised in this book are relevant to them as well. Thus, it is important to realize that an "ESL program model" is one that provides instruction to ESL students in English and includes an ESL component.

For a more in-depth discussion of dual-language programs, see Cloud, Genesee, and Hamayan, (2000).

Other school environments, which Helene will not discuss at length, have also been created for ESL students. One type in particular, *newcomer schools*, is worth mentioning; it constitutes a truly different and separate program for ESL students. Newcomer schools typically serve newly arrived students. These programs, although extremely diverse in character (Short, 1999), are typically available at the middle and high school levels, and will be referred to in Chapter 4, which deals with teaching ESL at the secondary level.

See p.71 for newcomer schools.

What Aspects Should Be Considered in Examining Program Models?

Frameworks

Curriculum Coordination

As discussed in Chapter 2, several studies suggest that ESL instruction is most beneficial to ESL students when the instruction is academic in nature and coordinated with the grade-level curriculum. For each program model, the ways in which this coordination is accomplished are examined.

Social Integration/Stigmatization

The basic human need to feel a part of a cohesive group (Stevick, 1976, pp. 49–50, citing Maslow, 1970, Chapter 4) can affect students in different ways. In Chapter 2 we saw that this need to belong motivated some students to work diligently in ESL class in order to learn information that would help them participate with their native English-speaking peers in the grade-level classroom. For some students, however, the need to belong and "fit in" to their class may cause them to feel embarrassed to work with a "special teacher" at all, even if the lessons with that teacher will help them accomplish their goal of participating more fully with their grade-level peer group. Still other ESL students seem to welcome the break from the grade-level classroom routine and the opportunity to interact in a small group with their ESL peers. For them, belonging to the "ESL group" seems to be important and satisfying. Each program model is viewed in terms of these issues of belonging.

Scheduling Issues

Since ESL students in elementary schools spend most of their day in grade-level classrooms, the ESL teacher must figure out how to work within each class's schedule. This can be tricky if the ESL students are spread out among many different classes and grade levels throughout the school, requiring the ESL teacher to negotiate ESL instructional times with each grade-level teacher. The principles to guide the scheduling process will be discussed for each program model.

Teaching Facilities

Demographic changes can result in unexpected increases in enrollment for some schools. When this occurs, schools lack adequate space to accommodate all the different classes and programs. Logically, the grade-level classes must be given adequate classroom space first; then the remaining programs (ESL, special education, speech, etc.) are assigned to instructional spaces (not necessarily full-size classrooms). The issue of adequate facilities will be discussed as it relates to each program model.

3.1 *Issues of Placement*

Many elementary schools try not to assign all the ESL students from one grade to the same grade-level classroom. Instead, schools often aim for a more or less even distribution of ESL students throughout the grade level. A feeling among many grade-level teachers (and school principals) is that too many ESL students in one classroom may present instructional difficulties for that grade-level teacher.

> Think about the advantages and disadvantages of dispersing ESL students in this way with respect to (1) scheduling ESL instruction, (2) working with grade-level curriculum, and (3) language practice opportunities for ESL students. If possible, discuss your ideas in a small group. Can you come to a consensus regarding which way is better—to concentrate ESL students in one or two classes per grade level, or to have equal distribution among all classes?

What Are the Characteristics of Three Program Models— Pullout, Inclusion, and Team-Teaching—in Use Today?

Pullout Model

Helene Becker

> When I first taught ESL to elementary school children in 1982, I knew of only one way to proceed. I would take the ESL children out of their regular classrooms and bring them to my ESL classroom for English lessons for a half hour to an hour per day. I would form small groups, usually putting together children from the same grade and/or with the same English proficiency level. As mentioned in Chapter 2, I used a separate ESL curriculum based on grammar and vocabulary, not necessarily the grammar and vocabulary associated with the students' grade-level lessons. Because I used my own ESL curriculum, I did not have much need to communicate with the grade-level teachers.

Separating the two learning environments in this way tends to make both students and grade-level teachers assume that the short period of ESL pullout instruction is the learning for the day, and that the ESL student is just marking time in the grade-level classroom (Cummins, 1994). This type of traditional ESL pullout instruction, with little direct connection to the grade-level program, has been shown to be the least effective way to help ESL students achieve long-range success in school (Cummins, 1994; Thomas and Collier, 1995). In spite of this, the pullout model remains prevalent, probably because it is financially the least costly, especially if ESL students are gathered together from several classes so that one ESL teacher can teach a relatively large group of students (Carrasquillo and Rodriguez, 1996). The pullout model can be used effectively, however, if certain guiding principles are followed, as explained below.

Curriculum Coordination

When using a pullout model, coordination of the grade-level and ESL curricula can be accomplished by establishing ongoing communication between the ESL teacher and each grade-level teacher. This communication can come about in several ways. Regular meeting times can be set up; a communication form can be used; teachers can touch base every morning or afternoon in the office, teachers' lounge, or wherever teachers may congregate; or a combination of these approaches can be used. If the ESL teacher is working on a long-term unit with the ESL students, the teachers may need to communicate only periodically.

Depending on the number of grade-level teachers with whom the ESL teacher needs to make contact, communication with grade-level teachers can be unwieldy. Here is the situation I encountered recently when I taught ESL at Kanoelani Elementary School in Waipahu, Hawaii.

Helene Becker

> At Kanoelani there were about 50 ESL students in a school of approximately 950 students, making the ESL population a little more than five percent of the student body. The ESL students ranged in proficiency level from basic beginning to advanced, and of the 36 classes in the school from grades K–6, 24 of them (two-thirds) included ESL students. (Some of these classes had only one ESL student, while others had up to six.) There were two half-time ESL teachers (the equivalent of one full-time teacher), myself and my colleague.

> Since 24 classes in the school included ESL students, each of us had 12 teachers with whom to coordinate instruction. With about half of my 12 classes I used a pullout model of instruction, which meant that I needed to coordinate pullout instruction with six grade-level teachers. Bearing in mind that I taught only half-time, a full-time ESL teacher in my situation would have been coordinating pullout instruction with approximately 12 grade-level teachers.

> The grade-level teachers and I managed to communicate as best as we could, mostly by written communication via our school mailboxes, and in person when necessary. However, I found that the system functioned best when I was working with the ESL students on an ongoing unit or project, or when I had complete responsibility

for a certain subject, thus minimizing the need to communicate often. For example, one year there were several ESL students in grades 5 and 6 who, because of gaps in their education, had mastered math skills only up to grade 3. Their grade-level teachers felt that the students were missing too much knowledge to be able to understand their respective grade-level math lessons. The grade-level teachers and I decided that I would use the pullout model so that I could instruct the ESL students daily in math at their level and try to catch them up to their grade-level peers as quickly as possible. After our initial coordination meeting, since I essentially became the students' math teacher, the two grade-level teachers and I needed to communicate only a few times per quarter to discuss progress and report card grades. The pullout model allowed me to address the particular content and language needs of these ESL students.

As illustrated in the above example, pullout instruction can be effective in addressing the content needs (in this case, math) of ESL students by having the ESL teacher take responsibility for teaching a specific subject. It can also be used effectively to provide ESL students with background knowledge for an upcoming lesson in the grade-level classroom. Here is how a short note from a grade-level teacher (at the school described above) allowed me to help students acquire background knowledge for an upcoming grade-level social studies lesson.

See Chapter 2 for a discussion of background knowledge.

Helene Becker

The note I received from one of the fifth-grade teachers simply stated, "In social studies, we're starting a unit on explorers." Previously, the teacher and I had agreed that social studies was a good subject for me to work on with the ESL students since they had a difficult time understanding the information from the new, interesting (but challenging) social studies textbook.

The next time I saw my group of intermediate ESL students from her class I asked them what they already knew about the explorers. A few of them had heard of Columbus, but that was about the extent of their familiarity with the subject. It quickly became apparent that several of them did not know the names and locations of the European countries that played major roles during the time of the explorers. We worked on locating these countries on a world map and talked about possible routes the explorers might have taken on their explorations. We also learned the names of some of the explorers so that when the ESL students heard the names in a class discussion or saw them written in the textbook, they would already be familiar with them. Then, to challenge the students cognitively, I asked them to think of some reasons the explorers might have wanted to venture out to find new lands. Doing this kind of preview activity during pullout instruction provided an effective means for me to help students acquire background knowledge so that they would be better prepared to participate along with their peers in their grade-level classroom.

Arrange to observe a "mainstream" elementary-school lesson in one of the core academic subjects (math, science, social studies, or language arts). If you were using a pullout model of ESL instruction, how would you prepare your ESL students for the academic lesson you observed? What topics would you cover? How would you present the information?

The pullout model can also be used to teach a review lesson, where the ESL teacher can go over the classroom content in order to clear up problems with language and concepts (Snow, Met, and Genesee, 1992). Communication with grade-level teachers can be fairly impromptu if the content does not require extensive preparation on the part of the ESL teacher. For example, if ESL students are having difficulty understanding the science lessons and textbook, the grade-level teacher can send a note along with the ESL students to tell the ESL teacher which pages to review. If the ESL teacher keeps a copy of the science book in the ESL classroom and stays ahead of the students, he or she will already be familiar with the unit and can go over those pages with the students, clearing up any difficulties.

Snow, Met, and Genesee (1992), citing Hawkins (1988), describe an interesting example of how the ESL teacher can use ESL pullout instruction to review grade-level curriculum even if communication between the teachers is cursory:

> She [the ESL teacher] knew that the students were just starting a unit on the California mission system but did not know the specifics of the content to be covered. Each day in the ESL class, she asked the students to tell her about what they had learned in social studies. Different students volunteered answers. At times, there was confusion about certain facts, but usually this was resolved with the teacher and students arriving at a common understanding of the facts or events.
>
> After the question and answer session, the students practiced working with the information in different ways, such as writing short summaries or describing the chronology of events to their partners. Occasionally, however, the class could not reach an agreement about the details or events described in the social studies lesson. In these cases, the ESL class collectively developed a list of questions, wrote the questions down in their notebooks, and sought clarification of the information during the next social studies class. The following day [during ESL class], the ESL students used the notes they had taken in the social studies class and discussed the information in question (Snow, Met, and Genessee, pp.34–35).

This ESL teacher was able to use the pullout model effectively to reinforce the grade-level lesson and to engage ESL students in activities with academic focus such as participating in academic discussions and developing academic vocabulary. Students were also using learning strategies such as summarizing, note-taking, cooperating, and questioning for clarification.

Using the Native Language

In using a pullout model, if the ESL teacher knows the native language(s) of the ESL students in a particular group, the native language can be used to help students learn grade-level content. For example, as a preview to a lesson in which the ESL students will participate in their grade-level classroom, the ESL teacher could explain essential lesson concepts and facts in the native language before students try to understand the more detailed version in English. In this way they are already familiar with the essential points and may find it easier to follow those points in English. In fact, during their grade-level lesson in English, they may be able to concentrate on learning the language associated with those essential points along with the points themselves.

Working with Beginning-Level Students

See Chapter 8 for a discussion on helping grade-level teachers develop effective instructional practices for ESL students.

The pullout model can also be effective in working with ESL students at the beginning levels of English proficiency. In the pullout setting, the ESL teacher can help students acquire survival oral proficiency and initial reading and writing skills. At this early stage in the students' English language development, even though it may not be possible to coordinate the ESL instruction with the grade-level curriculum, the ESL teacher still needs to communicate with the grade-level teacher; the ESL teacher can be a valuable resource for the grade-level teacher regarding how to work with ESL beginners in the grade-level classroom setting and how to help them adjust to their new culture.

Social Integration/Stigmatization

In using a pullout model, the ESL teacher needs to be aware that some students may feel stigmatized by being separated from their class for "extra help." As suggested by Krashen (1981 and 1982), affective variables such as attitudes and feelings can affect success in language acquisition. That is, a student's attitude can have a strong effect on his or her openness and willingness to learn. A student who is not open to learning will have a strong "affective filter" that can block out the instruction.

From my own experience, and that of many colleagues, it seems that a negative reaction to learning in an elementary school pullout situation is more common in older children (grades 4–6) because children at that age (and older) tend to be concerned about appearing "different" in front of their classmates. In contrast, in the lower elementary grades, some students jump up with excitement to greet the ESL teacher at the door. This is not to say, however, that all children in grade 4 and above resist ESL pullout instruction, or that all children in grade 3 and below welcome it. Rather, the ESL teacher needs to be aware of the possibility of negative feelings (at any age) toward being singled out and isolated from one's peer group, and take steps to mitigate the problem if it arises.

Negative or disruptive student behavior may indicate that students are indeed angry, embarrassed, or in some way uncomfortable about participating in ESL pullout instruction. If that is the case, the ESL teacher may want to encourage students to discuss their negative feelings, and perhaps make changes to accommodate student needs. For example, it may be that students are uncomfortable about having the ESL teacher appear at their classroom door to call them to ESL class; perhaps the students can go to the ESL teacher's room on their own. This is a relatively simple change that may alter student attitudes. In addition, through discussion and experience, if students become aware that their ESL class is helping them succeed in their grade-level class, they may come to welcome their pullout instruction.

Else now addresses the broader issues surrounding negative attitudes toward ESL instruction.

THE NEGATIVE FEELINGS THAT HELENE DESCRIBES are often due to the way the larger society perceives bilingualism and the existing attitudes toward people who are from linguistically diverse backgrounds. In the United States, bilingualism is seen as an aberration. We forget that bilingualism is the norm in the rest of the world, and that the majority of the world is bilingual (Crawford, 1992). Because the majority of U.S. Americans, especially those who hold positions of power, are monolingual, speaking two languages is seen as the exception rather than the rule. Additionally, since the majority of bilingual people in the United States come from minority groups with low prestige and socioeconomic status, bilingualism is not highly regarded or valued by the mainstream population. Thus, the education of ESL students is typically seen as a compensatory program rather than enrichment. As many researchers have pointed out (Cloud, Genesee, and Hamayan, 2000; Collier, 1995), perceiving a program as enrichment is a key element in creating an effective instructional program for language-minority students and in helping them develop proficiency in a second language.

Thus, it is essential that the whole school begin to see the presence of ESL students as a potential for enrichment for all students. ESL students must be valued for the rich funds of knowledge they bring to the school milieu and the diverse ways of doing things and communicating that monolingual native English-speaking students may not be familiar with (Moll, 1995). When schools equalize the status of all language backgrounds and value the cultures that all students bring with them to the school, they take a significant step toward creating an effective learning environment for all students. Thus, a question that must be discussed within each school is how to change the whole school ethos so that students who are developing proficiency in two languages are valued, and bilingualism is seen as an asset for all students rather than a burden.

A Strong Bond

In certain cases, especially with beginning-level students, when employing a pullout model, a strong relationship can develop between the ESL students and the ESL teacher. In the grade-level classroom, a newly arrived student who speaks little English may feel isolated and frustrated especially if no one else in the class speaks the student's native language. The student may have left behind close family members and friends in the native country and may be experiencing culture shock. Since the grade-level teacher has a large group of students to teach and may not be able to give adequate individual attention to an ESL student, the ESL student may feel lost at times. Since the ESL teacher often instructs a relatively small number of students at one time, and may be particularly sensitive to the needs of ESL students, the close, nurturing relationship that can develop in a pullout ESL class may help lessen the anxiety of newly arrived students and may hasten their adjustment to school and to the new culture. As stated earlier, this sense of security and harmony in the ESL learning environment can have a positive influence on the language acquisition process (Krashen, 1981, 1982 and Stevick, 1998). I recall a situation in which I found out years later how significant this special bond could be.

Helene Becker

During my second year as an elementary ESL teacher in the West Hartford Public Schools, an ESL student arrived from French-speaking Canada. Marie was the only fifth-grade beginning-level ESL student at that time, so I saw her individually for about 45 minutes daily. After that year, I was on leave teaching in Italy, and did not see Marie again until she was a high school student. She attended the high school where I had resumed teaching ESL in the district, and although she no longer needed ESL instruction, she would stop by my classroom to chat. Several years later, the day before she graduated, she handed me a card in which she expressed gratitude for the help I had given her when she first arrived in the United States. She told me how much she valued the special relationship we developed when she came here as a fifth-grader:

> You were the only person I could talk to, and when I found out you were going to Italy, I cried. It meant so much to me to have someone in the school who understood how hard it was for me and who could explain things that I didn't understand.

In my experience, this special bond with ESL students develops readily in a pullout situation (although it certainly can be as strong when teaching through another program model). The pullout model may provide some ESL students with a haven where they feel safe and better understood. For students such as Marie, this haven and special bond with the ESL teacher can be important for their adjustment to a new culture.

Else discusses another advantage of the pullout model.

Else's Perspective

ANOTHER SIGNIFICANT ADVANTAGE that ESL teachers have in a pullout model is the long-term relationship that they are able to develop with their ESL students. This advantage has not been mentioned much in the literature, probably because it is just being recognized in the U.S. American elementary-level educational system, which is based on an annual shift in teachers. Each year, as students advance grade levels, they receive their instruction from a different grade-level teacher; this prevents these teachers from keeping track of students over a period of years. In contrast, ESL teachers are likely to see the same students over a period of two to three years. Schools in other countries, such as Italy and Denmark, are set up in such a way that all teachers follow their students for at least two or three years. Some schools in the United States are beginning to experiment with this model, and many are finding it very effective (Atwell, 1987).

Because of this instructional continuity with a pullout model, the ESL teacher often holds key developmental information about students that others in the school do not have. ESL teachers should play a key role in placement and evaluation decisions; they are the ones who can determine if the instruction offered to a student is developmentally appropriate, and they are the ones who can informally assess how students are progressing over the years. As more and more schools move toward a more comprehensive assessment model instead of the traditional norm-referenced testing model, teachers' evaluations of student performance should begin to play a more central role in the placement and promotion of students (Genesee and Upshur, 1996; Hamayan, 1995).

For a discussion of comprehensive assessment models, see Chapter 5, pp. 122–126.

Scheduling Issues

When ESL students are pulled out of their grade-level classroom for ESL instruction, obviously, they are missing some grade-level instruction. Therefore, it makes sense to schedule ESL pullout instruction only during a block of time when one of the following conditions is met: The ESL students cannot benefit significantly from the concurrent instruction in the grade-level classroom; the concurrent grade-level activity is enhanced for the ESL students if done separately with the ESL teacher; the activity in the grade-level classroom can be conveniently made up by the ESL students at another time. If none of these three conditions is met, ESL students should not be removed from their grade-level classroom during that block of time, for although they may benefit from their ESL instruction, they will lose out on other instruction. Examples of these three conditions are discussed below.

Condition 1: Students Cannot Benefit Significantly from the Grade-Level Instruction.

You may recall an earlier example where the benefits of pullout instruction were discussed for several fifth- and sixth-grade students whose math level was considerably below their grade level. I worked with them in a pullout situation so that I could help them fill in the gaps in their math knowledge. I scheduled their ESL instructional time at the same time that their respective grade-level classes were having their math lessons; since the ESL students could not benefit from the grade-level math lessons, it was an appropriate time period for their ESL pullout math instruction.

Condition 2: Instruction Is Enhanced if Done with the ESL Teacher.

Some activities in the grade-level classroom are beneficial to ESL students but can be enhanced with the ESL teacher in a pullout setting. For example, if students have a regular time slot in their day where they choose and read books on their own, the experience can be enhanced by doing the activity in the ESL classroom.

In the smaller group setting, the ESL students can take turns reading their books to the ESL teacher or to each other, and can use the books as springboards for discussion and other activities. For ESL students, this kind of active reading can improve their oral, reading, and cognitive skills, and increase their vocabulary.

Condition 3: The Grade-Level Activity Can Be Conveniently Made Up.

Some classes have blocks of time where students have an opportunity to do catch-up work, or to do a quiet activity on their own. If no other time can be found for ESL instruction, this "free time" can be used, as long as the ESL students can manage to do their catch-up work at another time or at home.

Grade-Level Instruction Not to Be Missed

Blocks of time that should *not* be used for ESL pullout instruction are those instructional periods during which ESL students can participate meaningfully. The benefit from participation does not necessarily have to be linguistic; the activity could be beneficial in affective ways, such as promoting a sense of belonging to their grade-level peer group, or promoting a sense of accomplishment and self-esteem. These positive feelings can contribute to students' acclimation to school and to future academic success (Scarcella, 1990).

ESL students at any language proficiency level can usually participate meaningfully in physical education, art, and music classes, because the lessons tend to be context-embedded (Chamot and O'Malley, 1987) and the activities are usually hands-on. In physical education class, for example, even if ESL students do not understand all the instructions, they can watch first and then join in. They are exposed to lots of natural language in a relaxed and fun context, which can promote language acquisition (Stevick, 1998, Chapter 10, explaining assertions of Lozanov). In music class ESL students can hum along or sing the words to a song even if they have not yet fully mastered the meaning of the words. At the very least, they have the opportunity to hear and repeat the sounds and rhythm of the English language. In art class, ESL students can often participate by seeing a sample of a finished product and watching their classmates proceed. In fact, I have seen many talented beginning-level ESL students do exceptionally well in art, and even assist their native English-speaking peers with projects. Since ESL students can experience success in these subject areas as well as a sense of belonging to their native English-speaking peer group, they should not be deprived of participation. By similar reasoning, they should not be deprived of their recess break; it is during this "free time" that ESL students can develop friendships and use language for true communication.

3.3 *NEGOTIATING WITH GRADE-LEVEL TEACHERS*

Imagine the following situation: You are meeting with a grade-level teacher in order to arrange ESL pullout instructional time for the four ESL students in her class. She wants you to take them during their art time; she does not want them to miss any of the core academic subjects, and she feels that art is not a priority. You believe it would be better to take them during their language arts time so that you can work on language arts at the students' own level. If you have a colleague available, role-play this discussion between the ESL teacher and the grade-level teacher. If not, write down the reasons you would offer the grade-level teacher for pulling out the ESL students during language arts time rather than during art time.

In addition to meaningful participation with grade-level peers in hands-on subjects such as physical education, art, and music, many ESL students—especially those above the beginning level—can participate meaningfully, at least to some degree, during core academic instruction. The breadth and depth of this participation depends, in large part, on the grade-level teacher's use of instructional strategies that are effective in helping ESL students understand content (Cummins, 1994). For example, a grade-level teacher who regularly uses maps, pictures, charts, diagrams, and other visual aids to make content comprehensible promotes meaningful participation on the part of ESL students in the class. The ESL teacher can assist grade-level teachers in this effort by listening to their questions and concerns and sharing teaching strategies. If, because of the expertise of the grade-level teacher (and suggestions from the ESL teacher), the ESL students are participating meaningfully in lessons of a particular content area in their grade-level classroom, they should not be pulled out at that time for ESL instruction. The ESL teacher should attempt to find another time for ESL instruction, or offer to provide ESL assistance in the grade-level classroom using one of the other program models described in this chapter.

See Chapter 8 for specific suggestions for assisting grade-level teachers.

See Appendix C for strategies to share with grade-level teachers.

Scheduling Flexibility

Scheduling ESL instruction does not always work out neatly so that the ESL teacher is able to pull students out of their grade-level class for ESL instruction at the perfect time for the ESL student, grade-level teacher, and ESL teacher. For instance, several students in different classes and grades may all need to have their ESL instruction in the same time slot. The ESL teacher needs to look at many variables together and have some alternatives in mind when negotiating with each grade-level teacher. The ESL teacher also needs to be flexible so that the ESL schedule is not immutable. There may be times when a special class or school event conflicts with ESL time. In these cases, the ESL teacher needs to defer to these special events so that ESL students are not deprived of these experiences with their peers. The ESL teacher can be helpful during special activities by offering to assist the grade-level teacher and/or students as needed.

Else's Perspective

THE POINT THAT HELENE MAKES IN THIS SECTION is very important: what the students are pulled *from* is just as crucial as what they are pulled *to*. The best ESL teacher and the best ESL teaching strategies cannot make up for the core curriculum that students forfeit and for which they will be held accountable. Students in third grade or higher, who have very limited proficiency in English and do not receive any instruction through their native language, are most vulnerable to this loss of access to the core curriculum. Thus, one of the biggest difficulties of the pullout model, from the student's perspective, is that the student is always being deprived of something else that is just as crucial as learning English: learning the curriculum. As Helene states, she has tried to choose the least of all evils, that is, the academic subject areas that the students are least likely to benefit from if they remained in the grade-level classroom.

Despite ESL teachers' best efforts, what the students are pulled to is not always most effective in promoting critical learning. Even if the ESL teacher has a homogeneous group of students, it is a challenge to teach abstract concepts through a language that students simply do not understand. To use the ESL standards as a framework (TESOL, 1997; see Chapter 2 for a description), beginning-level ESL students need to learn to use English for everyday social interactions, and to develop the language for classroom survival, before they are able to learn new concepts through that language.

The reason that pullout is not the most effective program to teach ESL students is that these students come to school with a set of goals that is somewhat more extensive than their English-speaking peers. In addition to the mastery of the grade-level curriculum, these students must develop a high enough level of proficiency in the language of instruction to be able to learn new concepts through that language. This characteristic of beginning-level ESL students, especially those beyond second grade, is ignored in most schools. Very few schools give these students the additional resources they need to fulfill the requirements of school. A few schools have begun to offer regularly scheduled and budgeted after-school instruction and summer school for students who are significantly lower in academic achievement. If we were to develop programs purely from the students' perspective, we would have add-on, rather than pullout, programs.

Teaching Facilities

Since the most desirable and well-equipped classrooms are usually assigned to full-size grade-level classes, ESL teachers often have to contend with a less than adequate teaching environment. In schools without sufficient classroom space to accommodate the various educational programs, the ESL teacher may have to do pullout instruction in a closet, bookroom, cafeteria, office, hallway, or other non-classroom area, which can be too small, noisy, stuffy, hot, or cold. The space may also lack a chalkboard or suitable desks and chairs. These deficiencies can have a negative effect on the quality of instruction and on the attitude of the students.

State-of-the-art ESL classrooms—complete with computers, an abundance of resources and supplies, and brand-new furniture—do exist. However, from talking to numerous ESL colleagues through the years, it seems that these situations are the exceptions rather than the rule. Here is a description of an instructional area in which I once taught.

Helene Becker

A few years ago in Hawaii, my ESL "classroom" was a small office that I shared with the other ESL teacher and the physical education teacher. Even though we all tried our best to keep our small room neat and uncluttered, it was bursting with desks, file cabinets, bookshelves, tables, chairs, teaching materials, and sports equipment. The office was located inside the students' cafeteria which, other than lunchtime, was used as a music classroom. Depending on the time of day, I heard children either talking and laughing during lunch or playing musical instruments and singing during music class. My ESL "classroom" was not an ideal language learning environment! Therefore, when I conducted pullout instruction, I usually opted to teach in the corridor outside the children's classroom rather than in my "classroom." When it was time for annual testing, I had to search around the school for a quiet, suitable space. Fortunately, the principal and vice principal were accommodating; each vacated her own office on more than one occasion so that I could test my students in a quiet environment.

The following year my ESL colleague and I were moved to a large, bright, newly-built portable classroom that we shared with two speech teachers. We divided the space so that we could all teach comfortably and without much distraction. The ESL children loved coming to the new, bright classroom—it made them feel special.

In my situation there was a sincere effort on the part of the administration to accommodate the ESL program (for example, during testing periods) and to find a more suitable space as soon as one became available. If the facilities assigned to the ESL program are considerably inadequate, the ESL teacher needs to seek alternatives so that the ESL students do not suffer. If no solution is found, one of the other program models described in this section should be considered.

THE SITUATION THAT HELENE DESCRIBES is unfortunately quite common for ESL teachers. However, it is simply not acceptable. According to the TESOL access standards (TESOL, 1997), students should have access to (1) an environment that is safe, attractive, and free of prejudice, (2) computers, computer classes, and other technologically advanced instructional assistance, (3) a positive learning environment, and (4) full delivery of services. These are simply not possible when students are placed in closets or open spaces where interruptions are frequent and the noise level is too high.

3.4 *PULLOUT MODEL: SUMMARY*

As shown in this section, the pullout model can be used effectively to help ESL students learn both language and academic content. However, there are certain drawbacks and difficulties. The teacher below talks about her experience—both positive and negative—with the pullout model of instruction. Use her story as a springboard for discussion with a colleague; then write a brief statement under each category in the chart below, summarizing your ideas about the pullout model.

	The pullout model can be used effectively if...
Curriculum coordination	
Social integration/ stigmatization	
Scheduling issues	
Teaching facilities	

Jean Hill, Whiting Lane Elementary School, West Hartford, Connecticut

ESL services at my school are all pullout during the time period that the mainstream class is doing reading and language arts. With the intermediate and advanced students I work on activities that help support classroom curriculum. I conference with the classroom teacher in order to see what they are doing. Most of the time I work with the students on the writing process, reading in content areas, and social studies units. For example, I just worked with the third-graders on the West Indies.

I see the beginners in grades three, four, and five twice a day. In the morning we do reading—sometimes I read stories to them and sometimes we use phonics-type readers as a springboard for working on sounds and spelling. In the afternoon we do language learning through hands-on projects such as planting tulip bulbs, cooking brownies, etc., or we use an ESL textbook to work on writing.

I like the pullout program because the students really get a chance to speak and interact. I have a big classroom equipped with four computers, all kinds of visual aids, and a rug space for the little ones to sit on. I also have volunteers who come in a few times a week to work with students on specific skill areas. I can work on extended projects and play noisy games with them because I have my own classroom.

The pullout program model has its drawbacks. I don't like the fact that the students are isolated from their classmates. Some seem OK about it, but I don't think all of the older ones like going to a "special" teacher. It's difficult to communicate with the classroom teachers—sometimes days will go by before we can meet. They are all so busy. Even if we do meet, they sometimes change what they were going to do on short notice, so I think I'm supporting classroom curriculum when in fact I'm doing something totally different with the kids. But I guess that's OK; they're still learning.

Inclusion Model (also called pull-in or push-in model)

With an inclusion model, ESL students are instructed by the ESL teacher right in their own grade-level classroom. Because of this, concerns associated with the traditional pullout model—a lack of coordination between the ESL and grade-level curricula, and the isolation of ESL students from their grade-level peers—

can be avoided. In addition, since the students are not being taken away from their grade-level classroom to learn English, the grade-level teacher may take more ownership of the ESL students (Torres, 1994) and realize that the education of ESL students is a shared responsibility. This may eliminate the tendency for some grade-level teachers to have the ESL students merely mark time in the grade-level classroom until the next pullout ESL lesson is scheduled.

Having the ESL teacher work in the grade-level classrooms, however, does not automatically mean effective ESL instruction. As with the pullout model, the ESL teacher needs to follow certain guidelines in order to provide ESL students with the assistance they need to learn language and to succeed in school.

Curriculum Coordination

As with any program model in an elementary school, when using an inclusion model, effective instruction requires coordinating the ESL and grade-level curricula so that ESL students are learning their content subjects along with learning language. In this model, since the ESL teacher works in the grade-level classroom and can converse with the grade-level teacher before beginning the ESL instruction, communication regarding curriculum can be clear, detailed, and up-to-date. The ESL teacher, therefore, is able to zero in on the immediate needs of the ESL students.

The ESL teacher can help ESL students gain access to the grade-level curriculum in similar ways as with a pullout model, either in a separate area of the classroom or while the ESL students remain at their seats (depending on the activity). Specifically, the ESL teacher can provide and add to students' background knowledge in preparation for a grade-level lesson, reteach or review a topic with which the students had difficulty, or teach a modified form of a grade-level lesson or unit. However, since the ESL teacher is present in the grade-level classroom instead of being isolated in a separate classroom, an inclusion model allows for last-minute changes so that the ESL students' immediate needs can be addressed. Here is an example of how this last-minute communication can help ESL students be successful in their grade-level classroom. This ESL teacher in Hawaii explains how she retaught a math lesson.

> The second-grade teacher and I decided to use an inclusion model for the two ESL students in her class. When I entered the room, she would let me know in which areas the students needed assistance that day. Our goal was to have the students continue to increase their language base while keeping up with the second-grade work.

> The two students, Princess and Glory, were born in Hawaii but spoke little English when they entered school as kindergartners (they spoke Filipino languages—Ilokano and Visayan, respectively). By the beginning of second grade both had fairly good oral communication skills, but Princess was having a difficult time with reading, writing, and math. Glory had occasional difficulties but did quite well, in general.

> Depending on their needs on any given day, I would work either with the two girls together (at Princess's desk area), or with Princess alone. When I came to the classroom at the scheduled time (three times per week for a half hour each time), the grade-level

Joy Ishihara, Kanoelani Elementary School, Waipahu, Hawaii

teacher would have instructions ready for me. During their morning language arts and math time, one or both of the girls would usually have difficulty with some aspect of the lessons or could not correctly complete an assignment. Most of the time, Princess had difficulty with math concepts; she needed reteaching of the concepts and lots of guided practice. I remember one particular day, for example, when the class had just learned the monetary value of coins—penny, nickel, dime, and quarter—and how to add different coins together. Princess could pretty much remember the names of the coins but not their values, and had guessed at the answers on her practice worksheet (most of the answers were incorrect). Using play money, for the entire half hour I worked with Princess (Glory didn't need help on this topic) to help her learn monetary values and add combinations of coins together. By the end of the session she was able to correct most of the work on her worksheet. I was able to use the ESL time to reinforce math vocabulary (penny, nickel, etc.) and academic concepts (monetary value of coins, addition) directly related to her success in the second-grade classroom.

We continued using this model during the entire year and saw good progress with both students. Princess received the help she needed so that she could keep up with her grade-level work, and Glory received help on an "as needed" basis. At the end of the third quarter marking period, Glory received an award for academic achievement; at the end of the last quarter, Princess received an award for "most improved" in the class.

I decided to find out how the grade-level teacher in the above situation felt about the effectiveness of using an inclusion model with her ESL students. She commented:

The ESL instruction complemented what I was trying to accomplish in the classroom. When one or both of the children were falling behind, the ESL teacher was able to provide the extra assistance the child needed to keep up with the class. With a classroomful of active second-graders, I would have had difficulty providing this help on a regular basis.

I liked the fact that the program was so flexible. I knew I could decide that day where the help was needed and not have to worry that I was interrupting a preconceived ESL lesson plan.

3.5 *CIRCUMSTANCES AFFECTING SUCCESS*

The inclusion model allows the ESL and grade-level teachers to coordinate curriculum quite easily. But the model does not always allow for lesson preparation on the part of the ESL teacher. In the second-grade classroom described above, preparation on the part of the ESL teacher did not seem necessary; however, in other circumstances, it might be. Think about how the lack of time to prepare might be a problem in certain situations such as the ones described below. Discuss with a colleague (or, if you are working alone, jot down some ideas) how each of these circumstances might make it difficult or impossible to use an inclusion model in the way it was used in the second-grade classroom described above:

- The ESL group is large, containing seven or eight students.
- The class is upper-elementary fifth or sixth grade.
- The grade-level teacher tends to forget when ESL instruction is scheduled and often seems surprised when the ESL teacher appears at the classroom door.

Else's Perspective

AS HELENE MENTIONS, depending on how it is executed, the inclusion or push-in model of ESL instruction, may not be completely free of the disadvantages of the pullout model. The students are often pulled aside so that the ESL teacher can work with them separately, which means they are still missing some of the instruction being delivered by the grade-level classroom teacher. The inclusion model used in this way has diminished negative effects to the extent that ESL students are less likely to be singled out as being in need of special instruction and they are more likely to focus on the same activities as the rest of the class.

As far as the effectiveness of the inclusion model is concerned, it is still the perception of this "special" instruction that makes a difference. If bilingualism is not seen as an asset within the school or larger community, the special attention paid to ESL students is likely to be seen as compensatory. If the ESL students are not perceived as a source of enrichment to the rest of the school by virtue of their additional language and culture, their perceived status will inhibit learning. As advocates of language-minority students, it is essential that we attempt to change this perception among our colleagues, the administrators, and even the larger community in which the school resides. Ideas and suggestions for treating ESL students' bilingualism as a valuable— and valued—asset are described in Cloud, Genesee, and Hamayan (2000).

The problem of singling out ESL students can be resolved by using the ESL teacher as a resource for all students rather than only for ESL students. In the best inclusion classrooms I have observed, the ESL teacher works primarily with the ESL students but also assists any student who needs help. This not only keeps the ESL students from being singled out, it also raises the status of the ESL teacher and defines her or him as a teacher for all; by doing so, in turn, this raises the status of the ESL students who are associated with that teacher. This may take away somewhat from the attention that ESL students need, but any academic shortfall is more than compensated for by the social benefits.

What do you think about the ESL teacher assisting non-ESL students? See Investigation 3.7, p. 60.

Assisting ESL Students During a Lesson

In addition to working with ESL students in the ways already mentioned, when using an inclusion model, the ESL teacher can assist ESL students by helping them participate in a grade-level lesson as it is occurring. In this way, ESL students do not miss any of their grade-level instruction; the ESL teacher is there to help make the instruction more comprehensible.

The ESL teacher can assist ESL students during a grade-level lesson in a variety of ways:

- Working in a small group setting with the ESL students sitting together, the ESL teacher can help them complete the same task that the rest of the class is completing.
- Circulating among the ESL students while they are working individually at their seats, the ESL teacher can help them complete the same task that the rest of the class is completing.
- Working separately with the ESL students, the ESL teacher can modify the grade-level lesson or assignment so that it is more suitable for the ESL students. For example, if the grade-level assignment is for students to read and discuss a three-page chapter in a social studies textbook, and then write a three-paragraph summary, the ESL teacher can help the ESL students read just two pages of the textbook (a more manageable assignment). Then, the ESL teacher can orally summarize for the students the information in the remaining page. The students can write a shorter summary, and if they have not yet acquired enough English to write it on their own, they can write the summary together as a group effort. If this lesson is part of an ongoing unit, the ESL teacher can attempt to locate alternative reading material for future sessions so that the ESL students are able to glean the same information as the rest of the class, but from reading material at their current reading level.
- Working in a small group setting with the ESL students sitting together, the ESL teacher can help ESL students understand a lesson presentation by displaying keywords, sketching pictures or symbols, pointing to pictures or words in the textbook, or quietly saying simplified keywords for the students. The ESL teacher can even do these activities in front of the room so that all students (not just the ESL students) can benefit from the ESL instruction. If the ESL teacher knows the native language of the ESL students, he or she can translate some of the keywords of the lesson into the native language in order to aid comprehension.

When the ESL teacher assists the ESL students with the grade-level lesson in these ways, the ESL students can immediately see how the ESL teacher is helping them be successful with their academic work. The grade-level and ESL teachers also see immediate results as the ESL students are able to participate in doing their academic work.

Else adds another perspective regarding ESL instruction with the inclusion model.

Else's Perspective
ANOTHER WAY FOR THE ESL TEACHER TO WORK in an inclusion model classroom is to deliver some of the instruction herself or himself to the entire class. If this is done on an extensive basis, it may be referred to as the team-teaching model that Helene describes in the following section. However, there is a place for some short-term team-teaching even in a push-in or inclusion model where the ESL teacher is clearly seen as someone who comes in occasionally to help a few students. There are advantages to having the ESL teacher participate in the workings of the entire class once in a while rather than simply working with a small number of ESL students all the time. In the section on team-teaching later in this chapter, Helene discusses the major advan-

tages, including the fact that the grade-level classroom teacher can see teaching strategies modeled by the ESL teacher that are especially appropriate for ESL students. When the ESL teacher uses sheltered instruction techniques, the grade-level classroom teacher can not only see how this is done, but also that these ESL strategies are beneficial for the entire class, not just the ESL students.

Another advantage relates to the issues of status that I discussed in an earlier commentary. When the ESL teacher helps only the ESL students, that teacher is perceived as someone who can only assist small groups of students, and at best, the few students who are in need of compensation. However, when the ESL teacher directs the whole class, that teacher's status changes to someone who can teach everyone. The perception by students that the ESL teacher can teach the important parts of a lesson to all students will raise his or her status in the eyes of the entire school population. By association, the status of the ESL students will change, too.

Familiarity with the Grade-Level Environment

Besides being able to coordinate the ESL curriculum closely with the grade-level curriculum, when using an inclusion model, the ESL teacher has the opportunity to experience firsthand the academic demands of that particular grade level. This allows the ESL teacher to gear the ESL instruction appropriately to help students meet those demands. In addition, being in the grade-level classroom gives the ESL teacher firsthand knowledge of the learning environment in a particular classroom. The ESL teacher can use that knowledge to help the grade-level teacher make the grade-level classroom "ESL-friendly." For example, the ESL teacher can reinforce strategies that are helpful to ESL students. He or she could say, "That weather chart with pictures is really good for the ESL students' comprehension and vocabulary acquisition," and make suggestions about additional strategies, such as, "When you ask Maria to do something, you might want to have her repeat the instructions back to you in her own words. This way you'll know if she understands. It's also good practice of her speaking skills." Rather than being isolated in the ESL classroom with little notion of the learning environments in the individual classrooms, by working in the grade-level classroom, the ESL teacher is in a position to help grade-level teachers make language and content more accessible to ESL students.

See Chapter 8 for a further discussion on promoting effective instruction in grade-level/content-area classrooms.

Working with Beginning-Level Students

Just as with the pullout model, the ESL teacher can use an inclusion model to instruct beginning-level ESL students in basic survival language, by gathering them in a separate area of the classroom. However, if the ESL instruction is completely different from whatever else is going on in the grade-level classroom, it may be less distracting for the ESL students if they are taught using a pullout model. Furthermore, if beginning-level students are dispersed among several classes in a grade level, they can be gathered together for instruction; this way they can receive more ESL sessions per week than if the ESL teacher were to go into each individual classroom separately.

Since an inclusion model can be implemented in so many ways, if both the grade-level and ESL teachers are flexible, ESL instruction can be altered continually depending on the particular lesson and the needs of the ESL students.

Here is further comment from Else on the inclusion model.

Else's Perspective

THE INCLUSION MODEL IS MORE SUITED TO STUDENTS who have attained quite a high level of proficiency in English. As Helene mentions, if the disparity between the ESL students' proficiency and the language level used in the classroom is too great, the help that the ESL teacher can give inside the grade-level classroom is of limited benefit to the student. At the risk of being repetitive, I should point out again the need to give students, especially those who are at the beginning levels of English proficiency, add-on help that supplements rather than supplants grade-level classroom instruction.

Some states or school districts offer varying levels of ESL support depending on students' English proficiency level. For example, in Illinois, school districts can opt for a part-time program for ESL students who have attained a certain level of proficiency in English but whose proficiency level is not high enough for them to survive in a grade-level classroom with no support at all. The inclusion model that Helene discusses is appropriate for students who only need, for example, to verify the meaning of a word, or to make sure that an idea is phrased correctly. Chicago Public Schools has also recently formalized the possibility of gradually decreasing ESL support rather than "exiting" students abruptly once they meet the criteria for English proficiency (Chicago Public Schools, 1998). After a student is assessed as being English proficient, he or she can continue to receive part-time support in the content areas, typically from an ESL teacher who comes into the grade-level classroom and does what Helene describes. Provision for a gradual increase in higher levels of language proficiency makes much more sense than the traditional termination of support once the student has reached the district-determined criterion of proficiency. Figure 3.1 below depicts the changing levels of support and grade-level instruction that a student may receive as a function of his or her proficiency in English.

See Chapter 5 for a discussion on exit criteria.

Figure 3.1: Changing Levels of ESL Support

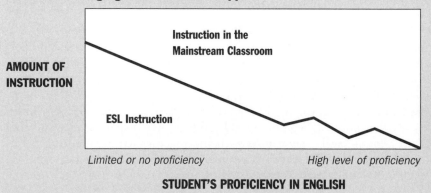

Thus, it is appropriate to use a combination of the models that Helene describes in this chapter based on individual student needs. The inclusion model is particularly useful at the higher levels of proficiency, and can serve as a safety net for students even after they have been identified as being English proficient. By continuing to give the students partial support on an as-needed basis, we avoid the misguided notion of "exit" from the ESL "program" when the student attains a certain score on the district's language proficiency test.

3.6 *OUT IN THE FIELD...*

Find out if the inclusion model is being used by elementary ESL teachers in your geographic area. If so, ask to observe an inclusion lesson. During the lesson, watch for the following:

1. What is the grade-level teacher teaching the class (that is, what is the content objective)?

2. What is the ESL teacher doing?

3. Jot down some examples of the content and language the ESL students are learning. Are they able to understand and participate in the lesson? Is the lesson working? How do you know?

4. How is the ESL lesson related to the grade-level lesson?

5. Is there anything in this lesson that you would do differently?

After the lesson, interview the ESL teacher and/or the grade-level teacher and ask the following:

6. How does the ESL instruction help the ESL students succeed in the class?

If possible, discuss your answers with a colleague. What have you learned about using an inclusion model?

Social Integration/Stigmatization

For some students, receiving ESL instruction right in their grade-level classroom may eliminate the embarrassment of being pulled out for instruction. For other students, an inclusion model may *increase* their feeling of stigmatization; they would rather go to a separate classroom for ESL instruction than be instructed separately right in front of their classmates. To help avoid this problem and to foster a positive attitude on the part of ESL students, the ESL teacher can enlist the support of the grade-level teacher as illustrated in the example below.

> When I taught ESL at Kanoelani Elementary School in Waipahu, Hawaii, one of the grade-level teachers in particular helped to promote this positive attitude: Whenever I entered the teacher's first-grade class to instruct my ESL group, the teacher gave me an enthusiastic welcome and then asked the entire class to greet me (chorally) as well. Her enthusiasm was infectious—students would

Helene Becker

often hear my footsteps as I approached their classroom door and they would say with excitement, "Here comes Mrs. Becker!" The teacher would periodically remind all the students how lucky they were to have another teacher in the room helping some of them to learn. As a result of the grade-level teacher's enthusiastic cooperation, several non-ESL students wanted to know why they weren't allowed to work with the "special teacher"—they were envious of the ESL students!

If there are negative feelings about working with the ESL teacher in the grade-level classroom, it is important to listen to students' concerns, and make adjustments if necessary. For example, if the grade-level and ESL teachers can arrange the schedule so that other small groups of students are working in the classroom at the same time that the ESL teacher is working with a small group of ESL students, there need not be any distinction made between the ESL group and the other small groups.

Investigations

After you have done Investigation 3.7, re-read Else's opinion on p. 55 about ESL teachers assisting non-ESL students.

3.7 *INCLUDING NON-ESL STUDENTS IN INSTRUCTIONAL GROUPS*

When I work with a group of ESL students in the grade-level classroom, the teacher sometimes asks me to include some non-ESL students in my group. Generally, these are students who are having academic difficulties and can benefit from the preview or review work I am doing with the ESL students. Think about the advantages and disadvantages of including these students in the ESL group. Compare your ideas with those of a colleague.

Scheduling Issues

When the ESL teacher meets with each individual grade-level teacher to set up ESL instructional times, the two teachers first need to decide on the purpose of the ESL instruction. If the ESL teacher will be mainly previewing and reviewing grade-level lessons, then the same guiding principles apply to an inclusion model as to a pull-out model: Students should not have ESL instruction during a time slot when they would miss a beneficial grade-level activity (unless the activity could easily be made up at another time). In the earlier example with Princess and Glory, ESL instruction was scheduled during the time that the rest of the class was doing "recreational reading." This activity could be made up at another time during the school day or at home, if necessary. On the other hand, if the ESL teacher will be assisting ESL students with grade-level lessons as they are occurring, then the ESL and grade-level teacher need to decide during teaching of which academic subject this kind of assistance would be most beneficial to the students. However, since the ESL teacher must consider the needs of all the ESL students in various classrooms, each following a different daily schedule, it is not always possible to work in a particular classroom at the best time of day for the ESL students in that classroom. For example, the ESL students in a particular class may need assistance with science lessons as they are occurring, but due to schedule demands, the ESL teacher may not be available during that time period. In that case, the grade-level and ESL teachers need to find another time when perhaps the ESL teacher could help ESL students understand their science instruction by previewing or reviewing the lesson instead of being there as the lesson is occurring.

Teaching Facilities

When the ESL teacher works in a grade-level classroom, if he or she is working separately with the ESL students in a corner of the room, it is possible for students (and teachers!) to get distracted by one another's activities. If, however, the ESL instructional time is scheduled when the rest of the class is also working in small groups, this problem is minimized.

Since the ESL teacher and each grade-level teacher need to collaborate continually on instruction and also share classroom space, an inclusion model requires them to be flexible and have a good working relationship. More than in a pullout model, in an inclusion model, the grade-level and ESL teachers must work closely together to address instructional issues for the benefit of the ESL students. Because of this need for pedagogical dialogue, if the grade-level and ESL teachers remain flexible and open-minded, this model can be professionally stimulating and rewarding.

If the teachers have dissimilar teaching styles, there is potential for conflict. When I taught ESL at Kanoelani Elementary School in Hawaii, I had a minor problem in one situation.

Helene Becker

> In one of the sixth-grade classes, the ESL students would work with me while the rest of the class was doing some quiet seatwork. The grade-level teacher did not allow any student collaboration during this seatwork; he wanted the students to work individually. As I worked with the ESL students (usually on make-up work they needed to complete), I wanted them to practice their listening, speaking, and reasoning skills, so I encouraged them to consult and help each other. I was worried that the grade-level teacher would be annoyed that my group was making noise, but he seemed to be OK with our low voices in the corner. I always felt a bit uncomfortable, though, allowing my ESL students to make "noise" in that classroom.

If the two teachers in the room cannot come to an agreement on such issues, pullout instruction could be considered.

3.8 *INCLUSION MODEL: SUMMARY*

Effective inclusion instruction means more than simply "including" the ESL students in the physical space of their grade-level classroom. Guidelines need to be followed for ESL students to get the most benefit possible from the usually limited time that the ESL teacher is present in each grade-level classroom. This teacher in Connecticut talks about how she manages to create a positive learning situation for her ESL students while recognizing that there are certain potential problems when using this model. Use her story as a springboard for discussion with a colleague; then write a brief statement under each category in the chart below, summarizing your ideas about the inclusion model.

	The inclusion model can be used effectively if...
Curriculum coordination	
Social integration/ stigmatization	
Scheduling issues	
Teaching facilities	

Teachers' Voices

Lillian Rausch, Charter Oak Elementary School, West Hartford, Connecticut

In my school our service delivery model is inclusion (except for the beginners, whom we pull out). I go into the classroom and work with an individual or small group in a corner of the classroom, usually during language arts/reading time. The classroom teacher decides on the area to be covered, and I bring my adapted lesson and materials into the classroom and work with the ESL students on it. The other children are doing a similar lesson at their level with the classroom teacher.

The good thing about inclusion is that the children do not feel different from the other students because they are studying pretty much the same thing as their peers right there in their own classroom. Another benefit is that I can help other students who are not ESL students, but who learn better in a small group setting with modified materials. If my ESL group is small, I will always add a non-ESL child if he or she needs the help.

The difficulty with an inclusion model is working out the scheduling; going into all classes during their language arts/reading time is a problem since I am just one person! This requires great flexibility on the part of the classroom teachers. Another problem with inclusion is that it requires all of the ESL students (or as many as possible) who are in the same grade to be in the same class. Otherwise, there are too many classes to cover, and I would have to switch to a pullout model. As a result, some classrooms end up with a large number of ESL students. The teachers in each grade with the majority of the ESL students really have to enjoy working with them, or it becomes a difficult situation for everyone. Fortunately, in my school, most of the teachers like having the ESL students in their classes, so it isn't a problem.

Investigations

3.9 PLACING ESL STUDENTS IN ONE CLASS PER GRADE

As the teacher above states, if all the ESL students in one grade level are placed in the same grade-level classroom, the inclusion model works well because the ESL teacher does not have to divide his or her time among too many classes. However, can the number of ESL students in one grade-level classroom become too large? Do you see any potential problems for the grade-level teacher? for the ESL students in the class? for the non-ESL students in the class? What complaints might parents have?

TEAM-TEACHING MODEL (ALSO CALLED CO-TEACHING MODEL)

Some elementary schools with large percentages of ESL students have hired ESL teachers to team-teach (or co-teach) with grade-level teachers. For several hours per day (as opposed to the few hours per week typical with a pullout or inclusion model), the ESL teacher teaches in the grade-level classroom as an equal partner with the grade-level teacher. Then, the ESL teacher may teach for a few hours per day in a different classroom with another grade-level teacher.

When an ESL teacher team-teaches with a grade-level teacher, the ESL students can get the support they need to be integrated both academically and socially into the "mainstream" of the school. The ESL teacher is there to ensure that the ESL students are involved in activities appropriate for their academic, linguistic, cognitive, and social development. The grade-level teacher, as well as the native English-speaking peers of the ESL students, becomes more responsible for supporting the learning of the ESL students, which has a positive effect on both the acquisition of English and the ESL students' sense of belonging to the mainstream society (Cummins, 1994).

Curriculum Coordination

The ESL and grade-level classroom teacher who are teaming can plan lessons together and decide how they will work with each other. At times they may both present information to the entire class, or they may divide the class in half for a particular lesson, the ESL teacher taking the ESL students (and most likely some non-ESL students) in his or her group. At other times, while one teacher is conducting a formal lesson, the other can give special assistance to ESL students (and others) as needed. There are many ways that the two teachers can structure the lessons to the benefit of the ESL students.

The ESL teacher teammate is able to present material to the ESL students (or to the entire class) using effective ESL strategies to ensure comprehension on the part of the ESL students. There is no need to coordinate the ESL instruction with grade-level instruction since there is no separate ESL instruction—it is simply instruction conducted by the ESL teacher. Furthermore, while the ESL teacher is teaching, he or she is simultaneously modeling effective ESL strategies so that the grade-level teacher can learn ways to teach the ESL students at times when the ESL teacher is working in another classroom.

When I taught ESL at Kanoelani Elementary School in Waipahu, Hawaii, I had the opportunity, on occasion, to team-teach lessons with a first grade teacher. Here is an example of how we worked together during a phonics lesson.

Helene Becker

> The grade-level teacher led the first part of the lesson in which students were asked to call out all the words they could think of beginning with the letter "r" as she wrote them on the board. During this part of the lesson, I carefully watched the expressions on the faces of the five ESL students in the class. Since these words were in isolation and not in the context of a meaningful story or conversation, I knew that the ESL children might not be sure of the meanings. When I detected confusion, I asked the class to re-explain the meanings of the particular words that the ESL students did not seem to understand, and to use the words in sentences. When the grade-level

teacher finished the presentation, I led the class in a game called, "Which word means...?" where I said (or mimed) the definition of a word and the students had to point to and say the word. For example, I said, "Which word means *this*?" and I proceeded to "run" in place. The students had to point to and say the word *run*. During this portion of the lesson, I paid particular attention to the ESL students to ensure that they understood the words. Afterwards, as students copied the list from the board, I walked around the room checking the ESL students' work and drawing little pictures on their papers to help them remember the definitions.

This team-taught lesson allowed the ESL students to benefit from a regular grade-level lesson with simple modifications to ensure the ESL students' full participation. Checking student comprehension frequently during the first part of the lesson and playing a comprehension game during the second part reinforced the lesson material for all students (not just the ESL students) in the class.

Teachers who team-teach have the flexibility to use different methods and student groupings in the classroom: One teacher can use suitable methods for a particular group of students while the other teacher can choose a different approach to meet the needs of another group, such as the ESL students. In addition, two teachers working together means opportunities to discuss and help each other with lesson strategies, materials, student discipline, and so forth. The two teachers can share decision making and provide individual attention to students as needed.

When the ESL teacher teams with the grade-level teacher, the ESL teacher can give input regarding the sequencing of concepts presented to the class. Obviously, some academic content can be taught more easily through hands-on and visual lessons, whereas other content is more abstract and requires more language to explain. It is easier for the ESL students first to understand lessons that lend themselves to concrete hands-on and visual demonstrations since less language is needed for comprehension. After they develop the language during that lesson, they can understand a more abstract related lesson.

Met (1994) illustrates how the sequencing of concepts from concrete to abstract can aid in comprehension of a science unit. For example, when teaching a lesson on the importance of proper nutrition in animals and plants, it may seem logical to first teach about the effects of nutritional food on human growth and well-being, since that personalizes the lesson for children. However, since children cannot actually see their own growth, it is probably better to present the information to ESL students about plants first, since they can actually see the results of good and bad nutrition on plant growth by growing plants in the classroom. After they have been exposed to the concepts and vocabulary in the context of a lesson using plants, they can then better understand a nutrition lesson regarding humans.

Social Integration/Stigmatization

The ESL students in a class where the grade-level and ESL teachers team-teach perceive themselves as "students" rather than "ESL students"; they are not singled out as "different." In fact, depending on the particular lesson and student needs, when forming instructional groups, students can be mixed and matched so that the ESL teacher's group may often contain several students who are not designated as ESL students. Furthermore, when a grade-level teacher and an ESL teacher teach together in a classroom, it promotes the notion that educating the ESL students in the school is not just the responsibility of the ESL teacher, but of all faculty and staff (Cummins, 1994).

Else extends the notion of status and stigmatization to the teachers in a team-teaching situation.

Else's Perspective

AS WITH OTHER INSTRUCTIONAL MODELS that Helene describes in this chapter, social issues are important for the success of a team-teaching model. Team-teaching can be effective only if the status of the two teachers is perceived as equal by the students, the other teachers in the school, and the administration. In many schools, since ESL teachers are perceived as having lower status than grade-level teachers, (usually because ESL is associated with lower-status minority students and with a compensatory rather than an enrichment program), it may be difficult for the team of two teachers to create an effective learning environment for students.

Having equal status in the classroom not only means teaching equally important academic subject areas and having equal time with the whole class, it also means having equal decision-making power within the classroom and playing similar roles in classroom management. The two teachers have to negotiate their roles with each other, and as Helene mentions later on, the personal relationship between the two is very important for the smooth functioning of the team. These issues are complicated enough in any team-teaching situation, but are compounded by status issues when one of the teachers is an ESL teacher, because ESL and grade-level teachers often do not see each other as equal peers. Thus, the personal relationship between the two teachers is as important as the perception of status among the teachers. The ESL teacher has to establish herself or himself as an equal peer to the grade-level classroom teacher vis-à-vis the rest of the faculty. A supportive and astute administration can help this status-raising process.

Scheduling Issues

For ESL students to benefit to the fullest extent from team-teaching, the ESL and grade-level teachers need to team-teach during academic instruction in which the ESL students need the most assistance. This may vary from classroom to classroom depending on the grade level, the difficulty of the curriculum and text materials, the teaching style and instructional methods employed by the grade-level teacher, and the needs of the ESL students. For example, the ESL students in a particular second-grade class may be struggling during math and during language arts instruction (perhaps they need a smaller group setting which an additional teacher in the room could provide), but the ESL students in a particular sixth-grade class may be having difficulty with the social studies and science lessons (perhaps they need more visual cues and hands-on experiences, which the ESL teacher could plan into the lessons). The ESL teacher should attempt to team-teach during the time periods when the combined efforts of two teachers will be of most benefit to the ESL students.

The team-teaching model works best when the ESL teacher teams up with only a few grade-level teachers. In this way, the grade-level and ESL teachers are able to work together as true teammates for much of the day's instruction. For this reason, true teaming situations are likely to be found only in schools with large percentages of ESL students. Otherwise, the school administration is unlikely to hire the number of ESL teachers needed to create true teams.

Teaching Facilities

In a team-teaching situation, obviously, the two teachers share the classroom space and resources. But more importantly, more so than in any other model, the two teachers must share teaching philosophies and must display a spirit of cooperation. When the teammates can work together well, the ESL students are in an optimal environment for learning language and content and for being integrated—both academically and socially—into the school environment.

CHAPTER SUMMARY

Since the ESL teacher typically works with a diverse group of students at different proficiency levels, with varied academic needs, and within the constraints of a limited number of hours allotted for ESL instruction, one type of program model may not be the best choice for all students. Input from grade-level teachers regarding program model choice is essential, since the type of program model used affects their teaching. For example, with a pullout model, the grade-level teacher must adjust to having the ESL students miss part of the classroom work. With an inclusion or team-teaching model, the grade-level teacher must adapt to working very closely with the ESL teacher.

In selecting a program model, it is important to be flexible. Since each model can be used effectively depending on the circumstances, the ESL and grade-level teachers need to evaluate each student's needs and make appropriate decisions.

Throughout the school year, it is sensible to remain open to the possibility of changing the program model, if necessary. The grade-level and/or ESL teacher may think that one model will be effective, but after instruction begins, it may become apparent that a different model may be more beneficial. For example, suppose that the grade-level and ESL teachers decide to use an inclusion model with a group of fourth-grade high-beginning level ESL students during the social studies time slot. However, if after a few weeks, the two teachers observe that, even with ESL assistance, the ESL students are not understanding the lessons and the textbook, the teachers should consider using a pullout model so that the ESL teacher could work with the students on similar content, but with more appropriate materials and methods of instruction. After a few months, when the ESL students have acquired more content-related language, the teachers may want to try an inclusion model once again.

In some school systems the choice of ESL instructional model is not made by the individual ESL teachers—the administration or districtwide ESL coordinator may make the decision for everyone. In other school systems, the ESL teacher may theoretically have a choice of models, but the hours allotted for ESL instruction may preclude some choices. For example, if two ESL teachers are hired to work in a school with 80 ESL students distributed in several classes in each grade, a pullout model—where children from various classes are grouped together for instruction—may be the only way to see all of the students at least a few times per week. If some of the students are at the beginning level of proficiency and, therefore, in need of ESL instruction daily, the instructional time remaining for intermediate and advanced students becomes even more limited, unless pullout groups are formed. No matter what one's philosophy and preferences, this may be the only possible choice in that situation.

And now some concluding remarks from Else.

Else's Perspective

IT IS IMPORTANT TO CONSIDER THE BASIS on which educational decisions regarding language-minority students are made in schools. Helene brings up some of the everyday issues, such as scheduling and teacher availability, that significantly affect the type of instructional environment we are able to create for our students. These issues are administrative factors, and although they determine whether or not it is possible to offer a specific instructional model, they need to be considered in the context of other, learner-based, issues. Learner-based issues that Helene also discusses, such as stigmatizing effects and language proficiency, are just as important, and cannot be ignored in the decision-making process. That is, educational decisions must be based as much on learning theory as on ease of administration. We need to ask, "What makes sense from the student's perspective?" just as readily as we ask, "Do we have/want to spend the resources to offer this type of instruction?"

The type of decision I describe above is typically made at the administrative level within a school, and teachers are rarely invited to participate in the decision making, although they are the ones who are most aware of the students' needs and their developmental progress. However, it is important to bring characteristics of effective instructional models into the communal consciousness of the school. If an instructional model that is not the most effective for students is chosen (perhaps justifiably, because of lack of resources or availability of teachers), the fact that it is not the most conducive model for learning must be acknowledged. The following criteria have been suggested for creating effective instructional environments for second-language learners (Cloud, Genesee, and Hamayan, 2000).

1. The instructional environment must encourage parental input regarding goals they have for their children.
2. Instruction must reflect high standards.
3. The instructional model must be supported by teachers and administrators.
4. Instruction must be developmentally appropriate.
5. Instruction must be student-centered.
6. Language and academic content instruction must be integrated.

For a discussion on the importance of parental input, see Chapter 7.

7. Teachers must constantly monitor and reflect upon the instructional model.
8. The instructional model must integrate the different components that make up a student's schooling.
9. The instructional model must aim for additive bilingualism.

3.10 *OUT IN THE FIELD...*

Find out which ESL program models are being used in your area. Interview an elementary ESL teacher and ask the following questions:

1. Describe the program model(s) you use to instruct your students.

2. Who decides which program model you should use?

3. What do you feel are the positive and negative aspects of using this (these) program model(s)?

If possible, discuss your answers with a colleague who has interviewed a different elementary ESL teacher. What did you learn about program models in "real" teaching situations? Did you find any of the information surprising?

Suggested Readings

In addition to the elementary school ESL program models discussed here, there are bilingual and dual-language program models. For an in-depth look at bilingual education, see Suzanne Irujo's *Teaching Bilingual Children (1998)*, a TeacherSource book. For a thorough treatment of dual language programs, see *Dual Language Instruction: A Handbook for Enriched Education* by Nancy Cloud, Fred Genesee, and Else Hamayan (2000).

For more on standards, see *Integrating the ESL Standards into Classroom Practice: Grades Pre-K–2*, edited by B. A. Smallwood (2000), and *Integrating the ESL Standards into Classroom Practice: Grades 3–5*, edited by K. D. Samway (2000).

4

ESL PROGRAM MODELS IN SECONDARY SCHOOLS

Secondary school-aged ESL students arrive in this country with varied academic backgrounds. Some have had extensive schooling in their native countries and are well prepared for the academic challenges ahead. Others arrive underprepared for grade-level schoolwork having had fewer than four years of formal education (Short, 1994). ESL programs in secondary schools must be able to accommodate the academically underprepared as well as the academically prepared ESL student. This chapter presents guidelines for designing and enhancing secondary school ESL programs in order to meet the wide range of educational needs of ESL students and promote their overall success in school.

 WHAT HELENE REFERS TO AS THE UNDERPREPARED STUDENT poses a special challenge for many teachers at the secondary level. These students have also been referred to in the literature as students with limited formal schooling (TESOL, 1997), underschooled or low-literacy students (Hamayan, 1994), and late-entrant students (Mace-Matluck, Alexander-Kasparik, and Queen, 1998). In addition to the second-language needs that other language-minority students have, these underprepared students have special needs that arise from their atypical school experience. Particularly, they lack school skills, and they come from backgrounds where literacy does not play as prominent a role as it does in our society. These two dimensions are vital to consider when designing instructional programs for these students.

These underprepared students not only need to learn the language of school but they also need to learn about school, as a topic of study. Regardless of the ESL instructional model used, a curriculum that incorporates the teaching of basic school skills needs to be developed and taught. Basic school skills—such as daily school routines and rules of behavior, lunchtime procedures, the way lockers function, class schedules, movement from classroom to classroom, the organization of departments—should be incorporated into the ESL curriculum. At a minimum, each underprepared student must be assigned a peer guide who can make sure that the student knows how to function within the school (Mace-Matluck, Alexander-Kasparik, and Queen, 1998).

On developing literacy through the native language, see Irujo, *Teaching Bilingual Children: Beliefs and Behaviors* (1998).

If, in addition to their lack of schooling, these students come from environments where literacy does not play a very significant role, their path to literacy must be planned carefully. As with school skills and knowledge about school, there is a need to begin with basic concepts of literacy. Many preliterate older students do not have the basic understanding of the functions and forms of literacy (Hamayan, 1994). They may not realize that written language can serve as a memory aid—as in shopping lists—or that titles and subheadings present the topic of what is to follow. The ESL teacher may have to guide these students through early literacy steps to help the basic skills of reading and writing emerge as naturally as possible. Skills such as the understanding of symbol-sound correspondence, word and sentence structure, and attributes of written text that schooled older students have already mastered may be quite foreign to the underprepared student. For many of these students, the most efficient way for literacy to emerge may be through the only oral language students know, their native language.

WHAT FACTORS PROMOTE A SUCCESSFUL PROGRAM?

As in elementary schools, ESL programs in secondary schools come in many different shapes and sizes. However, within their own individual structures and limitations, programs can use the following guidelines as a basis for developing effective educational plans for ESL students.

OVERALL EDUCATIONAL PROGRAM

GUIDELINE 1: ESL classes need to be viewed as only part of an overall educational program for ESL students.

This guideline can best be illustrated by describing my own experience 18 years ago in the West Hartford (Connecticut) Public Schools. At that time, the ESL classes were the entire ESL program rather than only a piece of a more extensive overall plan, as they are now.

Helene Becker

I was hired to teach ESL to high school students and was assigned to three ESL classes: Level I, Level II, and Level III. The 20 or so ESL students in the school had been placed in those levels by their respective guidance counselors based on how well they seemed to speak English (no formal assessment was done). Each student was enrolled in only one ESL class per day, even if the student had just arrived in the United States and spoke no English. The rest of the day the students had to fend for themselves in their content-area classes, trying to understand their teachers, most of whom had only minimal knowledge and experience with respect to ESL students.

ESL students were rather new to this suburban community, and it took time to establish a more complete program. Little by little, however, over a period of several years, the program expanded and improved. A second period per day of ESL instruction was added for the beginning-level students, a fourth level of ESL was offered, a daily tutoring program was set up and some content-area classes specially designed for ESL students—sheltered classes—were created. We enhanced the program in these ways because it was obvious from the start that simply offering ESL students one or even two ESL classes per day and expecting them to be successful in their other school subjects was unrealistic. In addition, my ESL colleagues and I worked with content-area teachers on developing teaching strategies to help ESL students succeed in content-area classes.

In addition to ESL instruction, ESL students at the secondary level need a carefully designed complete program that meets their individual needs. The program may consist of a combination of the following: ESL classes, sheltered content-area classes, mainstream content-area classes, electives, tutoring, and in bilingual settings, content-area classes taught in the students' native languages. The individual student program depends on the student's level of English proficiency, academic background, and interests, as well as the course options available at the particular school. Procedures for assessing student needs and placing students in classes should be systematic and easy to follow (a placement form or grid should be available) so that students are correctly placed in appropriate classes. In other words, in order for ESL students to meet with success in secondary schools, their daily overall programs—not merely their ESL classes—need to be carefully selected and monitored. The remaining guidelines in this chapter explain the various components that can contribute to an effective daily program for ESL students.

See Chapter 5, pp. 101–114 for a discussion on assessing student needs and placing students appropriately.

But before I continue discussing guidelines, Else explains a situation where it may be appropriate to separate ESL students for primarily ESL instruction.

Else's Perspective

THERE IS ONE SITUATION IN WHICH setting up a primarily ESL type of program may be appropriate, at least on a temporary basis. That is the newcomer school type of program that many districts are currently opting for. Newcomer schools are designed to help older students, especially those coming with incomplete formal educational experiences, acclimate to school life in the United States before they enter a regular school. Naturally, ESL is a primary component of the curriculum, as is an introduction to school rules and cross-cultural issues. However, students in most newcomer schools are not deprived of academic content areas, although the extent to which they are exposed to secondary level academic subjects depends on the students' English language proficiency and the availability of native language resources. Although the 86 newcomer schools that currently exist share some characteristics, they vary significantly from one another (Short, 1999). This variance is so great that it is very difficult to talk about newcomer schools as one type of model.

Newcomer schools vary as to location. In some districts the newcomer school is part of the main school building whereas in others it is in a separate location that may be quite a distance away from the main building. The schools vary as to the length of stay: Some districts allow students to stay as long as two years while in other districts students can only stay a few months. Newcomer schools also vary as a function of the portion of the day that students attend: Some are full-day schools and others offer a part-time program where students return to their home school for the balance of the day. The extent to which native language support is offered also varies from school to school.

Despite the increasing popularity of newcomer schools in the last five to ten years, we have little research evidence regarding their effectiveness. Some administrators argue that newcomer schools isolate students from native English-speaking peers, and therefore the students learn English at a much slower pace. Others argue that students who come lacking so many skills need the time with peers with similar needs to learn the basic ways in which school functions as they build basic skills in ESL. They argue that students need to learn school skills before they are thrust into the complex and demanding culture of a high school or middle school. As Short (1999) states, we still do not have enough research evidence to be able to draw any conclusions about the effectiveness of the model in general or about the different types of newcomer schools.

SHELTERED CONTENT-AREA CLASSES

GUIDELINE 2: ESL students should have the opportunity to take sheltered content-area classes so that they can simultaneously learn language and academic content.

In sheltered classes, ESL teaching strategies are used to teach both content subject matter and language so that ESL students have the opportunity to simultaneously learn academic subjects and English. This kind of class is beneficial to ESL students for two main reasons. First, since teachers of sheltered classes use teaching strategies specifically designed to help ESL students learn academic content, ESL students are ready to study academic subjects before they would be ready to study the same subjects in the "mainstream" (Snow, 1991). This means that ESL students do not fall behind their native English-speaking peers while spending time learning English and getting ready for content-area classes. Second, teachers of sheltered classes have two goals—teaching content, and teaching language. They know that they have to specifically teach the language that students need in order to learn the subject matter. Therefore, ESL students are in a learning environment where the emphasis is simultaneously on both of their essential needs—learning content and acquiring language.

Ideally, every "mainstream" content class should have a sheltered version so that after the first year of acquiring basic English skills, ESL students would have access to any and all classes they needed or wanted to take. Realistically, however, most school districts cannot afford to offer such a variety of sheltered classes. Each sheltered class requires financial resources to develop curriculum, obtain or create teaching materials, and hire and train teacher(s) to teach it. Most importantly, each class offered must be financially justified by having sufficient numbers of students to enroll each year. In schools with large numbers of ESL students to enroll in sheltered classes, more can be offered; with smaller numbers of ESL students, only a few sheltered classes are feasible. Nonetheless, whatever sheltered classes are offered should be taught by highly qualified teachers who are certified and/or trained in both teaching the content area and using ESL teaching strategies so that ESL students are exposed to the same level of teaching expertise as their native English-speaking peers.

Here is commentary from Else regarding the broader issue of funding for public education.

Else's Perspective

HELENE'S CONCERN ABOUT FINANCIAL RESOURCES is certainly understandable and its urgency should not be ignored. Funding for public education in the United States has diminished over the last few decades. However, we must remind ourselves that this decrease of financial support for education is not due to lack of funds. Rather, it is due to an increasing reluctance by politicians and the public at large to invest in public education. Despite the common political rhetoric, public education has not been a high priority for quite a few years (Kozol, 1991). Federal investment in education (as well as infrastructure and research) has continued to fall over the last three administrations as funding for the military and for correctional institutions has increased. According to Justice Policy Institute statistics, for every state job in higher education that was cut in California in the last decade, three prison jobs were created. To the extent that California is representative of other states, this is a disturbing national trend that is leading to some of the difficulties that Helene describes.

Funding for programs designed specifically to benefit minority students is a low priority within the department of education—hence the serious lack of resources that Helene refers to is something that most ESL programs face. Advocacy for better support for education must be an agenda for anyone with an interest in public education.

In deciding which specific subjects to offer as a minimum number of sheltered classes, the following considerations may be helpful.

Mathematics—Many people believe that since math is "mostly numbers," it is a relatively easy subject for ESL students. On the contrary, math lessons and textbooks can be difficult for ESL students because of the specialized vocabulary and concepts involved, including some everyday words with completely different meanings in a math context (such as *table, round,* and *root*) (O'Malley and Valdez Pierce, 1996). However, since math does rely somewhat less on literacy skills than other core academic subjects, even beginning-level ESL students can be successful in a math class if it is offered in a sheltered format where language is taught along with content. In schools with a considerable number of ESL students with gaps in their basic math knowledge, a sheltered basic math class should be offered at the very least. This class may give these students the foundation they need to go on and take "mainstream" math classes later on.

Science—School districts wishing to meet the needs of ESL students should offer at least one science class in a sheltered format (perhaps the first course in the school's regular science sequence). Since many concepts in science are concrete, require little prior cultural knowledge, and can be taught using a hands-on approach (through lab experiments and demonstrations), ESL students can do quite well in a sheltered science class, even if they have only studied English for one year. At the high school level, if students take the sheltered science class, in grade 10 and then two years of "mainstream" science, they can complete the three years of science study preferred by many universities. Since ESL students who start learning English relatively late (that is, in secondary school) can often compete better in the work world in math and science fields than in language arts and social studies fields (where native-like fluency in English is usually necessary), it is important to give ESL students as many opportunities as possible to take science (and math) classes.

English/Literature—English/literature classes (along with most social studies classes) tend to be problematic for ESL students since the coursework usually includes extensive reading and requires a considerable amount of cultural background knowledge. "Mainstream" teachers often wrongly assume that all students in their classes are familiar with everyday references to people and places as well as with common idiomatic expressions often found in literature. The teacher of a sheltered English class is aware of the need to teach specific cultural and linguistic information so that students can better understand the class discussions and text materials.

As discussed in Chapter 2, even beginning-level ESL students can read some literature in ESL class provided that short, relatively simple texts are used with lots of discussion, visuals, and so forth. By the second year, students can benefit from a literature class as long as it is in a sheltered format so that appropriate teaching strategies and materials are used.

Some school districts have also developed sheltered **transition English classes** to help prepare ESL students for the challenge of studying literature along with native English-speaking peers the following school year. In these transition classes advanced ESL students are given the same or similar reading and writing assignments as are given to students in the "mainstream" English classes, but in an ESL environment where students can receive the help and support they need. The following year (or semester) students should meet with success in (carefully chosen) "mainstream" English classes.

Social Studies—As mentioned above, the extensive reading and cultural background knowledge required in many social studies classes can be obstacles to ESL students' success in those classes. In fact, even after two or three years of studying English, ESL students can still have tremendous difficulty with "mainstream" social studies classes. Consequently, it is desirable to offer one or more social studies classes in a sheltered format. A sensible choice would be sheltered American history, since many ESL students are unfamiliar with the people and events that have shaped the present-day United States. The teacher of a sheltered American history class teaches the class with this assumption in mind. The teacher of a "mainstream" American history class, on the other hand, naturally expects students in the class to know something about significant people, places, and events in our past, since American history topics are taught throughout the elementary school years. Therefore, ESL students in the "mainstream" history class could be expected to be familiar with such topics as the Pilgrims, Native Americans, or the Revolutionary War, about which they may in fact know little or nothing.

The subject of American government can also present difficulties since the concepts are abstract and unfamiliar to many ESL students. School districts should aim to offer ESL students a sheltered American government class that can be taken after students have completed a sheltered American history class; teachers have found that the content of the sheltered American history class provides useful background knowledge for learning the content of the sheltered American government class.

Else's Perspective

ESL AND SHELTERED CONTENT-AREA TEACHERS HAVE a triple task ahead of them. They need to teach the specialized subject matter, the specialized language skills associated with each academic domain, and general learning skills (Cloud, Genesee, and Hamayan, 2000). Most frameworks that discuss integrated language and content instruction have incorporated these three goals (see, for example, Chamot and O'Malley, 1987, and Short, 1991). While content objectives are primary, especially in the sheltered classroom, language objectives must be in the forefront of all lessons. Three types of language objectives must be part of the lesson. The first of these is **content-obligatory language** that all students need to learn in relation to specific content-area topics. The second type is **content-compatible language** that English-proficient students have mastered but that the ESL student may not yet have picked up (Snow, Met, and Genesee, 1989). Finally, teachers can identify other, more general, features of language that may fit into a particular topic and take advantage of the context to teach those features (Cloud, Genesee, and Hamayan, 2000). For example, when teaching about the weather, it is easy to teach comparatives and superlatives. That is, **nontechnical vocabulary** can be highlighted and taught alongside the specialized terms.

Teachers should review content-area as well as second-language curriculum in their district in order to establish language objectives that are compatible with the content-area curriculum. They can also take guidance from the standards that have been developed in those content areas. In addition to any state or local standards that may exist, the national professional organizations that represent most of the academic content areas have developed standards in their area of specialty. Standards exist for Mathematics (National Council of Teachers of Mathematics, 1996), Social Studies (National Council for the Social Studies, 1997), and Science (National Science Teachers Association, 1997). Also, because of the prominent role that standards are currently playing in education, standards-based instruction is something that ESL teachers must familiarize themselves with.

The third goal I mentioned, developing general learning skills, is also important in that students can use those skills to enhance learning of all subjects. These broad learning goals include the acquisition and practice of study skills such as note-taking and research skills, learning strategies such as observation, and social skills needed in academic learning environments, such as working together with others to make decisions. These skills are

See the discussion of learning strategies instruction in Chapter 2, pp. 13–17.

highly correlated with academic success and can be taught directly to students whose cultural background or educational experience has not given them the opportunity to learn.

4.1 CONTENT-OBLIGATORY VS. CONTENT-COMPATIBLE LANGUAGE

As Else states above, teachers of sheltered classes need to think about both content-obligatory and content-compatible language objectives. For a better understanding of the difference, think about these objectives in the context of a sheltered class, such as basic math. Imagine that you were going to teach a lesson on the topic of adding fractions with unlike denominators such as $\frac{1}{2}$ and $\frac{7}{8}$. Think about the specific language you would need to teach during the lesson in order for students to understand the concept; make a list of these words and phrases. Which items on your list are content-obligatory—that is, they would probably be taught (or reviewed) in a "mainstream" basic math class as well? Mark these items "C.O." Which items on your list are content-compatible—that is, they would be taught in a sheltered basic math class but not in a "mainstream" basic math class because the teacher would assume that the students already knew them? Mark these items "C.C." If possible, compare your list with that of a colleague. When you are finished, jot down some of the nontechnical (that is, not math-specific), language you and your students would probably employ during the course of this lesson. Could you use this everyday language as a basis for teaching your students about some features of English? Which features?

ELECTIVE CLASSES

GUIDELINE 3: Beginning-level ESL students should take several hands-on elective classes.

As explained in Chapter 3 with respect to elementary school students, secondary students at the beginning level of English proficiency can also benefit from participation in hands-on classes such as art, music, physical education, wood shop, and cooking. Successful participation in these types of classes usually requires a lower level of English proficiency than participation in core academic classes. In fact, artistically, musically, or athletically talented ESL students have the opportunity to be highly successful in such classes. In addition, by interacting with native English-speaking peers in these classes, ESL students can practice authentic language and develop friendships. This integration of ESL students in the "mainstream" of the school may help ESL students feel more accepted and comfortable in their new cultural surroundings.

Most secondary schools require an accumulation of a certain number of these elective credits for graduation. It makes sense for ESL students to accumulate these credits early on in secondary school when they have not yet acquired the higher level of English proficiency needed to earn credits in core academic classes. Later on, when they have further developed their English skills, they can spend more of their school day in academic classes; their increased level of English proficiency at that later time may help them benefit more from the academic classes than if they had taken them sooner.

Else issues a warning, however, about ESL students taking electives.

HELENE'S SUGGESTION OF LOADING beginning-level ESL students' schedules in the first year with electives is excellent. We must do so, however, with a very clear long-term plan that incorporates higher-level courses in the following years. We must be careful not to let the electives be the most important features of the ESL students' first year or subsequent education plan. These students need to be aiming for the higher-level courses throughout their secondary school experience. Unfortunately, many teachers and administrators who are not experienced with ESL students and who lack training in second-language acquisition may mistake the beginning-level ESL students' inability to function in high-level courses for an inability to learn. Students who come with limited formal schooling, whom Helene referred to earlier in the chapter as underprepared students, are most prone to this misconception (Mace-Matluck, Alexander-Kasparik, and Queen, 1998).

NATIVE LANGUAGE SUPPORT

GUIDELINE 4: Native language support provides shortcuts to learning.

In many cases, an ESL program is part of a bilingual program in which ESL students receive instruction in academic subjects (that is, math, science, social studies, and literature) in their respective native languages while they are acquiring English through ESL instruction. As they acquire more English, they typically increase their load of academic classes taught in English and take fewer courses taught in the native language.

In schools where large numbers of ESL students speak the same native language, it is possible to establish a bilingual program. In this way, students can have access to content knowledge in their native language while they are acquiring English. Several studies by Thomas and Collier (1995) have shown that using the native language to teach content has a positive effect on students' long-term success in school. Furthermore, bilingual programs that actively promote literacy skills in the native language have a positive effect on promoting students' academic development in the second language—in this case, English (Cummins, 1994). Since learning subject matter can occur in any language, it does not matter which language is used to teach content knowledge. As students become more proficient in English, concepts they have learned in their native language are still in their body of knowledge; they will now be able to express their knowledge in English. Until their English skills are more developed, however, students will learn more efficiently and profoundly in their native language. It makes sense to take advantage of their already developed proficiency in their native language to teach academic content.

Nevertheless, in a school district with a relatively small number of ESL students or a heterogeneous ESL population, a bilingual program is usually not feasible.

Without a high concentration of same-native-language speakers, bilingual content classes would not have enough students enrolled in them. As mentioned earlier, since public school budgets do not typically allow for the hiring of teachers for classes that contain too few students, a bilingual program is not likely to be created unless there is a large enough enrollment of ESL students who all speak the same native language.

In many cases, however, students' native languages can be used to some degree to help them learn lesson material. If a teacher is proficient in the native language of some of the ESL students in the class, the teacher can offer to discuss the lesson with the students in the native language before or after class. Bilingual aides or volunteers can be of assistance in this way, or they can assist students in the classroom during the lesson, especially in a small group setting or on an individual basis. Native language support can also be offered at a tutoring center as described below in *Guideline 5*.

For an in-depth discussion of native language support, see Irujo, *Teaching Bilingual Children* (1998).

HELENE'S STATEMENT REGARDING THE IMPORTANCE of native language support for the ESL student who still has limited proficiency in English needs special attention. It is important for different reasons for students of different ages. For young ESL students, the native language needs to develop so that it can provide a strong foundation for second-language learning (Collier, 1995; Cummins, 1981b). Since younger students are still clearly developing their concepts, instruction in the native language can assure a smooth progression of that developmental process. The older ESL student may not need the native language to develop conceptually, since the significant stages of cognitive development are typically completed by puberty. However, for older ESL students, the native language is essential for gaining access to the academic subject areas. In many cases, it is the only way that a student will be able to comprehend abstract new concepts in the content areas.

Helene's advice to provide support in the native language whenever possible must be taken seriously. In fact, native language support must be provided in such a way that it meets certain criteria. First, native language support needs to be delivered in a systematic way. That is, a routine must be established for when the student receives native language support, who provides it, and in what contexts. Second, native language support should be provided on the basis of highest need. That is, it must be provided to the students who need it most, and in the areas in which they need it most. Finally, and most importantly, a long-term plan for native language support must be established. The most effective way to do this is to develop an individualized language use plan for students that specifies how native language support is to be provided over a period of three to four years. Although similar to it, this long-term language usage plan is not to be confused with the Individualized Educational Plan (IEP) that is required for students with special education needs.

Establishing a long-term individualized plan for secondary as well as elementary ESL students is crucial in that it can ensure a smooth transition from native language to English-only classes in the content areas. This transition is but one of several critical transitions that adolescents who enter U.S. schools with limited proficiency in English must negotiate (Lucas, 1997). The transition from native language and ESL or sheltered classes to English-only content-area classes can be particularly difficult and may result in students not being able to cope with the demands of classes and teachers (Saunders and Goldenberg, 1999; Lucas, 1997).

TUTORING

GUIDELINE 5: ESL students should have access to ongoing tutoring support.

Even if ESL students are able to enroll in several sheltered classes tailored to their linguistic and academic needs, in order to ensure their success, many need to have regular access to individual tutoring. Since ESL students come to school with diverse backgrounds, schools need to be prepared to assist a wide range of students including those who have had limited or interrupted schooling in their native countries and, as a result, may have low literacy or math skills—or both. Even if they now have the opportunity to attend school regularly, schoolwork can be a challenge because of gaps in their prior knowledge and education. Adding in the fact that their classes are conducted in a second language, it is easy to see how ESL students can become overwhelmed! A tutoring center can provide ESL students with the assistance they need to be successful when a homework assignment is difficult, when they do not understand the teacher's directions, or when they are just so overwhelmed that they do not know how or where to begin. If necessary, the tutors in the center can even act as liaisons between a teacher and an ESL student in order to clear up any misinterpretations or misunderstandings about assignments.

Students can be assigned to a tutoring center in lieu of a study hall. Depending on their schedules, this can be every day or a few times per week. Students should also have the opportunity for before- or after-school tutoring. They can receive help with their content-area coursework, and if they have time left over during an assigned tutoring period, they can practice or study English. The tutoring center can be stocked with study materials (books and stories to read, grammar worksheets to do, etc.) for this purpose. ESL students who have already exited from the ESL program and are enrolled in all "mainstream" courses can also be assigned to the tutoring center instead of a study hall so that they, too, can receive tutoring assistance as needed. The tutoring center can be staffed by ESL teachers, teaching assistants, community volunteers, university students, and peer tutors.

It is helpful to students if the staff in the tutoring center includes tutors who speak some of the students' native languages. In this way, students can get assistance with their assignments in their respective native languages, which can save time when discussing assignments or concepts and can lead to a deeper understanding of the lesson material. The native language help can also come from peers; students from the same language background can work on assignments together, discuss concepts, and offer explanations to one another using their first language.

Besides being a place where students can get help with academics, the tutoring center can serve as a home base for the ESL students where they can make friends and discuss concerns, difficulties and problems they may be having in their new academic and cultural environment. Especially in a big, impersonal high school environment, it is important for ESL students to have a place where they feel comfortable and welcomed. ESL students may even want to use the tutoring center to conduct some cultural activities for themselves or for the rest of the school. For example, in one school in which I worked, the ESL students organized a yearly international lunch where each student brought a typical food from his or her country to share with classmates and teachers.

I asked a former high school student of mine to talk about how the ESL tutoring center benefited her when she was an ESL student several years ago:

> The ESL tutoring center was very helpful to me as well as being a "break" during the school day. I was able to keep up with my homework and get assistance from a teacher on any unclear material that might have been taught in a specific classroom that day. I could get help with writing papers for my more difficult classes. It was also a time to socialize with the other ESL students which helped me feel less alone, especially in the beginning, when I just arrived from Portugal and hardly spoke any English.

TUTORING, WHETHER THROUGH A PEER OR AN ADULT, should be offered to every secondary-level ESL student. It is inexpensive and not very complicated to set up (Lucas, 1997). Tutors need to be trained, and they need to be given very specific tasks to complete with tutees. If the tutor assigned to the ESL student is a peer, reciprocal tutoring should be encouraged, so that the ESL student teaches his or her peer something that can be shared with the rest of the class. Since many ESL students come from culturally different backgrounds, they will have something interesting to share with non-ESL students. This is not bound to happen naturally, however; the teacher needs to set up the tasks and expectations in such a way that the English-proficient peer has to rely on information provided by the ESL student once in a while.

Another point to consider in setting up a peer tutoring system is the finding that the benefits of tutoring are far greater for the tutor than they are for the tutee (Heath and Mangiola, 1991). This means that, if given appropriate tasks, ESL students themselves can benefit tremendously from the act of tutoring another student.

Despite the all-around benefits to ESL students of tutoring from peers or adults, the most important thing to remember about tutoring is that it is never enough. In addition to the fact that tutoring should never occur without the prior planning or close supervision of a certified teacher, it should also never supplant instruction by a qualified certified teacher. For the same reasons Helene and I discussed under pullout models in Chapter 3, tutoring needs to occur as an add-on rather than in lieu of academic instruction.

4.2 ADVOCATING FOR AN *ESL TUTORING CENTER*

Suppose you want to organize an ESL tutoring center at your school, and you are trying to gain administrative support. Your principal believes that the center will benefit the ESL students, but because there are only 30 ESL students in the school, she is not ready to find space and hire staff. You realize that if you can convince the principal that an ESL tutoring center will benefit others in the school in addition to the ESL students, she might decide to allocate the necessary space and funds.

Think about ways that the center will also benefit "mainstream" students and even "mainstream" teachers. By yourself or with one or two colleagues, list the ideas that you would present to your principal to convince her that the center would be beneficial to the school as a whole.

COMMUNICATION AND COLLABORATION

GUIDELINE 6: *In order to ensure that the overall program for ESL students is effective, ESL teachers need to establish ongoing communication and collaboration with teachers of sheltered and "mainstream" classes as well as with guidance counselors.*

Once an ESL program has been established in a middle or high school, it is important to evaluate how well the various components are working, both individually and together. The teachers and counselors who work with ESL students need to meet periodically to discuss answers to the following questions.

Is there a sufficient variety of ESL and sheltered classes to meet student needs? Teachers and counselors need to discuss whether the ESL program as a whole is adequate or if additional ESL and/or sheltered classes are needed in order for ESL students to be successful in high school and to be prepared for post-secondary education.

Is each individual student's daily program suitable for that student? Because ESL students' needs are so diverse, it is difficult to predict if even a carefully thought-out daily program of classes will meet a particular student's needs. Therefore, it is essential to check that the program chosen is, in fact, appropriate for that student. Each student's progress should be evaluated continually and program changes should be made as necessary.

In my experience at the high school level, there were many cases where particular classes that we thought were suitable for certain students were found not to be so two or three weeks into the semester. In those cases, we tried to make class changes as soon as possible. Our standard procedure was to move the student into the supposedly more suitable class for a two-week trial period. At the end of the trial period, if the class seemed appropriate for the student, we officially made the change; if not, we looked for alternative solutions. In most cases, this flexible approach helped us to find the correct class for students. I remember one situation where we had to make several changes for a student during the school year. This is what happened:

Galinda, a student from Russia, arrived at our high school as an eleventh-grader speaking very little English. Although she had studied English in school for many years in Russia, she had had little opportunity to speak it. She scored high on our entry exam in the areas of reading and writing so we placed her in a high level of ESL (Level III) and various sheltered classes.

Within a few weeks Galinda began to speak in class and showed evidence of a higher degree of proficiency in oral English than she had demonstrated on her entry tests. Apparently, she had previously learned a considerable amount of English; she needed to be in an English-speaking environment for it to kick in as she became accustomed to hearing native speakers and began to feel more comfortable in her classes. After two weeks we changed her ESL class from Level III to Level IV and enrolled her in our transition English class, which prepared ESL students for "mainstream" literature classes. The wonderful teacher of that class was so impressed with Galinda that after a month the teacher suggested we enroll Galinda in a "mainstream" literature class. Since that teacher also taught a section of American literature, we decided to transfer Galinda to that particular section where she could get some extra attention, as needed, from the willing and dedicated teacher.

At the semester break we made the change; with hard work, and some assistance from the teacher, Galinda did quite well. She continued to amaze us all with her abilities and perseverance. The following year, when it was time to apply to college, we encouraged her to aim high. When the college acceptances came in, we all celebrated—Galinda was accepted with a scholarship to Yale University.

This kind of program flexibility (with the support of the school administration and faculty, which must allow and accept these midquarter class changes) helps students achieve their potential. Teachers must watch for signs that each student's program is appropriate, and if not, take steps to make changes. Just as we should not hold back students such as Galinda by having them stay in classes that are not challenging enough for them, we also should not keep students in classes where they become frustrated because they have not yet acquired the academic skills or language proficiency necessary to succeed in those particular classes.

Else's Perspective

FLEXIBILITY IN THE IMPLEMENTATION of an instructional model for ESL students is probably one of the most essential factors in the success of a program. In the previous chapter, Helene mentioned the importance of taking an experimental approach in setting up an instructional model and assessing the effectiveness of various aspects of ESL education for a group of students. She suggested that, based on that ongoing assessment, changes could be made as needed. Collaborative and collective troubleshooting and problem solving among all staff involved in the instruction of ESL students are the only ways to ensure that all students are receiving the education they deserve.

Many school districts have found that a close relationship with a university has served the purpose of program evaluation well. But rather than having the university researchers complete an outside evaluation, it is more effective to have the researchers collaborate with key school personnel on all aspects of the evaluation (Cazabon, Lambert, and Hall, 1993). Field-initiated research projects that teachers conduct with the help of the outside evaluator often yield valuable information about the program. Cazabon (2000) suggests some rules of thumb for program evaluation.

1. It is critical to engage everyone in the discussion: parents, the business community, staff, administrators, and university-based researchers.
2. A steering committee must emerge from the larger group of people whose responsibility it will be to define evaluation goals and how they are to be measured.
3. Multiple sources of information must be sought and used in the evaluation process.
4. The instructional program and the evaluation design must be seen as evolving, and individuals involved in either endeavor must be open to change.
5. Information that guides teaching will emerge over time rather than in one short-term study.
6. We must accept change as a natural consequence of the results of any investigation, research, or evaluation.
7. The information obtained from the evaluation must reach all those who have been involved in the process, including students.

Are ESL students encouraged to take as many "mainstream" classes as possible? Even though sheltered classes should be offered in as many academic subjects as possible, only ESL students who need such courses should take them; ESL students should be encouraged to take as many "mainstream" content-area courses as their level of English proficiency permits. Teachers and counselors need to evaluate individual student programs to ensure that ESL students are being challenged and encouraged to work at their full potential.

Have the ESL and sheltered teachers discussed their respective curricula with one another to ensure that they are complementing (if appropriate) rather than duplicating their efforts? Especially if a content-based curriculum is used in the ESL classes, the ESL and sheltered teachers need to decide which content will be covered in ESL classes and which will be covered in sheltered classes. For example, if ESL students are taking a sheltered American history class, the ESL teacher may want to include some geography and map skills in the ESL class curriculum to prepare students for some of the American history lessons. On the other hand, if ESL students are taking a sheltered basic math class, the sheltered math teachers may decide to handle all the ESL students' math language needs during the sheltered math class, allowing the ESL teacher to work on other language needs during the ESL class. Depending on the needs of the ESL students and the course

See Chapter 2 for a discussion of curriculum coordination.

offerings available, the ESL and sheltered teachers may want to coordinate their curricula, or alternatively, the ESL teacher may want to concentrate on preparing ESL students for classes they will be taking in the future that are not available in a sheltered version. These matters need to be discussed in order to make decisions that will be the most beneficial for ESL students.

See Chapter 8 for a discussion of providing professional growth opportunities for all staff who work with ESL students.

Is support—such as resource personnel, training, and materials—available for the ESL, sheltered and/or content-area teachers and counselors who work with ESL students? It is essential that those teachers and counselors who work with ESL students have adequate support and are sufficiently trained in pedagogy and cultural matters. Through discussions, it can be determined if the support currently being offered is sufficient, or if steps need to be taken to increase resources and enhance professional growth opportunities.

Have ESL, sheltered, and content-area teachers explored the possibility of team-teaching certain units and/or entire courses? In Chapter 3, the benefits of team-teaching in an elementary school were discussed. Specifically, it was argued that ESL students benefit when a grade-level and ESL teacher work together, the grade-level teacher contributing expertise in general teaching and content knowledge and the ESL teacher contributing ideas and expertise regarding ESL teaching strategies. ESL students in a secondary school setting can also benefit when teachers work together.

At a recent teachers' conference, I attended a session in which an ESL teacher from New Jersey talked about her team-teaching experiences in a middle school. First, she described the different team-teaching situations in which she has worked; then she talked about the benefits to both students and teachers. This is what she reported:

Judith O'Loughlin, Ho-Ho-Kus Public School, New Jersey

> I have team-taught with an eighth-grade English teacher and a seventh/eighth-grade social studies teacher. The English class was made up of about 15 "mainstream" and 9 ESL and/or special education students. Our usual procedure was to divide each lesson into parts or sections; then the English teacher and I took turns teaching the parts of the lessons we felt comfortable with. The "other" teacher wrote on the chalkboard, chimed in information, and played devil's advocate, asking for clarification. This latter activity eased the embarrassment of reluctant students who might not have wanted to ask questions for fear of looking stupid in front of their peers. It also opened things up for discussion.
>
> When the students were doing writing assignments, the English teacher and I were able to divide the class in half to consult with students and offer feedback in smaller group sessions. During free reading time we circulated to work with individual students to check on their comprehension. The English teacher did not have an ESL or special education background (I have both) so the techniques that I initiated seemed to be helpful especially to the ESL (and special education) students.
>
> The eighth-grade social studies situation was somewhat different; the social studies teacher taught the main part of the lesson, and then we broke into small groups to do reading, writing, and

computer activities/assignments. I had the ESL students in my group with other kids as well. The class consisted of about 25 students, seven of whom were ESL and/or special education students. The social studies teacher designed the tests; I either modified them for the ESL students or designed alternative tests, as needed.

In the seventh-grade social studies situation I did not actually work in the social studies classroom; instead, I developed a literature link to the geography units the class was studying and I worked with the ESL seventh-graders during a separate supplementary period. By reading literature (and recycling vocabulary from the social studies geography lessons) students had a better understanding of the connection between geography and people's lives and seemed to have more interest in both the social studies and literature lessons.

I believe that a team-teaching model is beneficial to ESL students for several reasons. First, they have an opportunity to learn from two different teachers with different teaching styles. If one teacher's style doesn't match well with a particular student's learning style, perhaps the other teacher's does. Second, the students can get more individualized assistance with two teachers in the room. Third, the students reap the benefits of the ESL teacher's knowing their vocabulary and language needs along with knowing appropriate teaching strategies to help them learn. The ESL teacher can model these strategies and techniques for the content-area teacher who can develop expertise in these areas, as well.

As teachers in a team-teaching situation we are no longer working in isolation and have the advantage of being able to bounce ideas off one another. I personally find that I am more creative when I work with someone else. Just as individual students see each of us differently, we see each student from our own personal viewpoint and can offer these unique perspectives when discussing student progress as well as problems.

There are some pitfalls to watch out for in a team-teaching situation. For example, teachers need to feel that they are sharing, more or less equally, the work of planning, marking papers, grading, and so forth, so that neither feels overly burdened with the workload. It is also important to match up teachers who have compatible personalities and teaching philosophies so that they are comfortable with each other in the classroom. The administration must show support for the team-teaching concept by providing some regular planning time during the school day at least a few times per week. In the beginning I needed to meet daily with my teammate, but after a few months we found that two or three times per week was sufficient.

IN ADDITION TO THE IMPORTANT FACTORS that Helene mentions, which contribute to the success of team teaching, the issue of the relative status of the two teachers must be taken into account. As discussed in Chapter 3, the perceived status of the ESL teacher as seen by students, other teachers, and administrators is very important. The ESL teacher must be perceived as having equal status to the content-area teacher, and must be seen as having equal decision-making power within the classroom and the school. The ESL teacher must be perceived as being capable of teaching components of the curriculum that are just as important to the functioning and success of the whole school as the core academic subject areas.

ESL teachers do not often enjoy this perceived status within the school community. Thus, it is essential that administrators and teachers collectively discuss this issue and plan ways to establish equal status among teaching staff.

4.3 *OUT IN THE FIELD...*

Team-teaching is becoming more prevalent as teachers recognize the potential benefits to students. Find out if any classes with ESL students are team-taught in your area. Perhaps you could get together with four or five colleagues and each take on the task of calling a different nearby secondary school. Each of you could ask if any content-area classes with ESL students are team-taught. If so, try to speak personally with one of the teachers involved in order to find out more information. You might want to ask the following questions:

1. What subject(s) are you team-teaching?
2. How many ESL students are in the class? How many "mainstream" students? Are there any special education students?
3. How are the two of you working together (that is, what does each of you actually do in the classroom)?
4. What do you perceive are the benefits to the ESL students in the class?
5. What problems or difficulties have you encountered using a team-teaching model?

Share your answers with the members of your group. Then, discuss your beliefs about team-teaching.

WHAT ARE THE COMPONENTS OF FOUR ESTABLISHED PROGRAMS?

This section describes ESL programs created by four school districts to meet the needs of their ESL students. I have chosen these particular programs because they represent four distinct program types: two high school ESL programs—one small program and one large program—and two middle school ESL programs—also, one small program and one large program. The sample programs demonstrate how the guidelines described in the previous section look in actual ESL programs.

The programs chosen are not perfect. However, they show how available resources (financial and professional) can be used to create quality educational programs for ESL students.

THE SMALL ESL PROGRAM IN A HIGH SCHOOL

High schools with relatively few ESL students (five percent or less of the student body) must usually offer a somewhat limited ESL program since the school cannot justify a disproportionately large financial allocation for a relatively small group of students. As mentioned earlier, school districts are reluctant to spend money on materials, classroom space, and especially teachers (the most expensive part) for classes that may consist of fewer students than "mainstream" classes and that serve a small proportion of the school population. Here is a look at an ESL program that one school district in suburban Connecticut has created to meet the needs of its ESL students.

Program Description

In any given year in this high school of about 1200 students, there are between 30 and 50 ESL students; they come from Puerto Rico and from various countries in Asia, Central America, South America, and Europe. Some of the students have a strong academic background in their native language whereas others have had only minimal schooling.

This ESL program consists of four levels of ESL classes, four sheltered classes (American history, American government, reading, and transition English), and an ESL tutoring center. The sheltered classes are taught by teachers certified in their respective fields with training in ESL teaching strategies. The ESL and sheltered classes tend to have relatively small numbers of students (between 8 and 20).

For a discussion of assessing students for placement in ESL classes, see Chapter 5, pp. 101–114.

Upon arrival in the school, each potential ESL student takes a placement test and is then assigned an ESL level, I through IV. This level determines the course of study in an eight-period day, as shown in Figure 4.1.

Sequence of Classes

As shown in the chart, Level I and II students are encouraged to take electives, whereas Level III and IV students are ready to pursue a program consisting of classes from all the core academic subject areas. The math sequence is such that students do not take geometry until they have reached ESL Level III; teachers in this school have reported that ESL students seem to need a higher level of English proficiency to understand geometry instruction than to understand algebra instruction. Since the health class also requires a high level of English proficiency, ESL students usually take it in their fourth (or, in some cases, third) year of learning English, instead of automatically taking it with their peers in tenth grade.

Figure 4.1: Placement Chart for Sample Small ESL Program in a High School

LEVEL I Student	LEVEL II Student	LEVEL III Student	LEVEL IV Student
ESL I	ESL II	ESL III	ESL IV
ESL I	Reading (sheltered)	Transition English (sheltered literature)	Transition English (sheltered lit.) or English (various choices)
Math (Algebra I or Prealgebra)	Math (Algebra II)	Math (Geometry)	Math (various choices)
Elective	ESL American History (sheltered)	ESL American Government (sheltered)	Social Studies (various choices)
Elective	Elective	Science (various choices)	Science (various choices)
ESL Tutoring Center	ESL Tutoring Center	ESL Tutoring Center	ESL Tutoring Center
Physical Education	Physical Education	Physical Education	Physical Education/ Health
Lunch	Lunch	Lunch	Lunch

American history and American government are offered in alternating years —otherwise, there would not be enough students enrolled to justify offering the classes. However, as mentioned earlier, since the American history class provides students with useful background knowledge for understanding the concepts in the American government class, students are at an advantage if they can take the American history class first. Nonetheless, since the school cannot offer both classes in the same year, students have to take whichever class is available that year; this is the reality in this small ESL program in a public high school setting.

Sheltered Class Options

When sheltered classes were originally created in this school district, it was decided that they were most needed in literature and social studies since classes in those subject areas were the most difficult for many ESL students; however, it is unfortunate that science is not also offered as a sheltered course. As mentioned earlier in this chapter, many universities prefer students to have three years of science study. In this ESL program, students who begin high school as Level I ESL students are usually unable to take a third year of science by the time they graduate.

Only four sheltered classes are offered, mainly for financial reasons, but also for philosophical reasons; some administrators prefer not to isolate ESL students in their own special classes. The ESL teachers have tried to convince administrators that it is best to provide ESL students with access to as many sheltered academic subjects as possible even though the students may be temporarily somewhat isolated from the "mainstream" (they do take "mainstream" classes from the very beginning in the form of electives and physical education, so they are always in the "mainstream" to some degree). Until ESL students acquire more English and can participate meaningfully in more of the "mainstream" classes, it is sensible to offer sheltered alternatives. This option is better than having the students wait two years until they are "ready" to take a "mainstream" class such as biology, which is not offered in a sheltered format.

Program Flexibility

Students enter the program at all different levels of academic and language proficiency. Therefore, a ninth-grader who comes to this school with a solid academic background and previous study of English might enter as a Level IV student, whereas a twelfth-grader with interrupted academic experiences and minimal study of English might enter at Level I. (Such a twelfth-grader, by the way, is usually advised to stay an additional year in high school in order to acquire more English proficiency, as well as academic proficiency, before graduating.) Either of them could take courses from a different column, if appropriate; the chart serves only as a suggested guideline. Since students are placed according to English proficiency levels and individual needs rather than grade levels, the ESL and sheltered classes are mixed with respect to student ages and grades.

4.4 *ANALYZING MIXED-AGE CLASSES*

In Chapter 2, it was mentioned that a mixed-age class sometimes presents difficulties in choosing suitable core literature materials. Can you think of other potential problems when there is a four-year age range in a high school class?

Since the rate of student progress is highly individual, especially in a diverse group such as ESL students, toward the end of each school year, ESL teachers and counselors carefully examine each individual student's progress, in order to advise students about course options for subsequent years. For example, some ESL students, especially those with strong academic backgrounds in their first language, may acquire English quickly and be able to enter almost all "mainstream" classes after only one or two years in this country. Others, especially those with interrupted schooling, may need tutorial assistance to succeed even in their ESL and sheltered classes. When advising students about course selections for the following year, teachers and counselors at this school generally follow the sequence guidelines, but they also try to tailor course selections to students' individual needs. For example, if necessary, students may take the sheltered reading class as well as the sheltered transition English class more than once, if at the completion of either class it is determined that the student is not yet ready to move on to a higher-level English class.

Summary

This ESL program seems to work well for the ESL students in this small suburban community. There is a low dropout rate among the ESL students and most of them progress successfully through the ESL and sheltered classes and on to "mainstream" classes. Of course, there is always room for improvement. But, considering the relatively small size of the program and its limited staff and resources, it is quite successful.

4.5 *EVALUATING THE SMALL ESL PROGRAM IN A HIGH SCHOOL*

Work with one or two colleagues and imagine that you are a team called in to evaluate the ESL program described above. Using the six guidelines discussed in the first half of this chapter, determine the strengths and weaknesses of this program, and see if you can make some suggestions for improvements. To organize the information, you may want to set up a chart such as the following:

Guideline	Rating	Comments/Suggestions
1		
2		
3		
4		
5		
6		

Rating scale: 1–5
5 = very strong in this area
1 = very weak or nonexistent in this area
0 = more information needed

If possible, discuss your results with another team.

THE LARGE ESL PROGRAM IN A HIGH SCHOOL

Since my own ESL teaching experience has been in relatively small ESL programs, I asked the district chairperson of a large ESL/bilingual program in Illinois to discuss the various components of such a program. As expected, this large ESL program offers many more courses than a smaller program is able to offer. In this particular school there is a concentration of Polish, Spanish, and Korean speakers; therefore, several content courses are taught in those languages (in other words, the school is able to offer a bilingual component to some ESL students).

Program Description

We currently have about 275 students in the ESL program, which is about 12 percent of the student body. The students come from Puerto Rico and from many different countries in Asia, Europe, and South America; a substantial number of students speak Polish (about 90 students) and Spanish (about 60 students). We have five levels of ESL. Once we determine students' levels, we place them in one of the following ESL courses: Beginning, Advanced Beginning, Intermediate, Advanced, and Advanced American English Skills.

David Barker,
Maine East
High School,
Park Ridge,
Illinois

Courses Offered

The Beginning-level students are in an intensive program taking only ESL for five periods per day. In these ESL classes, students do a wide variety of activities using many different materials. The goal is to acclimate them to American high school and to the broader American culture while giving them the English skills they need to survive in an academic and social environment. This five-period intensive program lasts about nine weeks, at which time students enroll in physical education and, usually, sheltered math, if they seem capable of succeeding. Since math classes are already in progress at this point in the semester, we place the ESL students in math classes where they already have some knowledge of the material. The goal is for these students to become familiar with mathematical terms and processes before they go on to more difficult levels the following year.

The Advanced Beginning-level students have enough English to get along somewhat in school. They usually take a total of three periods of ESL, a sheltered computer class, a sheltered math class, and physical education. We encourage students at this level to take art or music in order to provide them with a good learning experience that does not require high literacy skills.

The Intermediate-level students are enrolled in two ESL sections and whatever academic courses they need or want, although they may take sheltered sections of some academic subjects. The ESL staff monitors their course selections for graduation requirements and for appropriateness for future participation in postsecondary education.

The Advanced-level students are also enrolled in two ESL sections and whatever academic courses (including sheltered courses) they need or desire.

The Advanced American English Skills course is our transition class. This is one period per day. It covers composition and literature, providing, among other things, the kinds of experiences that native speakers get in a ninth-grade English class. It is also designed to prepare ESL students for future "mainstream" English classes in high school and college.

In their free periods, all ninth-grade ESL students are assigned to the resource room, where an ESL teacher is available each period to provide tutoring (in any subject). In our school, in the general population, only ninth-graders are assigned to study halls/resource rooms, but we also include all the Beginning level ESL students (in all grades) and any ESL students who are in danger of failing an academic subject. Other ESL students may drop in to the center for tutoring help, as needed, if space allows. ESL students can also get assistance by going to the math resource room (available to all students in the school) as well as by seeing their individual teachers in free periods or after school.

Skills Taught

The ESL classes at all levels include composition, literature, and language arts. At the Beginning and Advanced Beginning levels, a great deal of time is also spent on teaching the skills needed for success in math, science, and social studies. We are preparing students to succeed in their sheltered and "mainstream" content courses.

We have a computer lab and an audio/video lab that provide students with maximum opportunities for acquiring language skills as well as computer and technology skills.

Sheltered Course Options

Sheltered classes are available in the following content areas: math fundamentals, prealgebra, algebra 1, algebra 2, precalculus, physical science, biology, chemistry 1/physics 1 (a sophomore course designed to introduce students to lab work), chemistry 2, U.S. history, government, three computer-related courses, health, oral communications (required for graduation), and consumer education (required for graduation). (See Figure 4.2 for a list of courses.) For the most part, the sheltered classes use the same materials as the "mainstream" sections, but the ESL sections have only ESL students, and the terrific content-area staff who teach them are highly motivated to help ESL students achieve.

The most common criticism of sheltered classes is that they are watered down. They certainly cannot be exactly the same as the "mainstream" classes, due to students' linguistic limitations, but we try to teach topics and concepts at an appropriately high level. I often point out to critics of sheltered classes that when native speakers of English reach high school and enroll in U.S. history, they have been exposed to the subject at least twice before during their schooling. This is not the case for ESL students. It seems unfair to mix ESL students with native speakers and expect the ESL students to do OK.

Figure 4.2: ESL and Bilingual Course Offerings in Sample Large ESL Program in a High School

LANGUAGE

ES101	Beginning ESL
ES102	Advanced Beginning ESL
ES103	Intermediate ESL
ES104	Advanced ESL
ES50	Basic Language Skills (used in tandem with above to receive the credit for class)
ES20	Advanced American English Skills

READING

ES601	Beginning—ESL
ES602	Advanced Beginning—ESL
ES603	Intermediate—ESL
ES604	Advanced—ESL
ES60	Basic Language Reading (use in tandem with above classes to receive credit for classes)

MATH

2020	Fundamentals of Math—ESL
20201	Fundamentals of Math/Bilingual (Spanish)
2030	Pre-Algebra—ESL
20302	Pre-Algebra/Bilingual (Polish)
2240	Algebra 2 Soph.—ESL
22402	Algebra 2 Soph./Bilingual (Polish)
22403	Algebra 2 Soph./Bilingual (Korean)
22502	Algebra 1 Soph.—ESL
2480	Pre-Calculus–ESL
24802	Pre-Calculus/Bilingual (Polish)

FOREIGN LANGUAGE

4820	Spanish for Spanish Speakers 1
4830	Spanish for Spanish Speakers 2

APPLIED TECHNOLOGY

6960	CWT—ESL Reltd.
6970	CWT—ESL Training

RESOURCE/STUDY

4810	Resource/Study Hall

BUSINESS

5491/5492	Keyboard & Format—FSL
5761/5762	Understanding Computers—ESL
5771/5772	Computer Applications—ESL

SOCIAL SCIENCE

1010	U.S. History—ESL
10101	U.S. History/Bilingual (Spanish)
10102	U.S. History/Bilingual (Polish)
10103	U.S. History/Bilingual (Korean)
12321	Government/Bilingual (Spanish) also 90821 for Constitution Test
1232	Government—ESL
12322	Government/Bilingual (Polish) also 90821 for Constitution Test
14121	Current Topics in Economics/Bilingual (Spanish)

SCIENCE

3110	Physical Science—ESL
31101	Physical Science/Bilingual (Spanish)
3210	Phys. 1/Chem. 1—ESL
32102	Chem. 1/Phys. 1/Bilingual (Polish)
32103	Chem. 1/Phys. 1/Bilingual (Korean)
3330	Biology—ESL
33301	Biology/Bilingual (Spanish)
3670	Chemistry 2—ESL
36702	Chemistry 2/Bilingual (Polish)

ORAL COMMUNICATIONS

0861/0862	Oral Communications—ESL
08611/08621	Oral Communications/Bil. (Spanish)
08612/08622	Oral Communications/Bil. (Polish)
08613/08623	Oral Communications/Bil. (Korean)

HEALTH

86021	Health—ESL Sm.1
86022	Health—ESL Sm. 2
86023	Health/Bilingual (Polish)
86024	Health—ESL (or other Bilingual)
86025	Health/Bilingual (Spanish)

CONSUMER EDUCATION

8721/8722	Consumer Education—ESL
87211/87221	Consumer Education/Bil. (Spanish)
87212/87222	Consumer Education/Bil. (Polish)
87213/87223	Consumer Education/Bil. (Korean)

(Adapted and printed with permission from Maine East High School, Park Ridge, Illinois)

Summary

Schools with relatively large ESL programs can offer ESL students a wide variety of ESL and sheltered classes and, in some cases, content classes taught in the native language. By following the guidelines described in this chapter, such schools can create quality ESL programs that are suited to individual student needs and are effective in helping students succeed in high school and future endeavors.

4.6 *Supporting Sheltered Classes*

As mentioned in the discussions of both the small and large ESL programs, not all teachers agree that ESL students should have the opportunity to learn content through sheltered classes. Imagine that you are at a faculty meeting and the topic of sheltered classes is being discussed. You feel that more of them should be offered at your school, but some teachers disagree. Role-play an interaction with one of the teachers in the room who disagrees with you.

4.7 *Evaluating the Large ESL Program in a High School*

Evaluate this large ESL program by following the same procedure outlined in Investigation 4.5. Then compare the two programs. How are they similar? How are they different? What essential elements must all ESL programs, large or small, include?

In the Middle School

Many middle schools today have adopted the team concept; that is, each student in the school is assigned to a team made up of perhaps a hundred students and possibly five or six teachers (the exact numbers vary, school by school). Each team functions almost as a separate school, with core academic classes for the students on the team conducted only by the teachers on that particular team. The purpose of the team approach is to allow a small group of teachers to get to know the same group of students; thus, if problems arise regarding particular students, teachers can work together to devise solutions. In addition, the team approach creates a more intimate atmosphere for students and a greater sense of belonging in what might be a big, impersonal school.

In some schools, the team approach allows for flexible scheduling so that special programs, projects, and units can be accommodated. For example, if a team is planning a special program or teaching a special unit, the teachers may want to extend the time of a particular class period or combine two class periods (say, a social studies and an English class) to conduct an interdisciplinary lesson or series of lessons. A particular social studies class might normally meet Period 1 and a particular English class might normally meet Period 5. But because the teams operate independently, they can have the flexibility to shift the schedule around so that these two classes can meet back-to-back on a given day.

Because ESL teachers do not typically teach one of the required core academic subjects taken by all students on a team (unless all members of the team are ESL students), ESL teachers usually combine students from several teams and grades to form classes. This can be problematic since a special team activity or a change in schedule on a particular team may mean that the ESL students on that team miss either their ESL instruction or another subject scheduled at that time. For example, if the social studies and English teachers decide to team-teach an interdisciplinary lesson during a two-period time block, the ESL students who take ESL class during what is usually the English time slot, but is the math time slot for that day, might have to miss either their ESL lesson or their math lesson.

ESL teachers in middle schools have had to find creative solutions to these scheduling problems. Here are examples of how two middle school ESL programs have managed to work within the team model.

THE SMALL ESL PROGRAM IN A MIDDLE SCHOOL

I asked a middle school ESL teacher who works in a small ESL program to describe the program and how it works within the team model.

Program Description

We currently have about 70 ESL students in the program, which is about five percent of the total school population. The students come from a variety of language backgrounds, so we do not have a bilingual program. (We do have one feeder elementary school with a Spanish bilingual program, so we provide some content classes in Spanish only for those students.) We have three levels of ESL classes in which students are placed by English proficiency level, not by school grade. The levels are A (beginner), B1 (intermediate), and B2 (advanced). We also have a level LA which is for our low-literacy students. We only have two students at that level this year, so they are actually placed in the same classes as the A-level students with the teachers making some accommodations. Here is a summary of our program:

Lorena Garner, Fairfax County Public Schools, Virginia

Figure 4.3: Placement Chart for Sample Small ESL Program in a Middle School

Level LA Student	Level A Student	Level B1 Student	Level B2 Student
ESL A	ESL A	ESL B1	ESL B2
ESL A	ESL A	Elective	English
Sheltered "Fast Math"*	Sheltered Math**	Math**	Math**
Sheltered Social Studies	Sheltered Social Studies	Sheltered Social Studies	Social Studies
Sheltered Science	Sheltered Science	Science	Science
Physical Ed./ Health	Physical Ed./ Health	Physical Ed./ Health	Physical Ed./ Health
Elective	Elective	Elective	Elective

* Sheltered "Fast Math" provides students with a review of basic math. They move out of this course when they are at or near grade level.
**Students are placed in math classes based on math proficiency rather than English proficiency.

We also have ESL students at level C, but they have actually been exited from the program. However, since they cannot be expected to have already reached the reading and writing levels of their native English-speaking peers, they may receive special consideration on standardized testing.

Course Descriptions

As you can see from the placement chart, ESL students learn content from the start through sheltered classes. For this reason the curriculum in the ESL classes does not need to cover the specific content, learning strategies and vocabulary necessary for learning in each content area—from the very beginning, students are learning this in the sheltered content classes. Therefore, in the ESL classes, after students learn initial survival English, teachers can concentrate on the content area of language arts (reading, writing, literature).

The dedicated teachers on the ESL teams generally do not use text-books—they modify content-area materials so that they are comprehensible to the ESL students. Some of us speak other languages, so when possible we use the native language (in small group situations) to help students comprehend the coursework and succeed in school.

The Team Model

ESL students are placed on teams, but the beginning-level students are on teams in name only since they are placed only in ESL and sheltered classes (and, therefore, do not take academic classes with their "teammates"). We do not have enough students to form entire teams made up solely of ESL students in each grade, but we do put all the ESL students on only one team per grade (rather than dispersing them among all the teams in each grade) which helps us somewhat with scheduling ESL classes. We have to take the intermediate and advanced ESL students off their teams in order to offer them appropriate ESL and sheltered classes, but they take their "mainstream" classes with the other students on their teams. Sometimes this scheduling is difficult to work out since some ESL classes are made up of students from all three grades in the school (which means three different teams), but the administration in my school is supportive and we try to work things out—I know that this administrative support isn't as strong in all schools.

In our school, teams do not, as yet, practice flexible scheduling (also known as block scheduling). This is where teams can schedule whatever they want during a certain block of time during the day. The school is in the process of investigating the possibility for future years. I believe that block scheduling will interfere with the ESL program because ESL students are not fully on teams. Therefore, when a team decides to change its usual schedule to offer something different, ESL students may have no place to go. Their "mainstream" science class, for example, may be canceled in order to schedule an extra social studies class that day (a class in which the ESL students may not be enrolled because they take the sheltered version). Their ESL class may become a "bus stop" for them. I know this is the case in other schools.

Summary

As you can see from the Teachers' Voices section above, fitting a small ESL program into a team model is a challenge. But schools have found creative ways to do so, as long as teachers and administrators remain flexible and willing to accommodate the needs of ESL students.

The Large ESL Program in a Middle School

I spoke with an ESL teacher/administrator who works in the same school district as the teacher above, but in a middle school with a larger ESL population. I asked her to describe the ESL program and how it works within the team model.

Program Description

Our middle school program currently serves about 230 ESL students who comprise approximately 26 percent of the student body. Our school follows a team approach, which means that each student is assigned to a team with a set group of students and teachers. Each team functions almost as a self-contained school within a school (except that students venture outside the team for physical education and electives). This approach allows teachers to get to know the students on their team quite well, and they are able to keep a close watch on them and their progress. This is especially important during the middle school years, when students are growing up fast and are easily distracted and influenced.

We decided that the best way to provide a good education for the ESL students in our school was to create ESL teams for beginning- and intermediate-level ESL students. In this way we could specialize the course offerings to fit the ESL students' needs and eliminate the scheduling problems associated with including ESL students from different teams in ESL and sheltered classes. ESL students at the more advanced levels of English proficiency are on teams comprised of about half ESL students and half non-ESL students.

Our students come from a variety of language backgrounds, so we do not offer bilingual classes. We divide the students into the same levels as do the smaller programs in our district, and follow the same class placement guide (see Figure 4.3).

Summary

The ESL students in this middle school ESL program are fortunate to be on teams made up exclusively of ESL students. The ESL students do not have to be pulled away from their team (with the risk of missing work if the team schedule is altered) for ESL instruction. In addition, since the teachers on such teams teach only ESL students, the topics discussed at their teacher team meetings can revolve around the unique issues regarding ESL students. Even though ESL students are initially somewhat isolated from the "mainstream," they are put on "mixed" teams as they acquire more English.

4.8 *Teaching in a Small vs. Large ESL Program*

Would you prefer teaching in a small or a large ESL program? Why? List the advantages and disadvantages of teaching in each. If possible, compare your answers with those of a colleague.

4.9 *Being a Student in a Small vs. Large ESL Program*

The advantage of being a student in a large ESL program is obvious—there are more classes tailored specifically to meet students' needs. What about being a student in a small ESL program—what are some possible advantages?

CHAPTER SUMMARY

Effective ESL programs in secondary schools have some aspects in common, but differ in many ways, as well. Schools need to work with the resources they have to provide ESL students with as many pathways as possible to a good education. At the very least, schools need to offer ESL classes, as well as sheltered content classes in certain core subjects. It is essential to consider the entire daily program (not simply the ESL and sheltered classes) when designing or examining the effectiveness of an ESL program. By communicating with content-area faculty, the ESL staff can determine if ESL students are faring well in their content-area classes or if adjustments in course selection or sequencing need to be made. With continual evaluation and dedication, ESL programs of any size can provide ESL students with tools for success.

4.10 *Out in the Field...*

In order to get a broader perspective on ESL program models in secondary schools, arrange to interview a middle or high school ESL teacher. Here are some questions you might ask:

1. How many students are in the ESL program? What percentage of the total school population do they comprise?
2. Are most of the ESL students from the same language group, or are they from different language groups?
3. Are any content courses offered in the students' native languages (that is, is there a bilingual program)?
4. If not, is the native language used at all for instruction or reinforcement of instruction? When and how?
5. What are the typical courses taken by ESL students at the beginning, intermediate, and advanced levels of English?
6. What do you feel should be changed/deleted/added to the ESL program?

Share your answers with a colleague.

Suggested Readings

For more on standards, see *Integrating the ESL Standards into Classroom Practice: Grades 6–8*, edited by B. Agor (2000), and *Integrating the ESL Standards into Classroom Practice: Grades 9–12*, edited by S. Irujo (2000).

5

ASSESSMENT ISSUES

My first ESL teaching job was at a learning center where adults in need of ESL instruction appeared at our doorstep. We gave them a short oral placement test, and then assigned them to one of six ESL levels. We did not test their reading and writing proficiency because we did not deal much with reading and writing in our classes; the purpose of our ESL instruction was to help students acquire oral communication skills. At the end of a six-week session, we gave students another oral test. If they passed, they moved on to the next level; if they did not, they repeated their current level. When they completed all six levels, they "exited" from the program. We did not have to issue any official report card grades and we did not have to worry about how content-area teachers were determining grades for our ESL students—the students weren't taking any other classes. They were studying only ESL.

In elementary and secondary schools, assessment issues are much more complex than they are in an adult school such as the one described above. First, it cannot be expected that every elementary and secondary student in need of ESL assistance will appear at the ESL classroom—some may be reluctant to ask for help. Schools need to have a systematic means of determining which students are eligible for ESL instruction. Second, in an academic setting such as an elementary or secondary school, where students must acquire good literacy skills to have access to academic knowledge, reading and writing proficiency also need to be assessed. Third, because public schools are accountable to the local community, to parents, and to the students themselves, schools need to report on student progress. One important means of communicating information about student progress is through report cards; ESL teachers need to establish criteria for determining report card grades for ESL students in ESL classes, as well as assist grade-level and content-area teachers in establishing fair criteria for determining report card grades for ESL students in grade-level/content-area classes.

This chapter will explore these and other issues with respect to different types of assessments given to ESL students for a variety of purposes. It is essential that ESL teachers have a solid understanding of assessment issues since the results of assessments in a K–12 setting can have considerable impact on ESL students, from placement in specific classes and programs to admission and scholarship opportunities at universities.

By directing the attention of teachers to the issue of assessment, Helene is sending the important message that assessment is an integral part of a teacher's work. This is a point that needs to be made explicitly because assessment remains an uncomfortable zone for many teachers. Teachers often do not see themselves as assessors and are reluctant to participate in the assessment process. However, teachers have vital information about their students that can rarely be captured by formal tests. In addition, the personal and long-term information that teachers have about their students cannot be captured by assessment procedures administered by people who are strangers to the student.

Traditionally, assessment has been seen as a specialized field that is the domain of experts outside of the classroom. And perhaps formal standardized testing is such a specialization that it requires its practitioners to be knowledgeable in psychometrics and statistical analyses. However, recent changes in the nature of educational assessment and the philosophy and outlook that define educational assessment have resulted in a view of assessment that is very broad in scope (Hamayan, 1995). In the current view, assessment has been expanded to include much more than standardized testing. This broad-based definition of assessment includes informal and sometimes subjective information that teachers naturally collect about their students. This view of assessment, then, takes on a data collection approach in which information from several sources is considered.

These changes have also brought assessment into the classroom and have made it an integral part of instruction rather than a separate activity that takes place at predetermined points during the school year. Helene distinguishes between district-level assessment and classroom-based assessment. This distinction exists in most school districts; typically, the district-level assessment tends to be of the standardized formal type, while most teachers take a more informal and more holistic approach to assessment in their classrooms. Most educators relate district-level assessment to high-stakes decisions (August and Hakuta, 1997), and rarely do those decisions incorporate the results of classroom-based assessment. Despite the fact that classroom-based assessment yields valuable information about students, those more informal and sometimes even qualitative assessment practices are still perceived as being alternative (Hamayan, 1995). Helene's suggestions for alternative assessment options at the district level in a later section of this chapter are very useful.

A Positive View of Assessment

Assessment (used broadly in this book to mean any type of formal or informal test or evaluation of student skills, knowledge, ability, or proficiency) can reveal to us what students already know (or know how to do), and what they still need to learn. This positive view of assessment focuses on present knowledge and future learning rather than on deficiencies. In other words, since it is natural and expected that ESL students have much to learn in the way of their second language, just as young children have much to learn in the way of their first language, ESL students should not be considered deficient. In a K–12 setting, when beginning-level ESL students score in the low range on a language assessment (as expected), they are often labeled "limited" or "deficient" simply because they are not yet fluent in English (Genesee, 1994). But, in fact, ESL students bring much knowledge to school; the knowledge simply happens to be in another language and may be expressed through means of another culture. Rather than viewing assessment as a way of determining in which areas students are deficient, teachers need to see assessment as a means of determining how much students already know or what they can do, in order to help them build on this knowledge to further their proficiency in English and the content areas (Met, 1994).

TWO CATEGORIES OF ASSESSMENTS

It is helpful to divide the assessments used with ESL students into two general categories: program-level assessments and classroom-level assessments (Brown, 1996). In a K–12 setting, these assessments are generally referred to as *district-level assessments* and *classroom-based assessments,* respectively. District-level assessments are those that are given to all students in the ESL program for the following reasons: to make entry decisions, that is, to determine which students need ESL instruction; to make placement decisions so that students are placed in appropriate groups for instruction; to monitor progress after students have been in school learning English for a period of time; and to make exit decisions, that is, to determine if students are ready to function on their own without assistance from an ESL program.

Classroom-based assessments are those that are given by individual ESL teachers in their classrooms, such as weekly quizzes. The main purpose of classroom-based assessments is to guide instruction. These assessments allow teachers to determine the effectiveness of their instruction and to plan future instruction that will optimize student learning (Genesee and Hamayan, 1994). Another purpose is to determine on a regular basis if students are making progress. In addition, since most ESL teachers will need to assign report card grades at the end of a marking period (usually four times per year), another purpose of classroom-based assessments is to gather enough information to determine appropriate report card grades.

In this chapter both types of assessments, district-level and classroom-based, are discussed with specific emphasis on the issues involved in a K–12 setting.

WHAT ARE THE PURPOSES OF DISTRICT-LEVEL ASSESSMENTS?

ENTRY DECISIONS

Schools need to have a reliable, systematic method for determining which students need ESL instruction. Determining ESL eligibility for students who arrive in this country without any prior exposure to English is easy—we know they need ESL instruction! But for many students the decision is not clear-cut. Many students have had some exposure to English through prior schooling in their respective countries or through prior schooling in a different school district in the United States. In the case of kindergarten children, many have had prior exposure to English through preschool, peers, relatives, or even television. A mechanism is needed to determine which students require ESL instruction and which are proficient enough in English to succeed on their own in grade-level/content-area classes.

In any public school system, the procedure for determining if a student is in need of ESL services starts at school registration. All students, native and non-native speakers of English alike, must provide the following information. (For elementary school students, the parents usually provide the information.) The wording of the questions may differ from district to district, but the information sought is the same.

1. What language did the student acquire first?
2. What language does the student speak most often?
3. What language is spoken most often at home by family members/caregivers?

If the answer to any of these questions in this "dominant-language question-naire" is a language other than English, the student is evaluated for ESL services.*

This initial screening procedure came about as a result of a civil rights class action lawsuit initiated in 1970 on behalf of a Chinese-speaking student, Kinney Lau, and 1,789 other Chinese-speaking students in the San Francisco public school system. The students were failing in school because they could not understand the language of instruction (English) and no special program was provided for them. The legal case, *Lau v. Nichols*, went to the United States Supreme Court; on January 24, 1974 the Court ruled that public schools must identify students who are not proficient in English, and then provide them with appropriate English language instruction so that they can participate in the school program (Scarcella, 1990).

The initial questionnaire is just a start—it merely indicates which students are *potential* ESL students. It does not indicate the proficiency levels of students, or if in fact they need ESL instruction. For example, I have met students who answered "Spanish" to all three questions on the questionnaire, but who were highly fluent in both Spanish and English and hence, were not in need of ESL instruction. On the other hand, I have received questionnaires with "English" as the response to all three questions, but within a few days into the school year, it became evident that these were not in fact the accurate responses. A few years ago, that situation occurred at Kanoelani Elementary School in Waipahu, Hawaii. Here is what happened.

> One of the sixth-grade teachers told me about a boy in her class, Jerald, who did not seem to speak or understand much English. When she asked him about his background, she found out that he had recently arrived in Hawaii from the Philippines. When she alerted me to the existence of this child, I panicked at first, thinking that I had placed his dominant-language questionnaire in the "all English" pile

Helene Becker

---

*Some school districts do not automatically evaluate students for ESL services unless the answer to at least one and a half or even two questions is a language other than English. One and a half answers of "Spanish," for example, would be: 1. Spanish, 2. Spanish/English, and 3. English.

by mistake, causing the child to fall through the cracks and not receive any ESL instruction. I retrieved his questionnaire from the pile and found that he (or his parents) had, in fact, responded with "English" to all three questions. Nevertheless, upon meeting and talking to Jerald, it was clear that he could not speak much English.

I called Jerald's mom and discovered that she had responded with "English" on the form because she did not want Jerald to have ESL instruction. Although she did not say so directly, my impression was that she did not want him to be singled out as "different" (or possibly "stupid") because he did not speak English. I explained to her that many other children in the school were just starting to learn English, and that teachers and students alike enjoyed helping them progress. I explained that the ESL program would help Jerald learn English as well as his academic subjects more quickly than if he did not have ESL instruction. Reluctantly, she agreed to change her answers on the questionnaire and to allow Jerald to enter the program.

Parents' reluctance to acknowledge their child's need for ESL instruction can have other consequences. Else explains.

> **Else's Perspective**
>
> NOT ADMITTING THAT A LANGUAGE OTHER THAN ENGLISH is spoken at home is a phenomenon that many school districts encounter during intake procedures. This type of misinformation can sometimes have much more serious consequences than was the case with Helene's student. As a result of misinformation about the student's dominant home language, some students may be misdiagnosed as having a disability or a disorder, especially when they have just enough proficiency in English to appear fluent. Typically, the ESL or bilingual teacher takes it upon herself or himself to convince the parents that there is nothing wrong with putting the child in the ESL program, as Helene did with Jerald. And, as Helene asks you to do in Investigation 5.1, it is an excellent exercise to rehearse what you would say to parents to convince them of the value of ESL instruction.
>
> However, it behooves a school to go beyond this solution and to think of preventive measures that would avoid the situation in the first place. As Helene mentions, the reason that some parents feel compelled to say they and/or their child speak English when they really do not is to avoid having their child singled out as "different" or even "stupid." These attitudes probably stem from prevailing sentiments in the larger society. Not only is bilingualism not valued in the larger society, but most schools perceive linguistically and culturally diverse students as being in need of compensation. In schools where bilingualism is seen as an enriching experience, the phenomenon that Helene describes is less likely to occur. Schools where learning English as a second language is seen as enriching for students with a native language other than English are not likely to have parents hide the fact that their children do not speak English. When a school goes even further and begins to see bilingualism as a possibility

not just for language-minority students but for all students regardless of their linguistic background, parents are more likely to admit that a language other than English is spoken at home.

Featuring the ESL program as a source of pride for the school and as an instructional model that leads to bilingualism (rather than a program that leads to English monolingualism) will create an effective learning atmosphere that will enhance all students' lives (Cloud, Genesee, and Hamayan, 2000).

Investigations

5.1 *CONVINCING PARENTS*

If you work in a public school, you may encounter a situation similar to the one described above involving Jerald. Imagine that you are the elementary ESL teacher who is trying to convince a parent to allow his or her child to receive ESL instruction. The parent, however, insists on not allowing the child to participate in any "special program." How would you convince the parent that the child would benefit from ESL instruction? With a colleague, role-play this conversation.

Once a list of potential ESL students (that is, the students who responded with a language other than English to at least one of the questions on the questionnaire) has been compiled, the assessment process needs to be initiated to determine which students are actually in need of ESL instruction. For those students who *do* enter the ESL program, the results will serve as initial scores to which subsequent scores on the same or a similar assessment instrument can be compared as the student advances through the program.

Listening/Speaking Assessment

The first step in the process is usually a listening/speaking assessment. Several commercial tests are available for K–12 students, including the Language Assessment Scales (LAS), Language Assessment Battery (LAB), Maculaitis Assessment Battery (MAC), and the Basic Inventory of Natural Language (BINL). As a result of administering any of these (or other) listening/speaking tests, students are assigned a proficiency "level" or "score" that differs depending on the test (they do not all use the same system). For example, on the LAS, students receive an oral language rating from Level 1 (non-English speaker) to Level 5 (fluent English speaker). Most school districts who use the LAS consider a score of Level 4 as indicating that the student is "orally proficient."

Reading/Writing Assessment

The listening/speaking assessment is only part of the information needed in making entry decisions, since, as discussed in Chapter 2, oral fluency does not necessarily mean reading, writing, and academic fluency. In fact, students who appear fluent because they can "speak English," possibly even without an accent, can have great difficulty in school because grade-level teachers may assume that they can do academic work on a par with native speakers. I have encountered this assumption many times; I remember the following incident in particular when I taught in the West Hartford (Connecticut) Public Schools.

> Early in my career my school district did not include a reading/ writing component in the ESL entry assessment. (The district includes a reading/writing component now.) As long as students could speak English well enough on a listening/speaking assessment, it was assumed that they did not need ESL instruction.

> A new student, Caterina, enrolled in the sixth grade at my school. She was from Peru, but had been in the United States about two and a half years and had managed to pick up conversational English without an accent. She was not placed in the ESL program because she received a rating of "fluent" on her listening/speaking assessment.

> During the second month of school Caterina's teacher mentioned to me that Caterina was having some academic problems. It seemed that she was having a difficult time comprehending the sixth-grade content materials, especially the assignments in her social studies and literature textbooks, and she was often quiet and withdrawn during class discussions. Since the teacher assumed that Caterina was fluent in English when she enrolled in the school, the teacher surmised that Caterina either had some sort of learning problem, or was just not motivated to learn.

> Since Caterina spoke a language other than English at home, I offered to enroll her "unofficially" in the ESL program. Over time, with some assistance and more experience with the written language, Caterina was able to do better in school, but I regret that the school gave her signals that she was not doing as well as she should have been when, in fact, she was progressing as we should have expected through the stages of language acquisition.

Helene Becker

Fortunately, we have come a long way in our understanding of the language acquisition process. As mentioned in Chapter 2, it is common for school-age children to develop proficient conversational skills within two years of their exposure to an English-speaking environment, but they often do not acquire grade-level reading, writing, and academic skills for five to seven (or more) years (Cummins, 1984 and Thomas and Collier, 1995); hence, in order to decide if a student is in need of ESL assistance, we must evaluate more than just listening and speaking skills. Otherwise, we run the risk of skipping over students who need ESL instruction, and of well-meaning but misinformed faculty members assuming that the student has a learning disability or a motivation problem.

Another reason for assessing students' reading and writing skills, especially at the secondary school level, is that in certain cases, students may score low on a listening/speaking assessment, but have considerable fluency in reading and writing English. These students have usually studied English in their respective native countries, but may have taken courses that emphasized reading and writing and provided little exposure to spoken English. By assessing their reading and writing proficiency we can determine whether they are able to enroll in some content-area classes. Although these students initially may have difficulty understanding the spoken English in content-area classrooms, after a short period of exposure, many of them can keep up with the coursework. These content-area classes would not be accessible to them if we knew only about their beginning-level listening and speaking proficiency.

In summary, it is best to administer a reading/writing assessment to all potential ESL students, regardless of their scores on the listening/speaking assessment, since the score on one does not necessarily predict the score on the other. A reading/writing assessment also provides a baseline score to which later scores for that student can be compared. Possible exceptions are the young learners in kindergarten and first grade who are just starting to develop literacy skills. However, some commercial test companies have now developed reading/writing assessments even for these young learners in order to assess their preliteracy skills (recognition and formation of letters, awareness of sound-letter correspondence, etc.).

Except for the BINL, which is strictly an oral test, the commercial ESL tests mentioned above for listening/speaking assessment also have reading/writing components. Some school districts, however, as part of their entry assessment choose a reading/writing assessment designed for native speakers of English rather than one designed for ESL students. The rationale for using such an entry test is that the test will supposedly assess how well a particular ESL student can handle unmodified content material in a "mainstream" setting. If the student can attain a certain "passing score" on a test designed for native speakers of English, then he or she is probably prepared to do grade-level work without ESL assistance, and therefore does not need to enter an ESL program.

Determining a "Passing Score" on a Reading/Writing Assessment

Once a reading/writing assessment is chosen, it is necessary to determine a "passing score" on the assessment. In other words, what score do potential ESL students need to attain to demonstrate that they do not (or no longer) need ESL assistance? This critical score cannot be gleaned from a testing manual because it depends in large part on the educational setting in which the child is currently situated. In a school district in which teachers are knowledgeable and experienced in working with students from diverse language backgrounds, a student may not need to attain a score as high as a student in a school district in which teachers are less experienced in working with ESL students; that is, students can manage with less help (and for fewer years) from the ESL teacher if the grade-level/content-area teacher is adept at strategies that help ESL (and former ESL) students learn. Using this logic, the "passing" score on a reading/writing assessment should vary school by school within the district (or even classroom by classroom within the school!), but this is too impractical to implement in reality.

Other factors that may influence the determination of an accurate reading/writing "passing" score on an ESL assessment tool include the level of difficulty of the academic work presented to students in grade-level/content-area classes and students' individual work/study habits. For example, in a school district that emphasizes high academic standards, ESL students may need to reach a relatively high "passing" score in order to demonstrate that they can succeed in a grade-level or content-area classroom without ESL assistance. Additionally, in order to succeed in academic subject classes, students who have strong academic backgrounds in their native languages, who have good work habits, and who study at home daily may not need to attain scores as high as other students on an ESL reading/writing assessment; their perseverance will allow them to do well even if they have not yet acquired a "fluent" level of reading and writing skills.

The argument that a "passing" score on an ESL entry assessment depends on several variables may seem odd to some readers: Shouldn't ESL students enter an ESL program based on some objective criteria that work in any school district rather than determining what score works in a particular school district? In theory, the answer is "yes;" but in reality, there is great variation across (and even within) school districts regarding the skills students need to succeed at particular grade levels and in particular classrooms. Since it is the ESL teacher's job to help students succeed in their grade-level or content-area classrooms, for any given assessment instrument it is essential to determine a score that demonstrates that students can succeed without ESL assistance in a typical grade-level/content-area classroom in that particular school district.

Kathleen Bailey (1998) discusses an analogous situation in a university setting. In order for nonnative speakers of English to be admitted into the master's program for teaching English as a second language at the university in which she teaches, they originally had to attain a score of 550 on the TOEFL (Test of English as a Foreign Language). This score was chosen as the cutoff because other master's programs at that university used a score of 550 for admission and because some ESL master's programs around the country used that score. Bailey reports, however, that after two years, it became evident that students who received scores around 550 were floundering in the program. Apparently, the reading and writing assignments in this particular master's program were too demanding for students who received the minimum score. Subsequently, the score was raised to 600, which proved to be a more realistic cutoff score. Similarly, in a K–12 setting, it may be unwise to choose a "passing score" on an ESL entry assessment instrument (the score to indicate that a student can succeed in the regular grade-level/content-area classes without ESL assistance) based on information in test manuals or by examining what other school systems do. These are useful starting points, but it is more helpful to students to base the score on the academic demands in that particular school district.

One way to determine a "passing score" for a particular ESL reading or writing assessment is to administer the test to current ESL students, and then note the scores of those advanced-level ESL students who are generally succeeding with grade-level work and appear to be almost ready to exit from the ESL program. The score that those successful ESL students have attained should be the score that potential ESL students should attain to demonstrate that they do not need ESL assistance.

Several years ago in the West Hartford (Connecticut) Public Schools, we did such an experiment. We were considering adopting the LAS-Reading and LAS-Writing instruments as part of our entry (and exit) procedures in the elementary schools and we wanted to select appropriate entry/exit scores. The testing manual describes the possible scores on each test as follows:

Helene Becker

LAS-Reading	LAS-Writing
1 = Non-reader	1 = Non-writer
2 = Limited reader	2 = Limited writer
3 = Proficient reader	3 = Proficient writer

We wanted to know if a score of "proficient" was "proficient enough" to succeed without ESL assistance. Here is how we proceeded:

We administered the tests to all our current ESL students and then analyzed the results. We specifically looked at the scores of advanced-level ESL students who were doing well in their grade-level classrooms in the hope that we could choose an average of their scores as the entry cutoff score.

We found that all of these advanced-level ESL students received a score of 3 on both the reading and writing assessments. In other words, attaining a score of 3 (proficient) on both the reading and writing instruments was probably necessary before a student could be expected to function successfully in the grade-level classroom without ESL instruction. We then asked ourselves if a score of 3 was *sufficient* for success. In other words, how did the ESL students who clearly were *not* ready to exit from the ESL program do on the assessments? Did they also receive scores of 3 indicating "proficient," when, in fact, we knew they were not ready to exit from the ESL program?

To our surprise, some of these less-proficient ESL students *did* attain a score of 3 on the LAS-Reading assessment. Since several of the students who had attained a 3 could not keep up with grade-level reading demands in this school district, a score of 3 did not automatically mean that a student was ready to exit from the ESL program; that is, a score of 3 was *necessary* but not *sufficient* for exiting. On the writing assessment, however, a score of 3 was sufficient for exiting. In other words, in general, only the ESL students who seemed ready to exit the ESL program were able to attain a 3 on the LAS-Writing assessment. All the less proficient writers received scores of 1 or 2.

As a result of this informal experiment, we decided to adopt the LAS-Writing assessment, but not the LAS-Reading assessment, as part of our entry screening procedures. By doing our experiment, we discovered that the reading test was not an accurate indicator of who should enter the ESL program and who should not because several ESL students who were not doing well in their grade-level reading programs could attain the highest possible score (that is, 3) on the reading test.

We attributed our results to the fact that in this particular school system, native English-speaking students entered school with high preliteracy skills and tended to become very good readers. The classroom reading demands were quite high, putting the ESL students in a position in which they needed to read English well in order to keep up with their classmates. The LAS-Reading assessment was, therefore, too easy a test in this school setting.

As a solution, we decided to use as our ESL reading assessment, the same test that was used in the district to assess native-English speakers, the Degrees of Reading Power (DRP). In this particular educational setting, the DRP was a more accurate predictor than the LAS-Reading assessment of who needed ESL instruction and who did not. We retested our ESL students with the DRP to establish cutoff scores for entry into the ESL program at each grade level by using the average scores of the advanced-level ESL students. Another logical way to establish these cutoff scores is to use the average scores in the school district of the native English-speaking students on the test. If this method is used, however, the grade-level classroom performance of ESL students who attain these "passing" scores at each grade level should then be examined in order to see if these scores do, in fact, predict success for ESL students in the grade-level classroom. If not, these "passing" scores need to be adjusted.

Native Language Assessment

During the entry screening process, in addition to administering listening/speaking and reading/writing assessments, it is helpful to assess students' proficiency in their native language. This information usually provides insight about the student's degree of prior academic preparation. In addition, school records should be checked and parents should be asked about the student's prior educational experiences in order to find out if the student has had continuous or interrupted/minimal educational opportunities. If literacy skills in the native language are minimal, and/or if schooling has been sporadic or minimal, it can be anticipated that teachers will need to make accommodations within the ESL and grade-level/content-area classes.

Information regarding the native language fluency may also be useful later on if there is a suspicion that the student has a learning disability. Learning disabilities and other handicapping conditions are usually independent of a particular language; that is, if a child has a disability, it will most likely manifest itself in all languages the child knows (Cloud, 1994). Since determining whether an ESL student qualifies for special education classes is a complex process requiring many pieces of information, it is helpful to know if the child has manifested normal language development in the native language.

Some ESL students, especially young learners in the lower grades, lose a degree of native-language proficiency if they do not use the native language regularly, while they are learning English. For this reason, it is important to assess students' native-language proficiency when they enter a school district before any loss has occurred, in case the information is needed later on in their academic careers.

See Chapter 6, pp. 156–162, on detecting special education needs in ESL students.

In cases where a native language test is not available, at least an oral assessment can be conducted by having a native speaker interview the student (see Figure 5.1). This will help determine if the student has developed age-appropriate oral language. A native language writing sample can also be obtained to get an idea of the student's level of literacy. If no native speaker is available to conduct these assessments, perhaps the student's parents or an English-speaking relative can be interviewed about the child's native-language proficiency (see Figure 5.2). This kind of secondhand assessment should not be considered completely reliable, but it might be useful in the future as one piece of information among other pieces.

A. General Information

Student's Name _____ Date_____ Duration of interview_____
School_____ Grade_____ Interviewer's name_____
Language being assessed_____
Place of interview_____
No. of years of schooling completed in native country_____

B. Performance Rating Scale

NATIVE LANGUAGE PERFORMANCE CRITERIA	Good	Fair	Poor
• RESPONDS TO SIMPLE QUESTIONS AND/OR INSTRUCTIONS Indicators:	3	2	1
• GIVES ORAL DIRECTIONS Indicators:	3	2	1
• DESCRIBES PEOPLE, PLACES, OBJECTS, OR ACTIONS Indicators:	3	2	1
• SHARES INFORMATION, EXPERIENCES, OR OPINIONS Indicators:	3	2	1
	Score:_____		

COMMENTS:

(Additional comments may be written on the back of this sheet.)

C. Assessment of Student's Native Language Proficiency

Score:	If Total is:		Circle Number
This Rater_____	20 or above:	Proficient :	Level 3
Other Rater_____	14–19 :	Marginally proficient:	Level 2
Total_____	13 or less :	Nonproficient :	Level 1

COMMENTS ON ANY DIFFERENCES IN SCORES BETWEEN THE TWO RATERS:

(Adapted and printed with permission from a form used in the Hawaii Public Schools)

Figure 5.2: Home Interview for Assessment of Native-Language Proficiency

SCHOOL_____

STUDENT_____ LANGUAGE_____

NAME OF INTERVIEWER_____ DATE OF INTERVIEW_____

METHOD OF INTERVIEW: BY PHONE?_____ IN PERSON?_____

Mr. / Mrs. / Ms. _____
                              (name of person interviewed)

who is the student's_____was contacted.
                              (relationship to student)

According to the information provided, the *NLP rate is (3   2   1)

*Native-Language Proficiency

....

Sample Questions

1. How frequently does the student communicate in the native language at home?

   Does he/she speak the language: All the time?_____
                                      Most of the time?_____
                                      Not at all? _____

2. Does he/she understand and speak the native language fluently?

   A. If the student is fluent, then he/she is rated proficient and the NLP rate = 3

   B. If the student understands but hardly speaks the native language, the NLP rate = 2

   C. If the student can hardly speak or understand the native language,
      then he/she is rated non-proficient and the NLP rate = 1

(Adapted and printed with permission from a form used in the Hawaii Public Schools)

Math Assessment

Once a student has been assessed for English and native-language proficiencies, math skills should also be assessed. At the elementary school level this information helps teachers plan for appropriate instruction; at the secondary level, it helps counselors place students in appropriate math classes. The math assessment can be done in English as long as word problems are not used, or, if they are, an interpreter is provided for the student.

Entry Decisions: Summary

In order to identify accurately which students need ESL assistance and which do not, information must be obtained about each student's English proficiency skills in listening, speaking, reading, and writing. "Passing" scores on entry assessments need to be examined to see if students who attain them truly do not need ESL assistance. If possible, the student's proficiency in the native language also needs to be assessed, and information should be obtained about prior schooling. This information is helpful in understanding the student's present level of education, and in meeting current academic needs. Information about the student's native-language proficiency may be needed later if a special education evaluation is ever necessary. Math proficiency should also be assessed in order to find out what skills students have already mastered and what they still need to learn.

Else's Perspective

IT IS IMPORTANT TO NOTE that Helene uses quotation marks around the word "passing" when she refers to scores on English proficiency tests. Unfortunately, many districts and many teachers use this terminology to refer to levels of proficiency in the second language, but we must understand that it only perpetuates the mistaken notion that students who are not proficient in their second language are "failing." This notion presupposes that we know how long it should take for a student to become proficient enough to be able to follow the curriculum in English and to learn new concepts through English (Collier, 1989; 1995). There is much debate about this issue even among researchers, let alone among school administrators, school boards, and politicians. Even if we agree with the finding that it takes seven to eight years to develop enough proficiency in English (Collier, 1989), the significant individual differences in rate of second-language learning would make any standard time limit meaningless (McLaughlin, 1995).

The notion of "passing" a second-language proficiency test also presupposes that we know what a successful level of second-language proficiency is for a given group of students, and that we know what type of language behavior a successful second-language learner demonstrates. The only information we have available in those areas is the suggested set of standards that TESOL published (TESOL, 1997), and those should only be used as rough general guidelines rather than absolute criteria.

For more on programmatic issues, see Chapter 3.

The notion that there is a "passing" score in English as a second language is associated with yet another misconception. According to that misconception, when a student attains a certain level of language proficiency and is deemed to be English-proficient, it is no longer necessary to provide support to that student in the grade-level/content-area classroom. Again, the notion that students "exit" from an instructional "program" and enter another separate "program" is misleading. Rather, second-language proficiency (as with native-language proficiency) develops gradually and continues to develop over a long period of time. Thus, a "passing score" needs to be replaced by a range of scores that represent a transitional phase of language proficiency development in a student's long journey toward English proficiency.

Part of the responsibility for the current state of affairs lies with the publishers of the instruments commonly used to assess second-language proficiency. Most standardized ESL tests readily produce a score rather than a qualitative description of strengths and weaknesses for a given student. They do so because district-level assessment is rarely satisfied with a nonquantitative measure of second-language proficiency, and until single-faceted scores stop being the primary criterion for high-stakes district-level decisions, it will be difficult to change this perception.

5.2 *OUT IN THE FIELD...*

Call one of the public schools in your area to find out what assessment instruments are used to make entry decisions for the ESL program. If you already work in a public school ESL program, call a school in another town and find out what they use. If possible, talk to the ESL teacher and ask the following questions:

1. What skills are tested (listening, speaking, reading, writing, native language, math, other)?
2. Are the tests designed for native or nonnative speakers of English?
3. What are the entry "passing" scores on the various segments? Are these scores reliable in indicating who needs to be in the ESL program and who does not? How do you know?
4. What are the positive aspects of using these particular assessment instruments? What are the negative aspects?

See if you can obtain or borrow a copy of the instruments. Do you agree with the ESL teacher's evaluation of the instruments? Would you want to use these instruments? Why or why not? If possible, share your findings with a colleague.

5.3 *CHOOSING READING AND WRITING ASSESSMENT INSTRUMENTS*

In choosing reading and writing assessment instruments, schools sometimes struggle with the issue of whether to use instruments designed for ESL students or for native speakers of English. Think about the advantages and disadvantages of each and jot down your thoughts You may want to use a chart like the one below. Then compare your list with that of a colleague.

ENTRY DECISIONS: USING ASSESSMENT INSTRUMENTS DESIGNED FOR:

ESL students		Native speakers of English	
advantages	disadvantages	advantages	disadvantages

PLACEMENT DECISIONS

In elementary schools, depending on the ESL program model(s) used, the results of the entry assessments may or may not have an effect on the placement of ESL students in instructional groupings. For example, if the model is one that brings the ESL teacher into the grade-level classroom (inclusion or team-teaching model), all the ESL students in that classroom may be grouped together for instruction most of the time, regardless of the results on their entry assessments. In that case, the results of the entry assessments are not used to place students in groups, but rather to aid in planning instruction for the various proficiency levels within the group. For particular lessons, however, the ESL students may be grouped by proficiency levels; depending on the lesson and student needs, lower-proficiency ESL students might work with the ESL teacher while higher-proficiency ESL students work with the rest of the class. It is best to be flexible and focus on the needs of the ESL students instead of embracing a rigid grouping arrangement that might not be the best configuration for all students every day. If a pullout model is used and students are pulled out from various classes within the grade level, the results of the entry assessments can be used to group ESL students for instruction according to proficiency level within each grade level.

Coordinating
ESL curricula
with content-
area curricula
is discussed
in Chapter 2.

In secondary schools, since students are usually placed in ESL classes according to proficiency level rather than grade level, the results of the entry assessments can be used to place students appropriately. If there are enough ESL students in the program, the ideal grouping arrangement is by proficiency level within each grade level. In that way, the ESL teacher can coordinate the ESL curriculum more closely with the content-area curricula for that grade level. If native language assessments and academic records indicate that a number of students have had minimal or interrupted schooling, courses should be offered to meet these students' particular needs. Some schools have designed special "literacy" levels of ESL for those students who lack basic literacy skills.

In order to follow through on placement decisions, especially in a large high school, it is recommended to design a placement grid that lists the general content-area subject categories so that ESL teachers can simply fill in the specific suggested courses and hand the information to the student's guidance counselor. In this way, the recommendations are clear and mistakes are minimized.

MONITORING PROGRESS

The next important purpose of assessment at the district level is monitoring student progress. Schools need to have reliable, systematic methods for measuring student progress. In the classroom, ESL teachers should be monitoring student progress continually; however, it is also necessary periodically to use some objective criteria to assure ESL teachers, ESL students, and the school community (administration, other teachers, parents, etc.) that ESL students are making reasonable gains. Progress should be formally checked at least once a year.

Student growth in the areas of listening and speaking can be measured by using the same (or a similar) instrument as was used for the initial entry assessment. Since listening and speaking tests are designed specifically for ESL students, they work well in measuring yearly gains. Once a student reaches a score of "fluent" or "near-fluent" on a listening/speaking assessment, it is probably not necessary to retest listening and speaking growth yearly; the focus of assessment should then be on reading and writing.

When measuring growth in reading and writing, schools must be careful to use an appropriate test for measuring reading and writing gains *made by ESL students*. Standardized achievement tests designed for students whose first language is English will not serve this purpose except when testing students who are close to native fluency. For example, the Degrees of Reading Power (DRP) or the Reading Comprehension and Language sections of the Metropolitan Achievement Test (MAT) are used to monitor progress in some ESL programs, but the tests are designed to measure reading and/or writing skills of native speakers of English. While a high score on these tests indicates that an ESL student may be ready to exit from the ESL program, a low score does not accurately reflect the gains that less-than-fluent students have made. Since the test designers assume that the test takers are already fluent in English, the questions are not designed to differentiate among various levels of fluency. Therefore, there are often subtle distinctions on various vocabulary and reading items that will emphasize what an ESL student does not know, but will offer little information about what the student does know (O'Malley and Valdez Pierce, 1996). ESL students who have not yet attained native-like fluency in reading and writing usually receive low scores on these kinds of tests. Another type of assessment is needed if their gains are to be measured.

A sensible way to monitor yearly progress is to use tests designed for ESL students such as the LAS-Reading assessment and the LAS-Writing assessment. These tests will better reflect gains made by beginning- and intermediate–level students; once students achieve a score of "proficient" on these tests, they can then take a standardized achievement test to see if they are proficient enough to exit from the ESL program (see discussion below on exit decisions). Another way to measure yearly growth is to have students keep a selection of their work evaluated using rubrics in portfolios. The current year's work can then be compared to previous years' work to determine gains made.

For more on using rubrics, see pp. 122–124 and pp. 134-135.

EXIT DECISIONS

The decision to release a student from the ESL program should be based on an exit assessment as well as on the student's level of success in the grade-level or content-area environment. If it appears that a student may be ready to succeed in grade-level work without ESL assistance, an official assessment should be conducted to validate this conclusion. This validation is recommended so that students are not exited too early based solely on an ESL or classroom teacher's "sense" that a student can succeed in a "mainstream" environment without ESL assistance. It is logical to use the same assessment instrument as was used in the entry assessment, with the same "passing" score, since that score signifies that a student probably does not need ESL instruction any longer.

Attaining a "passing" score on an exit assessment, however, is not a sufficient criterion for exiting from an ESL program. Some students do attain the exit scores on an assessment, but are not doing well in their grade-level work. This can be due to a variety of factors, such as the difficulty of the work in that particular classroom, the availability of tutoring support, the grade-level teacher's skill and experience in working with ESL students, and the student's effort, study skills, and motivation. Test scores alone should not be used for making exit decisions so that students who still need ESL assistance, for whatever reason, are not exited too early.

One indicator of success in the grade-level/content-area classroom is report card grades in academic subjects. If a student reaches the required scores on an exit assessment, at that point the report card should be checked to see if the student is attaining satisfactory grades in major subject areas in "mainstream" classes. In most school systems this means a grade of "C" or higher. If the student has attained at least average grades in major subjects, then the ESL teacher needs to get input—from the grade-level teacher at the elementary level and several content-area teachers at the secondary level—in order to determine if, in fact, the student appears to be ready to function without ESL support. The ESL teacher can obtain this essential input from grade-level/content-area teachers by using a form such as the sample shown in Figure 5.3. By following this procedure schools may avoid exiting students too soon.

Exit assessments can be administered as part of a yearly monitoring system, but students at beginning and intermediate proficiency levels should instead be given an assessment that shows more moderate gains than those that are usually demonstrated on an assessment used to make exit decisions (as discussed in the previous section on *Monitoring Progress*). If students seem ready to exit from the program before the end of the school year, they can be tested sooner to see if they no longer need ESL instruction.

At the other extreme are students who do show some academic progress each school year, but even after years in an ESL program, may not be able to meet the exit criteria. These students usually fall into two categories: students with low-literacy skills, and students with handicapping conditions.

Students with Low-Literacy Skills

BICS and CALP are discussed in Chapter 2.

The first category consists of students who arrive in this country, usually at the upper elementary or secondary level, with minimal prior schooling. Although they may acquire social language (BICS) quickly, because of gaps in their education, it may take them many years, perhaps their remaining time in school, to catch up and acquire grade-level academic language and skills (CALP). These students may need to receive some ESL support until they graduate from high school. I remember one such student in my ESL class several years ago at Conard High School in West Hartford:

Teachers' Voices

Helene Becker

> Maria arrived in Connecticut from the Dominican Republic and entered the seventh grade. I met her two years later when she entered the ninth grade and enrolled in my ESL Level II class. She was an enthusiastic and determined young lady who wanted to do well in school. However, she was struggling in all her classes, including ESL, sheltered content classes, and basic math.

Figure 5.3: Evaluation of Classroom Performance Form: High School

Please return this form by ___/___/___ To _____
                          (date)   *(ESL teacher's name)*

English /Content-Area Teacher completing form _____ Course:_____
                                              (name–please print)

EVALUATION OF CLASSROOM PERFORMANCE FORM:
HIGH SCHOOL

ENGLISH AS A SECOND LANGUAGE PROGRAM

STUDENT_____ ID#_____
          (last)   *(first)*   *(middle)*

SCHOOL_____

INSTRUCTIONS TO THE ENGLISH/CONTENT-AREA TEACHER:
This student is being considered for exit from the English as a Second Language (ESL) Program. To help evaluate his/her overall achievement, please use the following scale to rate his/her performance in your class.

	CIRCLE APPROPRIATE RATING:					
	unsatisfactory		average		excellent	
ABILITY TO LEARN COURSE CONTENT Successfully learns content-area information	1	2	3	4	5	6
ACADEMIC PERFORMANCE Academic performance in class	1	2	3	4	5	6
STUDY HABITS Brings necessary materials to class, begins work promptly, listens to instructions, follows directions, and completes assigned tasks	1	2	3	4	5	6
CLASS PARTICIPATION Participates in class activities and discussions	1	2	3	4	5	6
COMMUNICATION WITH TEACHER Expresses ideas adequately, uses relevant vocabulary, and asks questions about assignments and the content area	1	2	3	4	5	6
COMMUNICATION WITH PEERS Expresses ideas opinions, interests; understands and is understood by peers	1	2	3	4	5	6
PREDICTION OF SUCCESS Chances for success in class without additional support in learning English as a second language	1	2	3	4	5	6

TOTAL POINTS_____

Other factors affecting student's performance or other comments: _____
_____
_____
_____

_____   _____
Classroom Teacher Signature   *Date*

(Adapted and printed with permission from the Fairfax County Public Schools, Virginia)

Her school records indicated that she had completed the sixth grade in the Dominican Republic. However, in her journal, she expressed that she had had very little education in her native country. She explained that in the rural area where she had lived, the teachers had not always shown up for work and the education system had been chaotic. She had gone to school fairly regularly through second grade, but her education after that was sporadic at best, and she did not learn much at all. She was impressed with our educational system and was thankful finally to be learning again.

Maria had to catch up on several years of missed academics. She progressed steadily and did quite well in her ESL and sheltered content classes. She was eventually able to take certain "mainstream" academic classes with modifications made for her. She needed ESL assistance in the form of formal classes and tutorial support during her entire time in school. She completed high school in four and a half years and is now attending community college.

If Maria had arrived in the United States earlier, perhaps by third grade, she might not have had the same kinds of academic difficulties she faced as a middle and high school student. She would have needed ESL instruction for several years, but she would not have started out so far behind academically. Perhaps, in that case, she would have been able to meet exit criteria even before reaching high school.

Students with Handicapping Conditions

The second group of students who may not meet the exit criteria, those with handicapping conditions, are usually also receiving assistance from special education teachers. Depending on the specific disability, some of these students may not be able to acquire enough academic skills to meet ESL exit criteria, even if they are exposed to an English-language academic environment at a very young age. It is best to work together with the special education teachers to decide on the most appropriate instruction for students with both ESL and special education needs. It may be appropriate to exit an ESL student who is receiving special education assistance if, after several years in an ESL program, the student's academic needs are now being adequately met by the special education teachers. ESL, special education, and grade-level/content-area teachers, along with the student and the student's parents, need to make this decision together.

Else offers important insights to encourage a shift in thinking about the concept of "exiting" ESL students.

THE NOTION THAT ESL IS A PROGRAM from which students graduate or exit is prevalent in most school districts. However, as I discussed in an earlier comment in this chapter and in Chapter 3, this representation of ESL services does not lead to an effective learning environment for students. I believe that this conceptualization of ESL services, as with other specialized student support services such as special education and assistance with reading and math for students who are

See Chapter 6, pp. 163–166, for more on appropriate instruction for ESL students with special education needs.

delayed in those areas, has become ensconced in our educational systems because of school funding models. Funding, at both the federal and state levels, is typically provided to schools under separate entitlement programs. Different administrators, and sometimes different teachers, are funded through different programs, and the resulting instructional support systems are seen as separate entities.

Rather than establishing exit criteria, which imply entry into and exit from a separate and finite program within the school life of a student, a continuum of services must be established. This continuum of services is then provided to students on an as-needed basis, and modified as the student's proficiency in the second language grows. As Helene suggests in the following section, continuing support is essential. As Helene also suggests, continued monitoring of students is needed in order to ensure that they continue learning new concepts in the grade-level/content-area classroom.

5.4 *ALTERNATIVE EXIT CRITERIA*

Suppose Charlene, an eighth-grade ESL student, has been in the ESL program since she started school in the United States in the first grade. She has been receiving special education services since the third grade. Charlene has a learning disability that prevents her from attaining the required scores on the ESL exit exams (standardized achievement tests in reading and language). Charlene would prefer not to go to ESL class any longer; she has come to feel embarrassed about being grouped with students who have only been in this country a few years but who consistently perform better than she does on reading and writing tasks. Along with a colleague, think of the factors you would consider in deciding whether or not to exit Charlene from the ESL program. See if you can organize your ideas to come up with alternative exit criteria for ESL students with special needs.

CONTINUED MONITORING

After exiting from an ESL program, students need to be monitored to ensure that they continue to succeed in their grade-level/content-area classes. Former ESL students should be monitored for at least one year, during which time the ESL teacher needs to obtain copies of students' quarterly report cards to make sure the students are maintaining at least a "C" average in their major content-area subjects. If not, the ESL teacher needs to meet with the appropriate grade-level/content-area teachers to determine how best to help these students maintain acceptable grades. These meetings could result in reenrolling certain students in the ESL program—either officially or, in some cases, "unofficially"—for help in a particular content subject or subjects on a short-term basis, until the grade(s) improves.

See Chapter 4, pp. 86–98, for examples of course options for ESL students in secondary schools.

Because middle and high school students enroll in distinct classes for each school subject, exiting decisions regarding ESL students do not have to be "all or nothing." For example, one ESL student could be enrolled in ESL Level IV, along with four "mainstream" classes, whereas another could be enrolled in ESL Level IV, two sheltered classes, and two "mainstream" classes. It is best to be flexible when advising students about their individual programs, suggesting that they choose demanding courses, but allowing them to retain some ties to the ESL program, even just for tutoring support, if that is what is needed for their academic success.

5.5 *FOLLOWING UP ON FORMER ESL STUDENTS' SUCCESS*

If you are currently teaching ESL, find out how well your former ESL students are succeeding in their grade-level/content-area classes. If you are not currently teaching ESL, find an ESL teacher who is interested in doing this study. Use a chart like the one below to gather data.

Name of Student	Exit Assessment Scores	Date Exited from ESL Program	Current Grades in Major Subjects	Generally, How is the Student Doing? *	Possible Reasons for Lack of Success

	POOR		AVERAGE		GREAT
*RATING SCALE:	1	2	3	4	5

If you find out that several former ESL students are not succeeding in their academic classes, try figuring out the reasons:

1. Are the grade-level/content-area teachers making sufficient use of ESL teaching strategies?
2. Are students exited too soon from the ESL program (that is, are changes needed in the exit procedures)?
3. Do these students exhibit sufficient effort and motivation?
4. Is tutoring support available for former ESL students?
5. Other reasons?

WHAT ARE OTHER ISSUES ASSOCIATED WITH DISTRICT-LEVEL ASSESSMENTS?

DISTRICTWIDE STANDARDIZED TESTING

School districts should consider exempting ESL students from official districtwide standardized testing until the students are ready to exit from the ESL program. Many school districts regularly administer standardized tests in math and English (and, in some cases, content-area subjects) to the entire student population at various grade levels. Typically, districts have policies that exempt beginning-level ESL students from these tests. However, after a certain number of years in an ESL program—usually between one and three, depending on individual school district policies—ESL students are required to take these exams. Because these tests are designed for students whose first language is English, ESL students who have not yet acquired native or near-native proficiency in reading and writing academic English tend to receive low scores on these tests. As discussed in Chapter 2, ESL students usually require at least five years (and often more) to attain grade-level academic proficiency. Logically, these districtwide standardized tests should not be administered to students who have not had sufficient time to acquire the necessary proficiency.

See the discussion of standardized tests on pp. 114–115.

Even if ESL students are academically prepared to take a standardized test in a particular content area such as math or science, they may do poorly, not because they do not know the material, but because of the complexity of the language used in the questions (O'Malley and Valdez Pierce, 1996). It is advisable to allow ESL students to acquire as much English as possible before requiring them to take official districtwide standardized tests, the scores from which become part of their school records and may be used inappropriately, causing ESL students to end up in classes where they receive instruction geared to their supposed inabilities (Freeman and Freeman, 1992). In addition, ESL teachers, and the ESL program itself, may be unjustly blamed for students' low scores. Furthermore, since the test results of individual schools and school districts are often made public and compared to one another, unfair and inaccurate conclusions may be drawn if ESL students are included in the test-taking pool.

Here is another point of view from Else.

Else's Perspective

THE ISSUE OF WHETHER OR NOT TO EXEMPT ESL STUDENTS from large-scale assessment is an important and contentious one. It has obvious pedagogical implications for students, especially at the school level, but it also has political and social implications for language-minority education in general, especially at the district, state, or national level (August and Hakuta, 1997). As Helene points out, many factors argue against inclusion of ESL students in district-level testing. Administrators may be reluctant to let the district norms go down because ESL students who are not proficient in the language of the test cannot adequately show what they know. From the students' perspective, taking a high-stakes test in a language in which they are not proficient can be frustrating and stressful. However, we also need to think of the potential disadvantages of exemption from testing of any identifiable group of students, especially one that tends to be disenfranchised.

By exempting language-minority students from high-stakes assessment, we run the risk of lowered accountability toward those students. If the performance of these students does not play a significant role in the general performance of the district or the state, the quality of services provided to these students may not matter as much. If this is a risk, then advocates of ESL students must ensure that their performance and their academic achievement are documented in alternative ways.

One way of doing this is to establish criteria and expectations for ESL students that would become benchmarks against which learning and achievement are assessed and their performance in school is interpreted (Cloud, Genesee, and Hamayan, 2000). These criteria and expectations can be established to some extent on the basis of general standards—such as the ESL standards developed by TESOL (1997)—but, ultimately, they need to be developed at the district or even the school level. This needs to be a long-term project that a school or district undertakes. Cloud, Genesee, and Hamayan (2000) suggest that teachers draw on at least three sources for identifying expectations of students:

1. School, district, and regional curriculum documents

2. District, state, and national content standards

3. Teachers' professional judgment of age-appropriate learning based on their cumulative classroom experiences

Thus, it is essential that the district be able to demonstrate to others that ESL students are learning as expected—in other words, for the district to show accountability toward these students and their parents.

DISTRICT-LEVEL ASSESSMENTS: ALTERNATIVE ASSESSMENT OPTIONS

In order to make entry, placement, and exit decisions, as well as to monitor student progress, besides using traditional tests for assessing students, some school districts have incorporated alternative ways of evaluating ESL students' English proficiency in the various skill areas. These alternative ways of assessing students are often referred to as **authentic assessment** because, unlike typical tests, they are based more closely on typical classroom activities. For example, as part of an entry assessment, rather than being asked to pick out the correct verb form or vocabulary word in a multiple-choice item, students might be asked to write a composition that would be evaluated using a **rubric**—a series of statements that describe student performance. A numerical value is assigned to each performance level in the rubric so that students' work can be scored.

Here is an example of a scoring rubric (Figure 5.4) for evaluating student writing; it contains six levels of performance:

Figure 5.4: Holistic Scoring Rubric for Writing Samples

Rating	Criteria
6—Proficient	• Writes single or multiple paragraphs with clear introduction, fully developed ideas, and a conclusion • Uses appropriate verb tense and a variety of grammatical and syntactical structures; uses complex sentences effectively; uses smooth transitions • Uses varied, precise vocabulary • Has occasional errors in mechanics (spelling, punctuation, and capitalization) that do not detract from meaning
5—Fluent	• Writes single or multiple paragraphs with main idea and supporting detail; presents ideas logically, though some parts may not be fully developed • Uses appropriate verb tense and a variety of grammatical and syntactical structures; errors in sentence structure do not detract from meaning; uses transitions • Uses varied vocabulary appropriate for the purpose • Has few errors in mechanics, which do not detract from meaning
4—Expanding	• Organizes ideas in logical or sequential order with some supporting detail; begins to write a paragraph • Experiments with a variety of verb tenses, but does not use them consistently; subject/verb agreement errors; uses some compound and complex sentences; limited use of transitions • Vocabulary is appropriate to purpose but sometimes awkward • Uses punctuation, capitalization, and mostly conventional spelling; errors sometimes interfere with meaning
3—Developing	• Writes sentences around idea; some sequencing present, but may lack cohesion • Writes in present tense and simple sentences; has difficulty with subject/verb agreement; run-on sentences are common; begins to use compound sentences • Uses high-frequency words; may have difficulty with word order; omits endings or words • Uses some capitalization, punctuation, and transitional spelling; errors often interfere with meaning
2—Beginning	• Begins to convey meaning through writing • Writes predominately phrases and patterned or simple sentences • Uses limited or repetitious vocabulary • Uses temporary (phonetic) spelling
1—Emerging	• No evidence of idea development or organization • Uses single words, pictures, and patterned phrases • Copies from a model • Little awareness of spelling, capitalization, or punctuation

(Adapted and reprinted with permission from O'Malley and Valdez Pierce, 1996, p. 22)

Speaking, listening, and reading can also be evaluated using rubrics designed for rating those particular skills.

Rubric-based assessments are useful because they can describe the different levels that ESL students pass through on their way to proficiency; therefore, they are authentic representations of the students' skills. Students themselves can get a clearer picture of their strengths and weaknesses from these assessments than from test scores (O'Malley and Valdez Pierce, 1996). Throughout the time students are in an ESL program, in order to monitor progress, their work with rubric forms attached can be collected in individual portfolios. The rubric forms can be updated each year and compared to those from previous years.

The Fairfax County Public Schools in Virginia has been experimenting with rubrics for evaluating oral and written proficiency. I asked an administrator in the ESL department to describe the rubric system that he and his staff are now using:

See p. 138 for more on student portfolios.

Keith Buchanan, Fairfax County Public Schools, Virginia

> Upon entry into our school district, students are evaluated at a central registration center for oral, writing, and reading proficiency in English, as well as writing and math proficiency in their native language. For the oral assessment, we have students answer some questions about themselves; then we have them do a story retell. We use an oral proficiency rubric to score their responses. For the writing assessment, we have students do a writing sample, which we score using a writing rubric. For reading, we first have students take the Qualitative Reading Inventory (QRI) test; if they score at the fourth-grade level or higher, we have them take the Degrees of Reading Power (DRP) test. (The QRI separates the lower-level readers better for placement purposes). From these assessments, a composite score is developed that is used by local schools for placement in appropriate classes. (Each school differs somewhat in course offerings, depending upon the size of the school's ESL population.)
>
> During their time in the ESL program, students develop a portfolio that is used for monitoring progress and for recommendations for exiting from the program. Teachers regularly update rubrics in oral, writing, and reading proficiency. As an additional aid in assessing reading proficiency, students take the DRP test yearly. When a student is possibly ready to exit from the ESL program, his or her latest scores on the oral, writing, and reading rubric forms are transferred onto an exit matrix (see Figure 5.5), which also contains ratings from the ESL and classroom teacher(s) of the "exit potential" of the particular student. The exit form is signed by the ESL teacher, the student's regular English teacher (they study regular English simultaneously with their last level of ESL), and a principal.
>
> Our exit procedures have evolved over the past couple of years to this rubric-driven system. They were developed by teacher groups and have been tested for consistency. They require a fair amount of work on the part of teachers, but I think that kids leaving the ESL program have an excellent snapshot of their strengths from these rubrics.

Figure 5.5: Exit Criteria Matrix High School Form: English as a Second Language Program

---

ENGLISH AS A SECOND LANGUAGE PROGRAM

STUDENT_____ I.D. #_____
       (last)   *(first)*   *(middle)*

INSTRUCTIONS: Please circle the appropriate matrix score (1–6) for each factor.

Writing Proficiency	1	2	3	4	5	6
Oral Proficiency	1	2	3	4	5	6
Reading Comprehension DRP Units	<15 units 1	15–25 units 2	26–35 units 3	36–49 units 4	50–59 units 5	60+ units 6
ESL Teacher Rating for Program Exit	not recommended 1	2	recommended 3	4	highly recommended 5	6
English/Content Teacher Rating	6–9 1	10–15 2	16–21 3	22–27 4	28–34 5	35–42 6
Principal (or Designee) Rating for Program Exit	not recommended 1	2	recommended 3	4	highly recommended 5	6

_____   _____
Signature of ESL Teacher Completing Matrix   Date

(Adapted and printed with permission from the Fairfax County Public Schools, Virginia)

5.6 WORKING IN A LARGE ESL PROGRAM

The school district described above has a large number of ESL students. With respect to assessment procedures, what are the advantages of working in such a school district?

5.7 USING AUTHENTIC ASSESSMENT FOR DISTRICT-LEVEL DECISIONS

Think about the advantages and disadvantages of using authentic assessment rather than standardized tests for making district-level decisions in an ESL program. Discuss your ideas with a colleague. Can you come to any conclusions?

5.8 OUT IN THE FIELD...

To supplement the information you found from doing investigation 5.2, it might be interesting to interview a different elementary or secondary ESL teacher at a school in your area to find out what district-level assessment procedures are being followed. The following questions can serve as a guide:

1. Describe the district-level assessment procedures used in your ESL program to make entry, placement, and exit decisions.

2. How do you monitor student progress from year to year?

3. What are the positive features of your assessment procedures? Which features would you like to modify or change?

After you interview the teacher, analyze the assessment procedures in terms of the principles suggested in this chapter. Do you have any suggestions to offer this school district regarding their assessment practices?

WHAT ARE THE ISSUES ASSOCIATED WITH CLASSROOM-BASED ASSESSMENTS?

PURPOSES

Although district-level assessments are a necessary component of an ESL program, classroom-based assessments (that is, routine assessments conducted by teachers in their classrooms) can have a far greater impact on the day-to-day instruction of ESL students. As expressed by Genesee and Hamayan (1994), "the primary purposes of [classroom-based] assessment are to identify the specific needs of individual students, tailor instruction to meet these needs, monitor the effectiveness of instruction, understand student performance in class, and make decisions about advancement or promotion of individual students to the next level of instruction" (p. 212). Since classroom-based assessments can have a significant influence on instruction, when used effectively, they can help optimize student learning. They can also be used to inform parents and the students themselves of the degree of progress students are making.

When we administer tests to our students in an ESL setting, we help them acquire test experience in a less threatening environment than in the grade-level or content-area setting. Besides preparing ESL students for instruction in the "mainstream," ESL teachers need to help students develop confidence and skill in taking the many kinds of tests they will encounter in their academic careers.

FORMAL AND INFORMAL ASSESSMENT

In order to use assessments in the classroom for the purposes mentioned above, ESL teachers need to assess their students often and regularly. Actually, while teaching, most teachers continually perform informal assessments of their students in order to guide the direction of the lesson in progress (Genesee and Hamayan, 1994). For example, by asking questions and observing student expressions and body language, teachers can judge whether students are "getting it" or not, and can alter the direction of the lesson accordingly. But in addition to this ongoing assessment, at the end of a lesson, series of lessons, or unit, it is prudent to conduct a more formal assessment, in order to be certain of student progress.

ASSESSING LANGUAGE, ASSESSING CONTENT

Assessments in the classroom should always be directly related to the objectives of the particular lesson or group of lessons (Coelho, 1994). ESL teachers need to be concerned with two distinct kinds of objectives—**language** and **content**. If a particular unit taught by the ESL teacher focuses on language, then the assessment needs to focus on language, as well. If the unit focuses on content, not language, then content should be the focus of the assessment. For example, if the ESL teacher has worked with a group of fifth-grade ESL students on a social studies unit about Native Americans, the assessment should test the concepts and information learned in the unit. In other words, students should receive a high score for expressing accurate information, even if the ideas are expressed in ways that are not grammatically correct. On the other hand, if students are explicitly taught how to express the answers grammatically, then grammatical accuracy can be assessed as well. For example, suppose one of the questions on the unit test was as follows:

> *Why were certain tribes of Native Americans always moving and following herds of buffalo?*

Suppose the student answered:
> *They need follow for get food.*

The student should receive most (or all) of the credit value allotted to this question because the information is accurate. Grammatical mistakes should be counted more than minimally only if the grammar associated with answering the question was emphasized and practiced during the unit or previous units. However, the ESL teacher can analyze students' grammatical mistakes on the assessment in order to plan future lessons aimed at helping students improve their use of language.

5.9 *ANALYZING TEST ANSWERS*

Ask an ESL teacher to lend you a copy of a test an ESL student has already completed (or if you are teaching now, you can use one of your own student's tests.) Examine the student's answers in terms of what the student already knows or can do well, and what the student still needs to learn or practice. How might this particular student's answers help you plan future instruction? In other words, what specific topics (content and/or language) would you need to address in order to help this student do better on a retest of the same material?

ESL Teachers' Role in Classroom-Based Assessment

When ESL teachers are in teaching situations where they conduct their own separate ESL classes, they have the responsibility for assessing student progress in those classes. However, depending on the particular ESL program and the level—elementary or secondary—ESL teachers may have only an indirect, yet important, responsibility for classroom-based assessments of ESL students. For example, in an elementary school setting, if the ESL teacher works in the grade-level teachers' classrooms, the grade-level teacher (not the ESL teacher) may have the primary responsibility for assessing the progress of ESL students. However, in order to ensure sensible decisions about assessments of ESL students in grade-level classrooms, the ESL and grade-level teachers should collaborate regarding assessment issues and decisions. At the secondary level, it is equally important for the ESL teacher to collaborate with content-area teachers regarding fair assessment practices in content-area classrooms. For example, ESL teachers need to discuss with content-area teachers the language/content distinction discussed above, in order to discourage content-area teachers from penalizing ESL students (especially beginning- and intermediate-level students) for language errors on assessments if the main objectives of the lessons are to learn concepts and information. ESL teachers can also suggest alternative ways to test ESL students, especially beginning-level students. For example, if available, perhaps an interpreter could aid the student during a test; or, instead of the student giving a written answer, perhaps he or she could make a visual or concrete representation of the material (Coelho, 1994).

The ensuing discussion in this chapter is meant to offer guidelines for the various distinct situations in which ESL teachers, either directly or indirectly, need to deal with classroom-based assessments of ESL students.

Typical Test Questions

Traditional assessments such as **multiple-choice** and **fill-in-the-blanks** tests have come under considerable criticism in recent years. Teachers have found that these types of test questions commonly test discrete skills and do not assess the full range of skills and abilities that teachers consider important and that are displayed in classrooms. For example, during typical lessons, students write compositions, work cooperatively to solve problems, share information, and integrate personal viewpoints—very little of which is assessed with these traditional types of questions (O'Malley and Valdez Pierce, 1996). However, especially for students above the beginning level of proficiency, as language proficiency grows, these typical test questions do give students an opportunity to show—to some degree—the progress they have made (Met, 1994), and do give teachers some valuable information to guide instruction. It is important to remember, however, that multiple forms of assessment will give a more accurate picture of student strengths, abilities, and progress, and no one type of assessment should be relied on exclusively. Teachers can increase the variety of assessments by including nontraditional instruments (described later in this chapter) as part of an assessment program.

For a discussion of alternative forms of assessment, see pp. 132–138.

In addition to the usual purposes of assessments, traditional types of tests in the ESL classroom serve the important function of exposing ESL students to the typical test questions they will encounter in grade-level and content-area classrooms. By familiarizing students with these questions in the ESL classroom, ESL teachers help students approach these questions in the "mainstream" setting with more experience and confidence. Including traditional assessments in the ESL classroom also gives ESL teachers the opportunity to teach strategies for answering the various types of test questions students are likely to encounter. Traditional test questions used in all types of classrooms (grade-level/content-area as well as ESL) include but are not limited to the following: multiple choice; fill-in-the-blanks and cloze passages; matching; true-false; short question/answer; and essay questions.

Else's Perspective

ONE WAY TO STRETCH THE INFORMATIONAL VALUE of restrictive-answer test formats (multiple-choice, true-false, matching, etc.) is to use them as a springboard for discussion and exploration. By using a think-aloud strategy, students can be prompted to examine their answers and to attempt to explain why they answered certain questions in a certain way. Through this process, teachers may discover that a student gave the right answer for the wrong reason and the wrong answer for the right reason. This revisiting and analyzing of answers will yield information about the process (why a specific answer was given) that led to a certain product (the score on the test). It can provide the teacher with insights about the student's proficiency or mastery of a content area that might not be obtained from the general score that a student attains on that test.

This technique is obviously quite labor-intensive and cannot be used with many students. However, it may prove to be quite useful in the following situations:

- When a student's performance on a test is unexpected (either too high or too low)
- For individual students whose language proficiency development and academic achievement are remarkably lower than their peers
- When a pattern of academic behavior that the teacher cannot understand is observed in a group of students

This post-testing think-aloud strategy can also be a useful tool for teachers who are conducting classroom research or who are systematically examining a question regarding learning and teaching.

GENERAL TEST-TAKING STRATEGIES

There are certain test-taking strategies that apply to all types of test questions. Some of these strategies may seem obvious, but certain students, especially those who have not had extensive school experience, benefit from explicit instruction in using the strategies.

First, ESL teachers need to help students understand the meaning and importance of *test directions*. Because of difficulty with language, ESL students can easily misinterpret directions. For example, if the directions say, "Put the items below in order of _least_ important to _most_ important," ESL students may not understand or may misinterpret the words _least_ and _most_ and may do the entire section incorrectly. Students should be told to read carefully all directions on the test and ask questions if they are not sure exactly how to proceed. ESL teachers can help students understand directions and demonstrate their importance by emphasizing them on ESL classroom tests. All teachers (ESL and grade-level/content-area) can aid ESL students in their understanding of test directions by modeling an answer in each section of the test so that ESL students can better understand how to proceed.

Second, ESL teachers should emphasize the need for students to *pace themselves on tests* and not spend too much time on any one question. Students should be told explicitly to skip over questions they do not know and return to them later. This gives them an opportunity to answer more questions correctly than if they waste time trying to figure out answers they do not know.

Third, ESL students should be taught that if a word bank is provided on a test, they should *put a check mark next to words they have already used*. Otherwise, for each item, some students may reread the entire list of choices instead of skipping over the words they have already used. This strategy helps students use their test-taking time more efficiently (Hamayan, 1994).

Fourth, students should be told to *check over their answers*, if time allows. Many students want to hand in their papers the moment they answer the last question, but teachers should discourage this practice. ESL students need to use the full time allotted to read over their answers and make final corrections.

Fifth, ESL students need to develop the habit of *answering all questions on a test* (if time allows), even if they have to guess. On most tests, leaving an answer blank will result in the student receiving no credit for that answer; guessing or giving a partial answer will give the student a chance to receive some credit.

Finally, students should be told to *look for answers to some questions right on the test*! Sometimes answers to one question are inadvertently stated in another question; experienced test takers know to be on the alert for this. Also, words that are needed to answer one question may be already spelled out correctly in another question. ESL students can sometimes correct spelling errors by being observant in this way.

Another helpful strategy (requiring the cooperation of the grade-level or content-area teacher) is to have the ESL students take their tests in the ESL classroom or with the ESL teacher present in the grade-level or content-area classroom. In this way, the ESL teacher can explain confusing directions and vocabulary words (without giving the ESL students any answers, of course). Another option is for the grade-level or content-area teacher to meet with the ESL students right before a test to clarify directions and to allow students to ask questions about vocabulary.

To get a sense of the challenges ESL students face when taking tests, try this activity. Borrow a content-area classroom test from a grade-level or content-area teacher (this can be a teacher-prepared or commercially made test). Analyze each set of directions and questions on the test in terms of the difficulties they might present to an ESL student. What could you do in the ESL classroom to help students gain skills useful for tackling this test? Do you have any suggestions for the grade-level/content-area teacher regarding changes to the test that might help an ESL student be more successful? Do any features of the test promote an ESL student's success on the test? If possible, share your findings with a colleague who has also done this activity.

Choosing an Appropriate Assessment

As mentioned earlier, when choosing a test format to assess the effectiveness of instruction and/or monitor student progress, it is essential to choose an appropriate assessment instrument directly related to the learning objectives (Coelho, 1994). Teachers need to consider if they want to assess content knowledge or language skills and design an assessment accordingly (Genesee and Hamayan, 1994). If the purpose of the assessment is to test language skills, then during classroom lessons, students need to be provided with sufficient language practice in the same (or similar) way they will be assessed. I personally learned this lesson the hard way—by providing students with one type of practice and then assessing them with a different type of assessment. My assessment instrument proved inappropriate and my students suffered the consequences. Here is what happened to me during my early years of teaching high school ESL students in Connecticut.

Helene Becker

> My beginning-level students had just finished learning how to form the past tense of regular verbs and they were now learning the forms for common irregular verbs. Over a period of a few days, I used pantomime and pictures to teach verbs such as *ate, spoke, sang, slept, went, got up, left, bought,* and *taught.* After considerable oral practice, including forming sentences with these words, I had the class copy a list of the words and sample sentences. I felt satisfied that the students had a good grasp of the material, so I decided to give them a short quiz.
>
> I announced the quiz and told the students to practice saying the verb forms at home just as we had practiced them in class. I also told them to read over the sample sentences they had copied from the board.
>
> The next day, when the students entered the classroom, I told them to take out a sheet of paper and write the numbers from one to ten. I then proceeded to pantomime ten different actions, pretty much the way I had done during the lessons. I wasn't out to fool them— I wanted them all to do well. After each pantomime, I asked the class, "What did I do?" The students then wrote the past tense verb to describe my action.

At the end of the day I was looking forward to correcting the quizzes because I was confident that my lessons had been effective and that my students had performed well. To my disappointment, however, I discovered that they had done quite poorly. In general, they seemed to know which verbs I was pantomiming, but they had spelled most of the words incorrectly. For example, some students wrote the word *spoke* as *spock*, and others wrote the word *sang* as *seng*. Since I was specifically testing them on the past tense forms, I felt that I had to mark the answers wrong if they had spelled the words incorrectly.

I reflected back on my lessons to see where I had gone wrong. After some thought I realized that the fault was not necessarily in my lessons, but rather in the assessment I had chosen. I realized that the majority of classroom time had been used to learn and practice the verbs orally whereas the assessment tested the verbs in written form.

During the lessons on the past tense the students had written each verb form only once or twice, when they copied the list of verbs and the sample sentences into their notebooks. That did not give them sufficient written practice to perform well on a written test. On the other hand, they had practiced *saying* each word at least ten times. I needed to either create an oral assessment, possibly by asking individuals to say the words as I pantomimed them, or give them more practice in writing the forms before I tested them with a written assessment. The assessment I had chosen—that is, a written assessment—was not appropriate to test the oral language that they had learned.

ALTERNATIVE FORMS OF ASSESSMENT

For the past decade there has been a lot of interest by ESL and grade-level/content-area teachers in alternatives to traditional forms of testing (O'Malley and Valdez Pierce, 1996). As discussed earlier, traditional tests do provide teachers with some useful information, but teachers have come to recognize that many kinds of traditional tests do not closely resemble the instructional activities in the classroom and therefore do not fully represent what students are able to do. Teachers have been searching for assessment tools that more closely resemble classroom activities and that will provide them with multiple forms of assessment. Using multiple forms of assessment, rather than using traditional classroom tests exclusively, allows the teacher (and student) to get a more accurate and complete picture of student strengths and accomplishments. This section discusses several alternatives to typical tests; as mentioned in the previous section on district-level assessments, many of these alternatives are called *authentic assessments* because they more closely resemble classroom activities and instructional goals than traditional tests (O'Malley and Valdez Pierce, 1996).

An authentic assessment consists of having students do a typical classroom activity and then scoring the students' performance of that activity. In contrast to traditional tests, where students may find out which questions they got wrong and how they did in relation to others in the class (A, B, C, D, or F), with authentic assessments, students learn their specific strengths, weaknesses, and areas for improvement.

Authentic assessment works best when students know ahead of time how they will be evaluated, and when they have the opportunity for self-assessment so that they reflect upon their own strengths and weaknesses. This promotes more active student participation in their own learning and progress. This self-assessment component typically consists of a checklist and/or written comments about their own work.

With authentic assessment ESL students do not have to be taught special strategies and tricks for being successful. Since these assessments are simply extensions of classroom activities, students use the same skills and strategies they use during classroom instruction.

Else's Perspective

ALTERNATIVES TO TRADITIONAL TESTING, which Helene calls authentic assessment, have also been referred to in the literature as "informal" assessment. However, as Helene makes clear later on in this section, it is essential that we maintain formality within any type of authentic assessment conducted in the classroom. The reason for formalizing authentic assessment is that, despite the increasing popularity of authentic assessment approaches, they are still considered "alternative" and unreliable. Although the effectiveness of authentic assessment approaches has been demonstrated (Gomez, Graue, and Bloch, 1991), their use for large-scale and high-stakes evaluation remains minimal (McDonald, 1993).

One of the problems with authentic assessment is that it often becomes the default alternative to traditional testing. It is everything that traditional testing is not. Thus, in addition to the requirement that Helene mentions—some level of formality in authentic assessment—we need to consider other criteria that these assessment approaches must meet. The following characteristics of authentic assessment procedures are essential (Hamayan, 1995):

- **Proximity to actual language use and performance**—Authentic assessment procedures include activities that have communicative function rather than tasks that have little or no intrinsic communicative value.
- **A holistic view of language**—Authentic assessment procedures are based on the notion that the interrelationships among the various aspects and skills of language cannot be ignored.
- **An integrative view of learning**—Authentic assessment attempts to capture, or at least takes into account, the learner's total array of skills and abilities.
- **Developmental appropriateness**—Authentic assessment procedures are based on appropriate cognitive, social, and academic developmental stages of the learner.
- **Multiple referencing**—Authentic assessment entails obtaining information about the learner from numerous sources and through various means.

In order for authentic assessment to become a viable addition to standardized testing, its users need to have conceptual clarity to ensure consistency. They also need to establish a mechanism of evaluation and self-criticism as they use different procedures. Finally, as Helene suggests, some standardization is necessary. Although the fiscal and logistic difficulties associated with authentic assessment are likely to prevent it from replacing standardized traditional testing, its role as a valuable source of information about second-language learners is unquestionable.

Authentic Assessment Tools

Observation

Observation simply means observing students during classroom instruction or activities. Using observation informally for assessment purposes is very familiar to teachers since teachers are continually paying attention to student utterances and behavior in order to gauge the effectiveness and success of a lesson. Using observation for more formal assessment purposes means planning and organizing the observations and devising systematic record keeping. Without formalizing the observations in this way, valuable information observed during lessons may be fragmented, disorganized, forgotten, or remembered inaccurately (Genesee and Hamayan, 1994).

Students can best be observed during instructional activities where they are working in pairs or groups. The ESL teacher can move from group to group making observations and filling in information on a *checklist* or *scoring rubric*. (A checklist is a list of items that describes what a student can either do or not do whereas a scoring rubric describes student behaviors and assigns a value to each.) All students do not have to be evaluated on the same day or doing the same activity. At times it may be useful to assess a group of students (rather than individuals) in order to get a general sense of how students are progressing.

Observation is useful for evaluating both language proficiency and content knowledge. For oral language, a rubric can be designed that describes characteristics at different stages of language development (see Figure 5.6 for an example). For content knowledge, teachers can design specific checklists or rubrics for different topics. For example, observation could be used to determine if students understand planetary movement in the solar system (using a model), if they can explain the water cycle, or if they are able to figure out how to solve a math problem (Genesee and Hamayan, 1994). When students are observed doing authentic classroom activities such as these, the assessment is often referred to as *performance assessment*.

With respect to both language skills and content knowledge, observation helps teachers evaluate students' production; observation may also be used at the same time to evaluate students' comprehension. For example, if students are asked to read an article and react to it orally in a group, the teacher can use observation to determine if the students understood the article (comprehension) and how well they can discuss their ideas (production). Teachers can also observe how well students exercise positive group behavior (turn-taking, listening skills, etc.).

Figure 5.6: Holistic Oral Language Scoring Rubric

Rating	Description
6	• Communicates competently in social and classroom settings • Speaks fluently • Masters a variety of grammatical structures • Uses extensive vocabulary but may lag behind native-speaking peers • Understands classroom discussion without difficulty
5	• Speaks in social and classroom setting with sustained and connected discourse; any errors do not interfere with meaning • Speaks with near-native fluency; any hesitations do not interfere with communication • Uses a variety of structures with occasional grammatical errors • Uses varied vocabulary • Understands classroom discussion without difficulty
4	• Initiates and sustains a conversation with descriptors and details; exhibits self-confidence in social situations; begins to communicate in classroom settings • Speaks with occasional hesitation • Uses some complex sentences; applies rules of grammar but lacks control of irregular forms (e.g., runned, mans, not never, more higher) • Uses adequate vocabulary; some word usage irregularities • Understands classroom discussions with repetition, rephrasing, and clarification
3	• Begins to initiate conversation; retells a story or experience; asks and responds to simple questions • Speaks hesitantly because of rephrasing and searching for words • Uses predominantly present tense verbs; demonstrates errors of omission (leaves words out, word endings off) • Uses limited vocabulary • Understands simple sentences in sustained conversation; requires repetition
2	• Begins to communicate personal and survival needs • Speaks in single-word utterances and short patterns • Uses functional vocabulary • Understands words and phrases; requires repetitions
1	• Begins to name concrete objects • Repeats words and phrases • Understands little or no English

(Adapted and reprinted with permission from O'Malley and Valdez Pierce, 1996, p.67)

Authentic Writing Tasks

As discussed in the section on district-level assessments, instead of testing students' writing skills by means of short-answer tests (multiple-choice, fill-ins, etc.), writing can be assessed by having students do a more authentic writing task. This can consist of their writing a complete paragraph (or several paragraphs) on a topic relevant to the current instruction in the classroom. Their work can be assessed by using a writing scoring rubric such as the sample in Figure 5.4 (p. 123). A scoring rubric can also be formulated to assess content knowledge through writing. As always, teachers should be careful to assess writing skills and content knowledge independently (using separate scoring rubrics), although the same writing sample can be used to assess both.

Although authentic writing tasks mainly require students to exercise their production skills, students may also need to use their comprehension skills, depending on the assignment. For example, if they are writing about a topic within a content area such as social studies, students may need to demonstrate comprehension skills of a prior reading assignment and/or class discussion in order to perform the required writing task.

Conferences, Dialogue Journals, and Learning Logs

In order to monitor student progress, teachers sometimes neglect to do the obvious—ask the students! Teachers can learn valuable information about student successes as well as difficulties by means of conferences, dialogue journals, and learning logs. Teachers can use this information to guide instruction so that students' learning needs are met.

Conferences are discussions with individual students, groups of students, or the entire class about any aspect of their learning or their work. For example, teachers can ask students to talk about the parts of a lesson that were particularly difficult and to share thoughts on what would make their learning easier or more enjoyable. Students can talk about strategies they used that were successful for learning and strategies that were not. Conferences in the ESL classroom can also be used to learn how students are doing in their grade-level or content-area classes and how the ESL teacher can help students do better in those classes.

Dialogue journals can be used for the same purposes as conferences, but the responses are in written form. They are called *dialogue* journals because students write down their thoughts and ideas and teachers respond to student entries (thus creating a written "conversation") on a regular basis (often weekly, rather than daily, to keep the task of responding manageable). Students should feel that they themselves can bring up topics or questions about anything, especially if they might not feel comfortable discussing the topic in front of the entire class. Because of the personal and private nature of journals, some students may be more open and honest when writing in a journal than when speaking during a class discussion or conference. Journals also give teachers an opportunity to informally assess student writing—although journal entries should not be graded or even corrected except when mistakes interfere with meaning. In those cases, teachers can respond with comments such as, "What exactly did you mean here?" In order for students to feel uninhibited and remain excited about writing in their dialogue journals, they should not feel that they are being judged in any way.

Dialogue journals can be used at times as **learning logs** in which students reflect upon their successes, needs, and learning strategies. For this purpose, teachers can structure student entries by asking a set of specific questions or giving students prompts related to their learning. Genesee and Upshur (1996, p. 123) suggest the following prompts:

This week I studied...
This week I learned...
My difficulties are...
I would like to know...
I would like help with...
My learning and practicing plans are...

Teachers can use this information to keep abreast of topics taught in the content areas, and then tailor ESL instruction to help students succeed in areas of difficulty.

Conferences, dialogue journals, and especially learning logs allow students to monitor their own progress over time. These methods of assessment encourage students to identify areas of difficulty, both linguistic and nonlinguistic, that may be interfering with their learning or academic progress. They encourage student involvement and investment in the assessment process. However, because the information gleaned from these methods of assessment is often honest and personal, these methods may not be useful for grading purposes. In fact, using these methods of assessment for grading purposes may subvert the advantages (Genesee and Upshur, 1996). As students communicate through conferences or journal writing, if they are being graded, they may concentrate more on their language use than on the central point, which is their message. Furthermore, they may tend to be less truthful.

Outlining, Classifying, Graphing, Map Reading, and Other Academic Tasks

Another way to assess student progress in language and/or content-area skills is to have students complete familiar written classroom tasks such as calculating the distance between two locations on a map or sorting a list of items into categories such as plant versus animal characteristics. By assessing students on work similar to what they have previously completed in class or for homework, teachers give students opportunities to demonstrate what they know instead of possibly "tricking" them with questions on traditional tests.

It is my belief that teachers should aim for all students to "pass" an assessment rather than hope for typical bell curve results where some students do exceptionally well and others do poorly. If teachers design assessments to more closely resemble classroom and homework activities, ESL students may have a better chance of performing well on assessment tasks. Using these familiar classroom activities as assessments may have the added benefit of demonstrating to students the importance of mastering these types of skills, which are needed for academic success in the grade-level/content-area classrooms.

The academic and learning skills needed for academic success, are discussed in Chapter 2.

Student Portfolios

A **portfolio** is a collection of student work that demonstrates student efforts, progress, and achievement (Genesee and Upshur, 1996). Portfolios usually also include student self-assessments and teacher assessments of the individual work samples in the form of checklists, rubrics, or written comments. Portfolios are useful with ESL students because, unlike scores on tests (such as multiple-choice or matching), they can provide a multidimensional perspective of student progress and growth over time (O'Malley and Valdez Pierce, 1996). Since teachers and students usually select items to be included in a portfolio, instead of highlighting what students cannot do, portfolios emphasize what students can do, and help students monitor their own progress (Freeman and Freeman, 1992).

It is logical to include in a portfolio work samples from the beginning of the school year to serve as baseline samples, with new samples added periodically. Items can be added monthly, or can be added weekly and then sorted through at the end of the month (Freeman and Freeman, 1992). The entries can be writing samples, social studies reports, math problems, science or art projects, or even audio- or videotapes of student work.

Because portfolios are (and should be) highly individualized and are principally useful for showing personal effort and progress (rather than achievement judged against a certain standard), some educators argue that they should not be used for classroom grading purposes (Genesee and Upshur, 1996). However, it is my belief that portfolios can be used for grading purposes, especially if effort and progress are included as part of the criteria for determining student grades. By examining a student's portfolio, a teacher can determine the effort the student has made as well as the gains made each marking quarter. The topic of including student effort and progress as part of grading criteria is discussed further below.

Effort and Progress

Since educators have recognized the need to assess ESL students by using multiple criteria, it can be argued that ESL teachers also assess students' effort and progress, especially for grading purposes. Because ESL students enter ESL classrooms with such varied previous educational experiences and proficiencies, it may not be possible for all students to perform well on classroom assessments. A student who may not have had sufficient prior schooling but is now spending many hours on schoolwork in order to catch up and succeed should be rewarded for those efforts; otherwise, the student may become discouraged and stop working hard. Therefore, even if a student receives low scores on traditional tests or even on authentic assessments, teachers should consider awarding at least some credit for effort and progress. **Effort** can be rewarded by giving students "credit" for keeping an accurate and up-to-date notebook, being punctual to class, behaving appropriately, coming prepared with all learning materials, doing homework assignments, contributing to group work (by providing charts, pictures, etc.), and so on (Coelho, 1994). **Progress** can be rewarded by noting a student's gains over the marking quarter even if the student's assessment scores remain quite low compared to the scores of other students in the class. ESL teachers can encourage grade-level and content-area teachers to include effort and progress in their assessments of ESL students.

Experimenting with Alternative Assessment

If you are currently teaching, try out at least one of the following means of alternative assessment: observation, authentic writing tasks, conferences, dialog journals. If possible, work with a colleague to do the following:

1. Plan how, when, and why (for what purposes) you will use your assessment.

2. If you choose observation or an authentic writing task, decide on a rating scale. (You may want to design something similar to the sample rubrics in Figure 5.4 or 5.6.)

3. After you do the assessment, write down your thoughts about using the assessment. What aspects were positive and what might you want to do differently the next time?

4. Share your thoughts and ideas with a colleague who used the same (or different) type of assessment.

REPORT CARD GRADES

Even though the primary reason for assessing ESL students at the classroom level is to guide instruction, some or all of the information gathered during assessments needs to be used to determine report card grades. Considerable thought must be given to the criteria used in calculating report card grades, especially at the high school level, since these grades can have a profound effect on a student's future with respect to college admission and even scholarship awards. As discussed earlier, in addition to establishing these criteria in their own classes, ESL teachers need to be proactive in helping grade-level and content-area teachers establish criteria for determining report card grades for ESL students in grade-level/content-area classes. Since ESL students are in the process of acquiring English, it is logical that they should not be rated in exactly the same way as their native English-speaking peers in the same classes.

Report card grades serve the important purpose of informing students and their parents about student performance in school. But determining report card grades for ESL students is often a sticky issue. How can teachers, both ESL and grade-level/content-area, give ESL students accurate yet fair report card grades in school subjects when the students are still in the process of learning the language of instruction? Because of the complexity and difficulty of determining accurate and sensible grades for ESL students, some teachers would rather not have to give report card grades to ESL students until they are proficient in English. However, since report cards are an integral part of school life, teachers cannot avoid using assessments for grading purposes. Consequently, ESL teachers need to give considerable thought to the issue of report card grades so that sound decisions can be made.

Grading Criteria

Not all teachers agree on the criteria to be used for determining report card grades for ESL students, especially in content-area classes. The controversy revolves around an issue discussed briefly in the previous section: When determining report card grades for

ESL students in ESL, sheltered, and "mainstream" classes, how much weight, if any, should be allotted for *effort* and *progress*, as opposed to true levels of *achievement*?

Achievement as Criteria

The arguments for assigning grades based on achievement alone are valid. O'Malley and Valdez Pierce (1996) argue that when other factors—such as effort, attendance, behavior, and attitude—are intermingled with achievement, students get a mixed message about their accomplishments: They may perceive that they have succeeded in reaching a certain level of achievement when perhaps they have not. An additional problem, they explain, is the great variation in grading from teacher to teacher: Some teachers may assign a small percentage of the grade to effort and similar criteria, while others may consider effort a large percentage of the report card grade. O'Malley and Valdez Pierce (1996) conclude by telling teachers, "Do not assign grades for effort and especially do not combine effort and achievement in a single grade" (p. 31).

Factors Other than Achievement

In contrast to the beliefs of O'Malley and Valdez Pierce, some ESL teachers do recommend using other factors besides actual achievement to assess ESL students. As mentioned earlier, although Coelho (1994) does not directly mention report cards, she suggests assessing students in part by observing if they are "coming to class on time, coming prepared, keeping notebooks up-to-date, keeping a vocabulary notebook, … and so on" (p. 322). Genesee and Hamayan (1994) also imply that other factors besides achievement should be included when grading ESL students: "Regardless of the specific grading procedures used in a district, it is important that all the information collected about students—qualitative as well as quantitative, …be used to formulate student grades" (p. 222).

In my personal experience I have found it sensible and necessary to include other factors besides achievement in formulating report card grades for ESL students. Over the course of many years, I have come to this belief based on the various factors described below.

Helene Becker

When I have taught my own separate ESL classes at the secondary level, in establishing a fair report card grading system for students in my ESL classes, I considered that my typical ESL class was made up of students from several different countries who had had widely diverse educational experiences. Some had had strong academic preparation from school in their native countries while others had had minimal academic preparation, the equivalent of a first- or second-grade education in their native language. Some students were fluent in a language that was closely related to English whereas others spoke a very different one that even employed a different alphabet. Some of my students came from cultures that put a strong emphasis on education while others came from cultures where formal education was less important. I asked myself, "How can I grade all these students with such diverse backgrounds fairly, knowing that their past experiences strongly influence their current academic performance?"

Earlier in this chapter I discussed Maria, a student from the Dominican Republic. As you may recall, Maria's records indicated that she had completed the sixth grade in her native country, but through information she wrote in her journal, I came to find out that she really had only completed the equivalent of a second-grade education. This explained why her reading and writing skills were extremely low, in any language. For example, she had no awareness of the difference between upper- and lower-case letters, a distinction important in her native language, Spanish, as well as in English. How was she going to keep up with the others in the class and pass her tests and quizzes?

After many years of experimenting with different systems, I designed one that was suitable in my teaching situation. For grading purposes, I decided to put considerable emphasis on each student's individual effort and progress in relation to himself or herself, rather than on each student's achievement in relation to an academic standard. I came up with the following report card grading system:

Report Card Grading System

Tests, quizzes, projects, and other assessments:	30% of grade
Homework:	30% of grade
Class participation:	30% of grade
Notebook:	10% of grade

Because this system was designed to encourage *maximum individual effort* on the part of students by rewarding them heavily for doing their homework, participating in class, and keeping an organized notebook, it also encouraged *maximum individual progress*. Since my goal was to encourage all students to do their best to learn the most they could, I felt that this report card grading system was consistent with that goal. In addition, if students were trying their absolute best, they could probably do fairly well on tests, quizzes, and other assessments.

Through the use of a system that heavily rewards effort, students are evaluated more on their own personal record than on their achievement compared to others in the class. This system encourages even a student such as Maria to work hard because her efforts are rewarded. Since students enter our schools with such varying degrees of preparation for accomplishment in our culture, I believe this method of grading is appropriate and encourages students to do their best.

If ESL and other teachers choose to grade ESL students solely on achievement, no matter how great student effort may be, I believe that some students may never achieve even passing grades. These students, faced with constant failure and frustration, are at risk for dropping out of school and never attaining the level of education of which they are capable.

I asked several elementary and secondary ESL teachers to discuss the criteria they used for determining report card grades for their ESL students. All reported that they rewarded effort and individual progress, to varying degrees. Here is a typical response, this from a secondary ESL teacher in Virginia:

Marilyn Bart,
Stuart High School,
Fairfax County
Public Schools,
Virginia

These are the criteria I use for evaluating ESL students in my ESL classes:

Report Card Grading System

Tests/projects/ writing assignments:	35% of grade
Classwork:	35% of grade
Homework:	30% of grade

Classwork includes participation, completion of assignments, preparation for class (bringing necessary materials), and behavior. Behavior includes cooperation and attitude, important for students' success in my class and in school in general. Homework is usually a reinforcing language activity; I give them a lot of credit for doing it because it is also so important for their success in school.

We realize that this system is not perfect because it does not always reflect the academic achievement of an individual student. But students are rewarded for valuable life behaviors such as perseverance and attitude. We all have students who work hard, but are having difficulty learning. These students usually pass as long as they make a concerted effort. On the other hand, we have students who do not show consistent effort, positive behavior, and cooperation in the classroom. Both of these students may receive a grade of "C" based on the criteria above, but for different reasons.

As the teacher above states, rewarding effort has its drawbacks, but not rewarding effort may have even more negative consequences in the form of discouraging and frustrating students to the point that they may give up.

ONE OF THE BIGGEST CHALLENGES FACING ESL TEACHERS is the grading of students who are developing their proficiency in a second language at the same time they are learning academic content. The issues that Helene brings up, such as grading for effort, are complex, and have emotional and academic implications for individual students and their families as well as political implications for language-minority students in general. In order to determine grading procedures more clearly and to evaluate the grading system that is being used, it might be helpful to consider the purposes that grades and student evaluation accomplish for different sets of people.

PURPOSES OF ASSESSMENT

The following are questions that different people might be interested in regarding the assessment of ESL students (Cloud, Genesee, and Hamayan, 2000):

Parents: Is my child learning what he or she needs to learn?

What is my child gaining by being in the ESL program?

Teachers:	Are students learning what I am supposed to be teaching?
	What needs to happen in order to improve student learning?
Administrators:	How do ESL students perform relative to others in the school?
Students:	What am I learning?
	How am I performing compared to what is expected of me?
	How can I make my learning more efficient?

It is also beneficial to examine the goals of assessment in order to ensure that the assessment procedures being used lend themselves to the type of information needed. Some assessment procedures may yield more useful information than others. Generally, assessment results are used to demonstrate to others that students are learning as expected. They also serve the purpose of monitoring student progress in order to plan appropriate instruction. As Helene mentions, the link between assessment and instruction must be strong. Assessment also serves the purpose of giving the teacher insight into students' learning styles, learning strategies, interests, and attitudes. These provide vital contextual information that can help the teacher in interpreting student performance and behavior. Finally, assessment should give students enough information to allow them to monitor their own learning (Cloud, Genesee, and Hamayan, 2000).

5.12 *FORMULATING REPORT CARD GRADING GUIDELINES*

What are your thoughts and beliefs about including effort as part of the report card grade? What about including individual progress, especially if the student is performing at a level below the other students in the class? What about a student who does well on assessments but puts in very little effort to improve? Consider the following situation as you formulate (or reformulate) your beliefs about these issues:

Suppose you have a ninth-grade student, Carolyn, in your intermediate ESL class. Carolyn has great potential and a strong academic background in her native language. However, she does class assignments and activities only reluctantly and completes very few of the homework assignments. Yet, she manages to do fairly well on classroom assessments.

At the end of the marking quarter, Carolyn earns the following grades:

Tests, quizzes:	B
Other classroom-based assessments (including contributions to group work):	C
Classwork (including behavior and attitude):	D
Homework assignments (half missing):	F
Notebook:	D

With a colleague, discuss how you would approach determining a report card grade (that is, how much weight you would give to each category) for Carolyn and your rationale behind your approach. Can you come to an agreement on her report card grade?

Collaborating with Grade-Level and Content-Area Teachers

If a school district has a high percentage of ESL students in many grade-level and/or content-area classes, "mainstream" teachers may have adapted their curricula, classroom assessments, and report card criteria to accommodate the abilities and needs of the students in the class. For example, the high school ESL teacher from Virginia who spoke earlier about her report card grading system adds,

> Since the high school in which I teach is 60 percent language-minority, the "mainstream" faculty is used to adapting curricula and grading practices to meet ESL needs. For the most part, many non-ESL [students] experience content-area difficulties, as well, so teachers are making adaptations for other students besides the ESL population.

Teachers' Voices

Marilyn Bart, Stuart High School, Fairfax County Public Schools, Virginia

In contrast, in a school district in which ESL students comprise a smaller percentage of the student body, grade-level and content-area teachers may need a special plan for determining report card grades for ESL students in their classes. Since ESL students in these situations probably do not have as much of an impact on the design of grade-level/content-area teachers' daily lesson plans and assessments, ESL students may perform lower on classroom assessments than in situations where teachers must adapt their plans more fully. Thus, grade-level/content-area teachers may be in a quandary about determining fair report card grades for ESL students, especially the first time ESL students appear in their classes.

I spoke with a recently retired elementary school ESL teacher from the West Hartford Public Schools in Connecticut, a district mentioned earlier with a relatively small ESL population (about five percent of the student body), to learn about her school's policy regarding report card grades for ESL students. I discovered that when she taught at the school, there was no set policy, and that each teacher devised his or her own system for grading ESL students.

> When I taught at Wolcott, each "mainstream" teacher in my school dealt with report cards differently. Some took into account the fact that the child was just learning English and wrote "ESL student" on the report card. Then, they graded the student only in areas that could

be graded (such as math, behavior, attitude, etc.) and left the other areas blank. Some indicated in the Comments section that the student was doing as well as could be expected given that the student was at the beginning or intermediate level (for example) of learning English, and then went on to write positive comments about the child.

It was probably easier to deal with report cards in the lower elementary grades (K–2). In the upper elementary grades (3–5), it became harder because of the academic expectations at that particular grade level. Again, most teachers were understanding of the process of learning a second language and were willing to adjust the grades. When the classroom teacher and I worked together to fill out the report card, I felt we could satisfactorily reflect the progress of the student.

There were things I wanted to change on the report card, but, in general, with sensitivity and understanding, a positive statement of progress—acceptable to the classroom teacher—could be made.

Judy Porter, Wolcott Elementary School, West Hartford, Connecticut

The teachers in this school, as in most schools, wanted to be fair and encouraging to ESL students. However, without some guidelines, there is a danger that eventually mistakes will be made and damage will be done. I came to this belief a few years ago, when I was faced with the following situation.

A few months into the school year at my new job, I found in my mailbox a copy of the report card of one of my fourth-grade ESL students. I had not asked for the copy, but it was the end of the first marking quarter, and I supposed that the classroom teacher wanted me to see how the student was performing in her various subjects.

Helene Becker

The student, Elsie, had come to this country from the Philippines about a year before, and was just beginning to feel comfortable speaking English. She was a shy girl and spoke very softly. Recently, however, her classroom teacher had reported to me that she had started to raise her hand in her classroom to answer questions. This was a big step, and I was very proud of her. Her reading and writing skills were quite typical for a literate (in her native language) fourth-grader learning a new language.

What I saw on her report card surprised and saddened me; her teacher had given her a "D" in both speaking and reading. If she were compared to the native English speakers in her class, I am sure she was doing "D" work or worse, but it seemed obvious that you could not compare her to her native English-speaking peers.

I spoke to her teacher and discovered that the school did not have any policy or guidelines regarding report card grades for ESL students. Each teacher decided for himself or herself how to evaluate ESL students. Some teachers, as in the case of the teacher above, used the same criteria they used for native English speakers, while others omitted grades altogether. Still others decided that "C" was a good grade for ESL students as long as they were showing considerable effort. The teacher who gave Elsie the "D's" did not mean any harm. In her eyes, Elsie was doing "D" work at this point in time, compared to her native English-speaking peers.

I went to the administration to express my concern about the harm done when a child receives a "D" simply because she is still in the process of acquiring English. How will a child interpret such a grade? She will probably feel that she is "stupid" in her new language and may give up putting in the effort. And how will her parents react to a grade of "D"? I explained that Elsie was doing as expected in reading and writing and was perhaps less verbal compared to other ESL students who had been here for about a year. But I also explained that the process of language acquisition was very individual, and that Elsie was doing well in her speaking progress now. In fact, given her current effort and successes, I would have given her an "A" or "B" in speaking, if I were judging her progress or comparing her to her ESL peers.

Elsie's grade-level teacher wanted to treat Elsie fairly, but at the same time she did not want to sacrifice the meaning or integrity of the grades she assigned. This sentiment is shared by many grade-level/content-area teachers with whom I have spoken. For this reason, it is important to be proactive and discuss with grade-level/content-area teachers the assigning of report card grades for ESL students before grading decisions are made. As a result of the situation with Elsie, the grade-level teachers agreed to raise for discussion at a teachers' meeting the issue of guidelines for determining report card grades for ESL students.

Grading Policy Guidelines for Grade-Level/Content-Area Teachers

Since it is not logical to use with ESL students a school's regular grading guidelines designed for students who are already proficient in English, it is necessary for schools to have a clear policy regarding grading guidelines for ESL students in grade-level/content-area classes. Schools might want to consider the following guidelines (adapted from the West Hartford Public Schools), which suggest three options. These guidelines can be used as a starting point for schools struggling with establishing grading policies for ESL students. These suggestions can be adapted for use in elementary or secondary schools.

Option 1: Letter Grade ("A" through "F")—Recommended when a student can attain a real "C" or higher. A grade of "D" should be given only when a student has not shown considerable effort.

Option 2: Pass/Fail—Recommended when a student cannot successfully complete all the work in a subject but can complete enough to justify a grade (and/or credit at the high school level).

Option 3: No Grade—Recommended when the student's level of English proficiency is too low to allow him or her to participate enough in a subject to justify a grade and/or credit. In these cases, teachers should make narrative comments describing progress and gains the student has made.

At the close of each marking period, after receiving input from the ESL teacher, and possibly from the ESL student, each grade-level/content-area teacher can determine which option is most appropriate for each student. For those students who show considerable effort but cannot yet attain at least average test and quiz grades, the pass/fail option should be used, because it does not have a negative connotation or effect on the student's school record while the student is acquiring

English. However, if the student does not do assignments, does not accept extra help when necessary, or does not participate in class in a positive manner to the best of his or her ability, the pass/fail or no grade options should not be offered.

At the secondary level, where students have more than one teacher, it is sometimes appropriate for teachers of the same student to select different grading options in the same marking period. For example, the social studies teacher may feel that an ESL student in his class is ready to receive a letter grade (option 1), whereas the English literature teacher may feel that the pass/fail option (option 2) is more suitable for this same student in her class. It is important to look at each class separately since each subject presents different kinds of challenges for ESL students, and one academic subject may be more difficult than another.

As students become more proficient in English, the grading option in each class can be adjusted, as necessary. It is important for the ESL teacher to communicate with grade-level/content-area teachers at the close of each marking period to ensure that the ESL students are being graded appropriately.

5.13 *OUT IN THE FIELD...*

Investigate the criteria used by ESL and grade-level/content-area teachers in your area to determine report card grades for ESL students in their classes. If possible, interview an ESL and/or grade-level/content-area teacher about report card grades. Here are some suggested questions:

To an ESL teacher:

1. How do you determine report card grades for your ESL students?

2. Do you collaborate with grade-level/content-area teachers in your school regarding report card grades for ESL students in their classes? What suggestions do you offer? Is there a school policy regarding report card grades for ESL students in grade-level/content-area classes? If so, please describe the policy.

To a grade-level/content-area teacher:

1. Regarding report card grades, what special considerations, if any, do you give ESL students in your classes?

2. Is there a school policy regarding report card grades for ESL students? If so, please describe the policy.

CHAPTER SUMMARY

With respect to district-level assessments, ESL programs need to establish precise, reliable, and consistent procedures in order to determine accurately: (1) which students belong in an ESL program (entry procedures); (2) in which classes/instructional groups students should be placed (placement procedures); (3) how much progress individual students are making yearly (monitoring procedures) and; (4) when students are ready to exit from the ESL program (exit procedures).

Districts need to decide which assessment instruments best suit their needs for these purposes. When assessing a student, it is important to get a total picture of student skills by assessing oral language as well as reading and writing skills. In addition to using traditional tests, school districts are finding the use of rubrics helpful in describing student levels of proficiency in these skill areas.

At the initial entry point, besides assessing students' English language proficiency, schools need to assess native language and math proficiency. At the other end, when students are exited, they must be monitored to ensure that their success continues.

Classroom-based assessments have multiple purposes, the most important of which are to guide instruction in the classroom and to evaluate student progress. In order to assess students accurately it is important to use a variety of assessment tools—both traditional tests and alternative assessments—and to match the assessment tool to the lesson objectives.

ESL teachers need to understand the complexity of evaluating ESL students in their ESL classes and to make decisions about how to determine report card grades. In addition, ESL teachers should collaborate with individual grade-level/content-area teachers regarding report card grades for each ESL student in their classes. A school or district policy helps to promote fairness without sacrificing the meaning and integrity of report card grades.

Suggested Readings

For an in-depth treatment of assessment issues in all types of ESL situations (including university settings), I recommend Kathleen M. Bailey's book in the TeacherSource Series, *Learning About Language Assessment: Dilemmas, Decisions, and Directions* (1998). For further reading specifically about traditional as well as alternative classroom-based assessments, I suggest *Classroom-based Evaluation in Second Language Education* (1996) by Fred Genesee and John A. Upshur. A thorough resource book on authentic assessment is J. Michael O'Malley and Lorraine Valdez Pierce's *Authentic Assessment for English Language Learners: Practical Approaches for Teachers* (1996). It includes many examples of reproducible authentic assessment checklists and rubrics for assessing language skills as well as content-area skills and knowledge. Finally, ESL teachers should read a short but valuable booklet entitled *Managing the Assessment Process* (TESOL, 1998). This 24-page professional paper offers guidance regarding assessment to teachers incorporating the *ESL Standards for Pre-K–12 Students* (TESOL, 1997).

6

SPECIAL EDUCATION
AND ESL STUDENTS

*If you were to walk into a special education classroom in a large
urban school district, you would probably find a disproportionately large number of ESL and minority students (Scarcella, 1990).
How did they get there? Do they all belong there? Are there some
ESL students who should be there but who are not?*

There are compelling reasons for ensuring that ESL students placed in special
education programs do, indeed, have special education needs. First, special
education is designed to serve students who have major disorders that interfere
with learning (Garcia and Ortiz, 1988). By placing an ESL student in a special
education program, we are labeling the student "handicapped;" we need to be
certain of the existence of a handicapping condition before the student is
assigned a potentially stigmatizing label.

Second, special education programs are expensive to run. They tend to have
small teacher-student ratios and strict requirements regarding meetings and
paperwork, which represent time and money. It is more cost-effective to educate
students in the "mainstream" rather than through a special education program;
consequently, it is wise to keep students out of special education when there is
no true disorder (Ortiz and Garcia, 1988).

Third, there is a question as to the usefulness of special education for some
ESL students. In at least one study of Hispanic students categorized as learning
disabled, after three years in a special education program, students actually
received lower scores than at the entry point on verbal and performance IQ
tests, and the same scores (that is, there was no improvement) on achievement
tests (Garcia and Ortiz, 1988). These results suggest that special education may
not always be the appropriate learning environment for certain ESL students, or
that the instruction offered in some special education settings does not always
meet the needs of ESL students.

At the other end of the spectrum, ESL students who have legitimate disorders
should have access to quality special education services. If schools cannot correctly identify these students, some may be deprived of valuable instruction that
could help them achieve their potential.

This chapter deals with the complexities of identifying and instructing ESL
students with learning and behavioral disabilities. Because some of the signs of
these particular disabilities are similar to characteristics of students learning a
new language, ESL students can be erroneously referred for special education

This chapter does not deal with the more easily detectable disabilities such as hearing, visual, or orthopedic impairment.

testing. For example, a student who speaks or writes with poor sentence structure may be learning disabled, or may simply be an ESL student in the process of learning English. If an ESL student is tested for learning disabilities, the results may tell us little, because the typical tests used are designed for middle-class, monolingual speakers and not for ESL students (Scarcella, 1990). At the same time there are ESL students who do have learning problems that go undiagnosed because there is no simple method to detect them in students who are learning a new language. It is essential that ESL teachers in elementary and secondary schools understand the complexities of diagnosing and teaching learning disabled ESL students so that these struggling learners may be identified and taught appropriately. In this chapter, a procedure will be suggested for identifying learning disabilities in ESL students, and recommendations will be offered for teaching ESL students who are found to be truly learning disabled.

Else offers a historical and political perspective on the issue of ESL students and the diagnosis of special education needs.

Else's Perspective

THERE IS A HISTORY IN THE UNITED STATES for associating bilingualism with disability or disorder. In the first half of the twentieth century, the question most frequently asked in the research was whether or not bilingualism has a negative effect on intelligence. And in fact, prior to the early 1960s, most research showed that children reared in a bilingual environment were handicapped in language growth and that their intelligence was impaired (Thompson, 1952). In contrast, more recent studies have focused on whether or not bilingualism has a positive effect on intelligence (Hakuta, 1986). As was the case with the earlier studies, the findings confirmed the question, and the majority of studies show that bilingual children have advantages over their monolingual counterparts (Peal and Lambert, 1962).

Several characteristics differentiate the two groups of studies. The earlier research was conducted with immigrant populations in the United States, and the more current work is coming out of Canada and Europe. The motivation underlying the earlier studies was clearly set in a different social context than current research. If we consider the status of bilingualism in the United States and contrast it with that in Canada and Europe, we can see that bilingualism in the United States remains by far the exception, whereas significant proportions of people (if not the majority) in Canada and Europe are bilingual. Bilingualism in the United States, even today, is typically associated with poorer disenfranchised immigrants, whereas in other parts of the world, bilingualism is expected of everyone regardless of citizenship, immigration, or socioeconomic status.

The different motivations underlying the early and current studies influenced the research methodology used as well as the interpretation of the findings (Hakuta, 1986). Statistical problems and confounding variables in the earlier research clouded the conclusions drawn from those studies (Gould, 1981). For example, lack of proficiency in English, the language of the tests used, obviously influenced the bilingual population's performance on the test, and yet this variable was often not controlled for. As Hakuta (1986) suggests, the question of whether bilingualism is linked to intelligence is misguided primarily because it ignores the social context within which bilingualism happens. However, the fact remains that bilingualism is still seen as an aberration in the United States, and many monolingual teachers and administrators habitually expect difficulties for students who are faced with learning English as a second language. I would venture to guess that the language-learning experience of these monolingual educators, which probably was limited to foreign language classes in high school, clouds their expectations for bilingual proficiency. Thus, Helene's observation—that special education classrooms, especially in large urban schools, have a disproportionately high number of ESL students—needs to be considered in light of the social and political context surrounding the education of students who have minority status within the school.

WHAT ARE THE ISSUES ASSOCIATED WITH REFERRING ESL STUDENTS FOR SPECIAL EDUCATION SERVICES?

OVER-REFERRING

Whenever a grade-level or content-area teacher says "I'm thinking about referring an ESL student for a special education evaluation," the ESL teacher needs to intervene. Since there are several characteristics that are normal and expected in ESL students, but that can also indicate a learning or behavioral disability, teachers can mistake these characteristics in ESL students for disabilities (Ortiz and Yates, 1988). Here is a summary of characteristics which may indicate a learning or behavioral disability and the reasons these characteristics are often seen in ESL students who do not have disabilities:

Figure 6.1: **Characteristics of Typical ESL Students Which May Be Mistaken as Signs of Learning or Behavioral Disabilities**

Learning Issues	Reason Difficulty Seen in Typical ESL Students
Academic learning difficulties	ESL students often have difficulty with grade-level academic language and concepts because it takes at least five years for nonnative speakers to display native-speaker-like functioning in academics (discussed in Chapter 2).
Language disorder	Lack of fluency is a natural part of learning a new language
Attention and memory problems	ESL students may have difficulty paying attention and remembering if they cannot relate new information to their previous experiences in their respective cultures.

Emotional/Behavioral Issue	Reason Difficulty Seen in Typical ESL Students
Withdrawn behavior	When students are learning a new language and adapting to a new culture, a "silent period" is normal. Also, this behavior might be appropriate in the student's culture.
Aggressive behavior	The student may not understand appropriate school behavior and language. Also, this behavior might be appropriate in the student's culture.
Social and emotional problems	When students are learning to live in a new language and culture, social and emotional problems develop.

The grade-level teacher who is thinking about referring an ESL student for special education services has usually noticed in the student one or more of the characteristics listed above. When it is pointed out that this characteristic is often seen in ESL students and that it is quite normal, the response may be, "But other ESL students I have had from the same country were not like that." The fact that the student appears "different" from others in his or her cultural group may be relevant when combined with many other indicators (as explained later in this chapter), but differences are to be expected, since progress in learning is individual and varied within any cultural group (just as with native speakers of English).

ESL students can also be over-referred to special education classes when teachers assume that student difficulties are caused by something within the student, rather than first examining external factors. For example, many ESL students struggle in school because they have previously had minimal or interrupted schooling, not because there is something intrinsically wrong with the students. As Cloud (1994) points out, "Students who do not possess an intrinsic impairment or disability but are undereducated or 'miseducated' cannot be considered *special education* students" (p. 244). ESL students might also be struggling in school because of other external problems such as poor nutrition, an unstable family environment, or frequent moving and changing of schools. Students who are experiencing academic or behavioral problems in school because of these external problems are not special education students.

Else's Perspective

HELENE'S POINT ABOUT THE NEED to look first at external factors first is crucial. When an ESL student has difficulties in school, it is much more likely that those difficulties are part of the normal second-language development process than that they are due to a long-term cognitive or perceptual disability or disorder. For that reason, it is recommended that external reasons for students' academic difficulties be considered first, and eliminated as possible causes, before starting an examination of intrinsic processing and learning ability. In order to eliminate the possibility that external factors may be responsible for academic difficulties, Hamayan and Damico (1991) offer a list of five questions;

answering "no" to all these questions eliminates the possibility that external factors are responsible for an ESL student's difficulties.

1. Are there any overt variables that can explain the student's being identified as having difficulties? These variables include test anxiety, or a teacher who has a pattern of over-referral of ESL students to special education.
2. Can the difficulties be explained by normal second-language learning processes? These include expected stages of second-language learning, patterns of second-language errors, and whether the student has had enough time to develop proficiency in the second language.
3. Can the difficulties be due to differences in cultural norms? Is the cultural context of school very different from the student's own way of interpreting and interacting with the world?
4. Does the student exhibit specific difficulties only in English (but not in the first language)?
5. Is there anything in the student's environment that makes academic achievement particularly difficult? For example, the type of instructional model that surrounds the student may lead to subtractive bilingualism, which may in turn lead to academic difficulties, or the student may come from an educational background that inadequately prepares him or her for school learning.

On disabilities in two languages, see p.161.

It is important that this type of questioning be made part of the everyday functioning of the school so that it becomes routine procedure. Only then will the mindset that initially sees bilingualism as a problem be changed.

A third reason we find an excessive number of ESL students in special education classes in many schools is that special education tests, including IQ tests, are not generally designed for a multicultural population in the process of learning English. Cummins (1984) points out that many teachers assume that ESL students are capable of taking such tests (in English) after one year in the United States. Although the student may have good oral skills in English (BICS), academic proficiency (CALP) takes much longer to acquire, and the student may do very poorly on such a test. Cummins adds that even testing in the native language (if such a test is available) can be problematic if the student is not enrolled in a bilingual program and consequently has not continued to develop cognitive/academic proficiency in the native language. If there is no strong promotion of the student's native language in school, he or she may have lost enough proficiency in the native language to render the results of the test invalid.

On BICS and CALP, see Chapter 2.

A fourth reason for over-referral relates to the quality of instruction that the ESL student may be receiving. If a student is not achieving at an expected rate, perhaps the fault lies in the teaching rather than in the learning. One should not assume that a student is learning disabled simply because he or she is having difficulty with some aspect of the academic curriculum (Scarcella, 1990). It may well be that appropriate accommodations have not been made in order for students learning a new language to have sufficient success with the curriculum.

A few years ago an ESL colleague of mine in Hawaii was faced with a typical situation: A grade-level teacher believed that one of the ESL students in her classroom had learning problems, but my colleague, who saw the student daily in an ESL setting, did not agree. This is what she reported:

Duc was a second-grader who arrived from Vietnam in the middle of the school year. He was an enthusiastic and playful child, even if he couldn't communicate much in English. I saw him for pullout ESL lessons every day, sometimes in a small group with other second-graders and sometimes by himself. Within a few weeks Duc began to talk and could answer my simple questions with one or two words. In short, he seemed to be a typical newly arrived student going through the stages of learning a new language and adjusting to a new environment.

About three months after Duc's arrival, when I came to pick him up at his classroom, his grade-level teacher pulled me aside. She was very concerned about Duc's lack of progress and his disruptive behavior in class. She was wondering if I had some of the same concerns and if I thought that he was showing signs of learning or behavioral disabilities. She reported that he was not paying attention a lot of the time and would sometimes distract other students in the class. When I asked her to tell me about some of the learning activities during which he was not paying attention, it became clear to me that the activities, in the manner in which she was conducting them, were probably at least part of the problem.

For example, she stated that when she read a book aloud to her students (who were sitting in front of her on the floor), in order to enhance comprehension, she would face the book toward the students so that they could see the pictures. However, after some probing, I found out that she did not point to the words and related pictures as she read the story so that Duc could visually "see" the meaning of the words. In addition, she did not make sure that Duc was seated up front and close to the book so that he could see the small words and pictures clearly. In short, she had not been doing many things differently for Duc because she had expected him to catch on by himself, as other ESL students in her class had done previously.

After further discussion, I discovered that the students to whom the grade-level teacher was comparing Duc had been born in the United States and probably had had quite a bit of exposure to English before entering school, even if they spoke a different language at home. In contrast, Duc was newly arrived to the United States and had had little exposure to English and American culture prior to starting school here.

The grade-level teacher also told me that when she had a few spare moments she worked individually with Duc on reading, using words from a "frequently used words" list. She found that Duc was not retaining many of the words that she considered quite easy (words such as *is, are, it, of, to, was,* and *they*). I pointed out that these words were in fact difficult for ESL students because they did not have any real meaning in isolation. I told her that I had had good success with Duc when he read some easy stories that had real meaning rather than words on a list that he didn't understand. He actually did quite well with these stories and was learning to read.

Fortunately, this teacher was willing to experiment with some simple accommodations, and Duc was able to make better progress. She and I began communicating regularly so that we could coordinate our efforts to help Duc learn English and benefit from content instruction in the classroom. Although Duc continued to be a challenging student that year, it was decided that a special education referral was inappropriate and the issue was eventually dropped.

UNDER-REFERRING

Under-referring of ESL students for special education evaluations occurs when teachers adopt the belief that an ESL student must study English for a certain period of time, usually one or two years, before it can be determined whether or not the student has special education needs. Some school systems have instituted policies that prohibit special education referrals for ESL students until this predetermined period of time has elapsed. When this is the case, ESL students who are in need of special help may be denied important services.

I suspect that, early in my career as an ESL teacher, some of my students' disabilities went undiagnosed because my colleagues and I did not know how to determine whether or not a student had a disability. Since we did not have any test we could administer to a beginning- or intermediate-level ESL student and we did not know what else to do, we just waited several years until the student learned more English and could possibly be tested in English. Even then the results of the tests were not completely valid since, as mentioned above, the tests were not designed for an ESL population. Here is a case I remember clearly.

> Several years ago, Tazlin, a shy, teenage girl from India, appeared in my ESL Level I class. She was a tenth-grader who had been in this country for about a year and had already taken ESL Level I at the high school across town. Her family had moved, so she had to change high schools. I decided to call the ESL teacher at her former high school to find out why Tazlin was repeating ESL Level I.

Helene Becker

The teacher told me the following:

> Tazlin had difficulty learning new information. When vocabulary or concepts were presented and practiced in the class, the other students eventually caught on, but Tazlin didn't. She couldn't pass any tests, even though she seemed to be trying quite hard. She usually did her homework, although most of the time it was incorrect. She had a much more difficult time speaking than the others in the class. I had to recommend that she repeat Level I; she would not be able to survive in Level II.

Jacqueline Werner,
Hall High School,
West Hartford,
Connecticut

Helene Becker

Within a few days, I concurred with my colleague; Tazlin had an unusually hard time learning. Given the fact that it was her second time through an ESL class (not a "mainstream" class) and she was still having difficulty, I suspected that perhaps she had some sort of learning disability, but I was at a loss as to how to find out. She certainly couldn't be evaluated by using a test meant for English speakers—she didn't speak much English. I doubted that my colleague and I could find a test in her native language (Hindi), and even if we could find one, who would be able to administer it? And if we found someone to administer it and we determined that Tazlin needed special education instruction, would the special education teachers be able to help a beginning-level ESL student? We ended up not doing anything, but we agreed to keep checking on her progress.

As I look back on my experience with Tazlin, I regret that at the time we did not have any formal process in place to evaluate her case. Perhaps by using other means of evaluation besides tests, we could have done some sort of evaluation and developed an educational plan that might have included special education services and would perhaps have helped her progress more quickly. I am happy to report, however, that she did start to catch on a few months into the school year and did finally pass ESL Level I. Unfortunately, at the end of the school year she announced that she was not returning in the fall—she was going back to India to get married. We were sorry to see her go; she was finally making some academic progress, had overcome much of her shyness, and seemed quite happy in our school.

WHEN SHOULD ESL STUDENTS BE REFERRED FOR SPECIAL EDUCATION SERVICES?

I have learned a great deal by trying to figure out how to help students such as Tazlin. Although I am convinced that there are no easy and precise answers, there are certain steps teachers can take to ensure that struggling students are assessed fairly for special education needs and receive proper instruction.

THE PREREFERRAL PROCESS

The purpose of a prereferral process is to examine the performance of an ESL student with suspected disabilities in the context of the current educational setting (Willig, 1986). It is a proactive process and seeks to avoid a referral to special education (Cloud, 1994). At a prereferral meeting, current or prior external factors that might be causing a student to have learning difficulties in the current educational setting, as well as possible internal factors, are taken into account. "An effective prereferral process can help distinguish achievement difficulties associated with a lack of accommodation of individual differences in regular classrooms from problems that stem from a handicapping condition" (Garcia and Ortiz, 1988, p. 2). Some schools have prereferral teams in place that routinely meet to discuss any cases that come up. Other schools call together the appropriate staff on a case-by-case basis. This could include the grade-level or content-area teachers, ESL teacher, social worker, principal, and any other staff familiar with the student. The ESL teacher should always be involved in the prereferral discussion in order to ensure that participants constantly keep in mind the complexities involved in evaluating a student who is learning a new language. Special education personnel (for example, special education teachers or psychologists) should *not* be involved in the prereferral process so that the focus at this stage is on finding ways to help the student *within the regular education setting*. The involvement of special education personnel tends to overshadow this intent and makes it easier to move students into special education (Garcia and Ortiz, 1988).

Topics that need to be addressed in a prereferral meeting include:

Student factors
- health status
- visual and hearing ability
- nutritional status
- socioeconomic factors
- home environment
- time in an ESL program
- prior schooling
- native-language proficiency
- English-language proficiency
- academic performance
- behavior patterns
- learning style
- adjustment to school

Current learning environment
- curricular accommodations made
- instructional accommodations made
- attitudes and qualifications of teachers
- ESL instruction available
- appropriateness of instructional program for this student

All of these factors, external and internal, need to be examined in order to determine what may be causing difficulties for the student. Information can be gathered from school records, teachers, parents, and the student. In addition, the student needs to be observed in the classroom in order to evaluate academic performance in the current educational setting. Teachers should also observe each other teaching the student, and then discuss whether the curriculum and instruction are appropriate, given the student's educational background and English-language proficiency.

After the information has been gathered and discussed, suggestions should be offered regarding alternative instructional methods and/or curriculum that may be more suitable for this student within the current educational placement (Willig, 1986). The purpose of these suggestions is to try to change any external factors that may be causing the student to have academic difficulties rather than first assuming that a condition within the student is the source of the problem.

For example, the sixth-grade math curriculum may be appropriate for sixth grade intermediate-level ESL students who have strong backgrounds in math in the native language. However, the curriculum may be inappropriate for a sixth-grade intermediate-level ESL student who has had interrupted prior schooling and therefore has not mastered fourth- and fifth-grade math concepts. In this case, the curriculum needs to be adjusted for this student so that he or she can learn the fourth- and fifth-grade math concepts needed in order to understand sixth-grade math. The student's lack of success with sixth-grade math does not indicate that the student has a learning disability; it only indicates that he or she lacks the background knowledge to benefit from the sixth-grade math instruction.

6.1 GATHERING INFORMATION

By yourself or with a colleague, design a questionnaire to be used to gather information prior to and during a prereferral meeting. Using the topics listed above, and any other topics you believe might be useful in obtaining relevant information, write the actual questions you would ask. After each question, make a notation as to where you would go to get the information (e.g., parents, grade-level teacher, student records, etc.).

6.2 MAKING SUGGESTIONS

Suggesting to a grade-level or content-area teacher that he or she needs to alter methods of instruction can be difficult! In order to promote good professional attitudes and relationships, the needs of the ESL students must be balanced with the sensitivities of the teacher who is being asked to do things differently in the classroom, perhaps after many years of teaching a certain way. During such discussions, ESL teachers need to choose words carefully.

Imagine that you are the ESL teacher at a prereferral meeting regarding a fifth-grade ESL student who is doing poorly academically in the grade-level classroom. You suspect that the student would perform better if the grade-level teacher used more visuals, gave students more hands-on opportunities, and allowed students to work more often in groups. Accommodations on tests also need to be made for the student (the questions need to be reworded using fewer complex structures). You are willing to demonstrate some instructional techniques for the teacher and to assist in the rewording of the tests.

With a colleague, role-play your interaction with this teacher during a prereferral meeting. Without causing the grade-level teacher to feel threatened or resentful, discuss the issue of making accommodations for the student.

In summary, schools need to have procedures in place for problem solving (a prereferral process) when ESL students are having learning difficulties. The goal of the process should be to make a sincere and persistent attempt to promote student progress within the regular education setting. The systematic, multifaceted approach for prereferral, suggested by Shernaz B. Garcia and Alba A. Ortiz (1988), in Figure 6.2 is a good starting point for schools interested in developing or improving their own procedures: As suggested in this model, a special education referral should not be initiated until all other possible explanations for the student's difficulties have been explored during the prereferral stage, and steps have been taken to help the student succeed.

Figure 6.2: Preventing Inappropriate Placements of Language-Minority Students in Special Education: A Prereferral Process

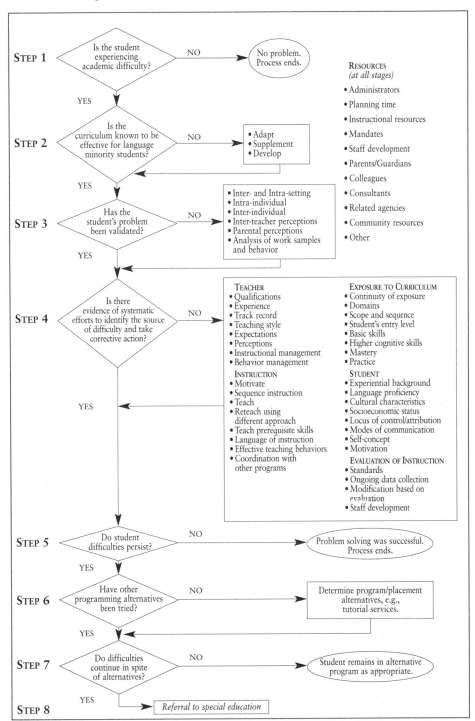

(Adapted and printed with permission from Garcia and Ortiz, 1988, p. 3)

THE SPECIAL EDUCATION REFERRAL PROCESS

After a sincere attempt has been made to alter the instruction to accommodate the needs of a struggling ESL student, if the problem persists, a special education referral should be initiated. As in the prereferral process, during the referral phase, the ESL teacher needs to be thoroughly involved so that typical characteristics of ESL students are not mistaken for indicators of disabilities, and participants in the process are continually reminded that an ESL student cannot be evaluated in the same way as a native speaker of English.

If a special education referral is necessary, a variety of evaluation methods should to be employed, with more emphasis placed on classroom assessments, work samples, student records, and observations, and less emphasis placed on standardized test results that may or may not provide any valid information. In summary, in order to make an informed decision as to whether or not a student has special needs, as much information about the student as possible needs to be gathered from as many people as possible.

In order to find out what procedures schools have in place to identify and assess ESL students with potential special education needs, I asked two educators to discuss the procedures used in their schools. It is interesting to note that both chose to mention under-referral of students as a problem rather than over-referral, even though over-referral seems to be the more widespread problem. The first Teacher's Voice is that of a third-grade teacher in a bilingual elementary school in Connecticut. Here is what she had to say about the procedures used in her school.

Sue Goldstein,
Regional
Multicultural
Magnet School,
New London,
Connecticut

The general procedure my school uses to determine if an ESL student is in need of special education services is similar to the procedure used for any child in the school. The classroom teacher or ESL teacher brings the case up to the TOPS (Together Our Pupils Succeed) committee, which is our child study team. At this prereferral meeting, we discuss strategies that might help the child improve. We try the strategies for a few weeks, and then we decide if there is sufficient improvement. If not, an official referral meeting is scheduled.

At the referral meeting, we talk about the issues of concern regarding this student. We also discuss the student's level of education in the native language (usually Spanish for our students) and the current level of English-language proficiency. We determine the student's language dominance by teacher observation and by testing the student with the LAS (Language Assessment Scales) in both Spanish and English. We then decide which testing instruments to administer and in which language(s). We use the test results as one part of the total student profile. We consider all the information we have gathered about the student to make a determination. It is often not clear-cut, but we do our best.

Most of the time our procedures for determining whether or not an ESL student needs special education services seem to work. However, sometimes the process moves too slowly because people believe that the student's difficulties stem from a lack of English-language proficiency rather than a learning or behavioral issue.

Last year two bilingual (Spanish/English) siblings who were having learning problems were placed in our bilingual program instead of being tested for special education. The parents were the ones opposed to the testing. This type of solution will not happen again while I am here—it did not help the children and we wasted a lot of time! When the children did not improve, they were finally tested (a year later) and both were diagnosed with learning disabilities. One child is in my class this year, and she is receiving one hour of special education help and a half hour of ESL instruction per day. I am happy to report that I am seeing some improvement. We all learned that placing children in a bilingual program in lieu of special education screening will not necessarily make the problems go away.

Before hearing from the second educator, let's examine the "choice of language" issue.

Choice of Language for Special Education Evaluation

This teacher brings up the issue of which language to use for a special education evaluation—the native language or English. Since a true disability exists across languages, the disability will manifest itself in both languages (Cloud, 1994). If resources are available (i.e., test materials and native-language testers), it makes sense to do the evaluations (both formal and informal) in the student's dominant or strongest language (not necessarily the native language); if the disability is not apparent in the dominant language, there is no disability (Willig, 1986). Testing in both languages, however, might help to verify the results. It should be kept in mind, though, that a student in an all-English program for one or two years may have lost academic fluency in the native language; therefore, it may not be appropriate to test such a student on academic proficiency in the native language (Cummins, 1984).

 THE QUESTION OF WHICH LANGUAGE TO USE for special education evaluation is often put in terms of a choice between the native language and English. Although Helene's warning about the use of either language when the context for its use is inappropriate must be heeded, it is always preferable to obtain information about the student in both languages. As Helene states, we should keep in mind that a student's fluency in the native language may have diminished over the years of not using it. Background information about the student must be used to interpret students' performance and to contextualize it. Background information includes such items as the type of educational experiences the student has had, the language in which the student has received instruction, the parents' literacy and educational background, and the number of years the student has been receiving specialized instruction in ESL. Thus, extensive data must be collected and used as a context for interpreting student performance.

Allowing students to show what they can do in both languages is particularly important if the purpose of the assessment is to find out what the student can do, rather than simply identifying the areas that pose particular difficulties for the student. This obviously poses logistical as well as psychometric challenges to a school district, especially when the human resources in a specific native language are scarce. However, the information obtained through the native language is invaluable and is certainly worth the effort.

The second educator is an ESL district chairperson in Illinois.

Teachers' Voices

David Barker, Maine East High School, Park Ridge, Illinois

The ESL teachers in my school have an excellent working relationship with the Guidance Department and Special Education Department. When any classroom teacher begins to suspect that an ESL student might have a learning or behavioral problem, we discuss the problem within the ESL department, take notes detailing the red-flag behaviors, and present this information to the Building Referral Team, which meets weekly. This team consists of the guidance director, the special education chair, the dean, a counselor, the nurse, the social worker, and the psychologist. At this (prereferral) meeting it is decided if a full case study (referral) needs to be done, or if we can offer some classroom strategies for teachers to try, if they haven't already tried them. Often we have built a strong enough case to indicate that we have compelling reasons for a full case study.

We have had a number of highly successful collaborations with special education, where we've managed to save some students from failing and perhaps dropping out of school. We have also had some dismal failures and some denials of service when we felt strongly that help was warranted. Currently, five ESL teachers are taking courses toward an ESL/Bilingual Education Learning Disability Endorsement in order to help us in what seems to be an area of growing concern.

Our recent successes with students have come from carefully documenting indications and behaviors that are problematic but seem unrelated to low levels of English proficiency.

The educator above describes a common situation—a prereferral meeting that includes members of the special education staff. However, as mentioned earlier, the focus of the prereferral meeting must remain on creating an appropriate learning environment within the regular education program, whenever possible.

The ESL teachers in this school district are to be commended for attempting, through college courses, to learn more about special education. It is desirable for ESL and special education teachers to learn as much as possible about one another's disciplines if ESL students with special needs are to be identified correctly and instructed effectively. The importance of fostering this mutual understanding is discussed further in the following section.

Frameworks

HOW SHOULD ESL STUDENTS WITH DISABILITIES BE TAUGHT?

If it is determined that an ESL student has a learning or behavioral disability, the ESL, special education, and grade-level/content-area teachers need to collaborate to provide appropriate instruction for the student. In this way, the collective talents and expertise of the teachers are used to the benefit of the student in need.

ESL teachers can share information about the language proficiency of the student and how that level of proficiency should influence instructional planning. In the same way, special education teachers can share strategies for teaching a student diagnosed with the particular learning disability in question. As with all special education instruction (for ESL and non-ESL students alike), lessons must respond to the student's specific disability in order to be effective (Cloud, 1994).

IN THE GRADE-LEVEL CLASSROOM

Professional sharing can take several forms depending on the needs of the individual students and the program models employed by both the ESL and special education teachers. At the elementary level, the ideal situation is for the student in need to stay in the grade-level classroom for as much of the day as possible, with the ESL and special education teachers working in the classroom for a period of time during the day, along with the grade-level teacher. Such collaboration allows the student to participate in the grade-level program with classroom peers and can provide valuable assistance to the student and/or grade-level teacher.

If a pullout model is used for the ESL and/or special education programs, the ESL and special education teachers can team-teach students designated as having both ESL and special education needs. If that is not possible due to schedule constraints, the teachers can confer to share expertise and ideas and to coordinate instruction. If necessary and/or appropriate, one teacher can do the actual teaching while the other can act as a consultant, offering ideas and strategies. The grade-level teacher needs to be just as involved in order to ensure that the special education and ESL instruction tie in with the instruction offered in the grade-level classroom. In this way, the student's program is less fragmented than if teachers "do their own thing" and hope that the instruction will all fit together nicely for the student (which it rarely does).

COLLABORATION AND CONSISTENCY

At the secondary level teachers also need to collaborate in order to share ideas about teaching methods and, as needed, behavior management techniques. Students benefit from consistency among teachers regarding academic and behavior expectations as well as enforcement of consequences.

Unfortunately, collaboration can sometimes be difficult, since it requires frequent meetings among busy teachers who may have different teaching styles and viewpoints. The bilingual teacher above from Connecticut comments here on this problem.

> When we decide that a student is in need of special education services, the ESL and special education teachers try to collaborate in order to program effectively for the student. Coordinating services, however, can be a problem. It's difficult for teachers to find time to get together to plan. And even if they find time, there are philosophical, methodological, and terminological differences that sometimes impede communication.

Sue Goldstein, Regional Multicultural Magnet School, New London, Connecticut

In order to provide optimum learning environments for students in need, grade-level, content-area, ESL, and special education teachers need to put their best efforts forward to learn from one another and develop expertise in each others' fields. As teachers collaborate and share expertise, they gradually gain knowledge and skills in one another's specialties; this can be accelerated through workshops and college courses. Teachers who are responsible for educating ESL students with special needs must extend their knowledge outside their primary fields of study in order to work together to provide the best possible education for students.

In the Fall 1996 issue of the Connecticut TESOL newsletter (pp. 1, 4–6), an ESL teacher, Hugh Birdsall, wrote about his successful collaboration with a special education teacher. The two teachers decided to work together to help Rosa, a struggling second-grade ESL student, learn to read. Here is a summary of their collaboration.

Hugh Birdsall,
Regional
Multicultural
Magnet School,
New London,
Connecticut

The ESL teacher, Hugh, reported that Rosa's grade-level teacher said "Rosa was not reading, was not even an emergent reader, and seemed to have no sight words at all." Hugh went on to say that "Although on her registration form Rosa's mother had indicated English as Rosa's primary language, since she was from an Hispanic background, she was sent to me…. After observing her in her classroom, I administered the LAS-Oral test for English proficiency and Rosa scored a 1—that is, she tested as a nonspeaker of English. I asked if I could work with Rosa for half an hour a day, four days per week."

Hugh came to find out that Rosa was already working with the special education teacher. Hugh learned that "Rosa wasn't deficient enough to qualify for mandated special education services," but the special education teacher decided to work with Rosa "on a non-mandated basis…. The fact remained that here was a seven-and-a-half-year-old who could not read." Hugh and the special education teacher were apparently determined to try to help Rosa.

Hugh shared an office with the special education teacher, which made planning together for instruction relatively easy. The special education teacher was also working with Arnie, another student from Rosa's class. Hugh reported that, "since…Arnie and Rosa were friends and were working on similar literacy skills, I [decided to] work with them both for my half hour, and then the special education teacher would work with them for the second half hour."

Although the ESL and special education instruction initially took place in the students' classroom, the teachers decided to switch to a pullout model: "The reading fluency demonstrated by their peers was clearly frustrating to them, and our presence in the class seemed to become more and more distracting to the other students. So, I began pulling [out] Rosa and Arnie with the understanding that they could occasionally bring a 'learning buddy' from the class, and that we would sometimes go back to the class to share some of the work we had been doing."

"During this period, [the special education] teacher and I consulted with each other daily on upcoming lessons, and [she] often tailored her follow-up classes to build on the work we had started during my half hour…[She] started sitting in on [my] classes. I believe that her presence and her input were crucial to the success of [our efforts]. We had formed a true partnership in learning…I also maintained a dialogue journal with their classroom teacher on the children's progress."

"Our first month-long project together...was a book which [Rosa and Arnie] took turns dictating to me. [They named it] *The Cat Superhero* and we shared the job of illustrating and coloring it. Once it was finished, they sequenced the pages and took turns reading it to me, to [the special education teacher], to their classroom teacher, to other students, and to their parents at home."

Hugh goes on to describe how he used their book to design some phonics activities, with which he had varying degrees of success. Subsequently, Rosa proposed the next book project, which they also shared with their grade-level classmates. The ESL teacher reported small but significant improvements in both Rosa's and Arnie's ability to read. At the end of the year, "Rosa and Arnie invited their entire class up to my office...to read their [new] book".

Rosa and Arnie were proud of the work they had accomplished; this was apparent in their eagerness to share their work with their classmates. Although progress was slow, by collaborating, the ESL and special education teachers were able to work together toward the common goal of helping struggling learners read. Hugh also reported that by the end of the school year, Rosa had made significant gains in oral language: "She scored a 4 [on the LAS-Oral Test]—that is, a high level of speaking and listening skills. Naturally, we still have a long way to go, but [the special education teacher] and I found this progress very encouraging."

Else discusses steps to ensure the collaboration of teachers who instruct students with disabilities.

◇ Else's Perspective ◇ AN IMPORTANT ASPECT OF THE INSTRUCTIONAL programming for ESL students who have been diagnosed as having a disability is the establishment of the Individual Educational Plan (IEP). The IEP for ESL students is very similar to IEPs written for monolingual students, with a few crucial additions (Cloud, 1994). IEPs for ESL students must specify issues regarding language of instruction. If the option to offer instruction in the student's native language is available, then the IEP must specify who teaches which content area in which language and how much special education intervention is provided in which language. In addition, if only ESL is available as a support, the IEP must specify how the ESL teacher works in collaboration with the special education teacher and the grade-level/content-area classroom teacher(s) to ensure the provision of services in the second language that are comprehensible to students. In that case, the IEP must specify how ESL strategies will be used and for which content areas.

As is the case with content area instruction for any ESL student, special education intervention is best given in the students' more proficient language. If the resources are unavailable in the native language, then the delivery of intervention must be sheltered in ways much like the sheltering of content-area instruction. In order for the intervention to be meaningful, it must be holistic and pragmatic (Hamayan and Damico, 1991).

CHAPTER SUMMARY

Research suggests that schools are placing a disproportionate number of ESL students into special education classes (Garcia and Ortiz, 1988; Cummins, 1984). Anecdotal evidence suggests that there are also ESL students who may be in need of special education instruction, but who are not receiving services. Both over-referral and under-referral are detrimental to ESL students. Those who do not have true disabilities should not experience the stigma of being labeled "handicapped" when, in fact, their learning or behavioral problem could be caused by external factors such as minimal or interrupted prior schooling or inappropriate or ineffective current instruction. On the other hand, ESL students who *do* have learning or behavioral disabilities should not be deprived of the special education instruction they need.

Identifying, assessing, and providing a proper educational program for ESL students with special education needs presents a considerable challenge. Grade-level, content-area, special education, and ESL teachers need to make decisions collaboratively, based on a comprehensive study of the student and external factors with little emphasis on special education test results. The teachers involved must learn about one another's respective fields and work together to provide the proper educational program for ESL students with special needs. The ESL teacher must remain vigilant to ensure that those involved in decision making are sensitive to the nature and needs of second-language learners.

Else's Perspective

WE MUST TAKE HELENE'S CAUTIONARY WORDS regarding the placement of ESL students in special education programs seriously. A special education label, no matter how delicately we phrase it, carries stigma. This is a matter to be taken seriously for any child; for the ESL student, who is all too readily seen as being in need of compensation for not being English-proficient, it is an even more serious issue. The task of identifying special education needs in ESL students, particularly in areas such as learning disabilities, is extremely difficult. Even with the best and most extensive assessment one can do, ultimately, we have to guess whether a student has a disability or not. We can only hope that we have made as accurate a guess as possible.

Some of us find it particularly difficult to live with guesses because the system within which we work does not allow us to change our guesses very easily. Once a child has been identified as being a "special education student" it is very difficult to remove that label. The fact that "programs" (such as ESL, special education, Title I) function separately and sometimes independently makes it even more difficult to provide services outside the categorization model that is common in most schools. For all these reasons, we must be cognizant, as Helene points out, of the tremendous challenge that faces us in the area of special education for ESL students.

6.3 *A MINI-CASE STUDY*

Have you ever taught a student who you (or other teachers) suspected might have a learning or behavioral disability? If not, try to find a colleague who has. Discuss or write about these issues:

1. What characteristics of the student led you or other teachers to believe that the student might have a disability?

2. What steps did you or other teachers take to meet the needs of this student before a formal special education evaluation was done?

3. Was the student referred for special education services? How was the evaluation done?

4. What was the outcome of the referral?

5. What was your role in this entire process?

6. What instructional program was developed?

7. Did the instructional program prove to be appropriate (that is, did the student show signs of improvement)?

Suggested Readings

I recommend a valuable resource book, Roseberry-McKibbin's *Multicultural Students with Special Language Needs* (1995) which contains reproducibles intended to help identify, assess, and instruct ESL students with special needs.

For more on ESL and special education issues, see Nancy Cloud's article, "Special education needs of second language students" in Fred Genesee (ed.), *Educating second language children*, (p. 243-277) (1994), and J. Echeverria and A. Graves's, *Sheltered Content Instruction: Teaching English-Language Learners with Diverse Abilities (1998).*

7

INVOLVING PARENTS

There is great variation in the degree to which parents participate in their children's education. Their involvement may be influenced by such factors as their awareness of the importance of participating, their knowledge of ways to participate, their available time and energy, and their sense of being accepted within the school community. In this chapter, it will be argued that parental involvement can have a significant impact on a student's success in school; therefore, ESL teachers need to make serious attempts to encourage such involvement for the benefit of ESL students. Reasons will be offered for the seeming reluctance of some parents to become more involved, and suggestions will be made for helping parents take a more active role in their children's education.

Parents can be involved in their children's education in several significant ways. From a very young age, even before their children are old enough to attend school, parents can have an impact on their children's current and future learning by regularly reading and conversing with them. These seemingly simple activities can have a profound effect on children's literacy and cognitive development. When children are old enough to enter school, continuing these activities can further promote their literacy and cognitive development. The advantages of reading and conversing with children are apparent whether the parent uses the native language or English. In fact, it will be argued that, in many cases, using the native language rather than English is preferable.

As their children enter school, parents can be involved on a daily basis by providing assistance, if possible, with homework assignments and with reviewing the day's classwork. Parents can regularly ask their children to talk about what they learned in school and their reaction to it. Parents can participate in parent-teacher meetings, open houses, and other school functions. They can be in contact with their children's teachers, discussing any concerns as well as offering and receiving suggestions regarding their children's academic, social, and emotional growth.

WHY IS PARENTAL INVOLVEMENT SO IMPORTANT?

EARLY INVOLVEMENT AT HOME

By the time most children start kindergarten, they have already developed an intricate linguistic system in their native language. They acquire language primarily through interaction with parents and other adult caretakers who elaborate and extend the one- and two-word utterances that young children initially make. Children's utterances become longer and more complex until, at around age five, their language approximates that of adults (Brown, Hammond, and Onikama, 1997).

Children who come from homes where there is extensive adult-child verbal interaction are more successful in school. Several researchers have found that when children are reared by adults who engage them in frequent, caring conversation, the children demonstrate better cognitive, linguistic, social, and emotional development (Brown, Hammond, and Onikama, 1997, citing "Proceedings," 1997; Martinez, 1981; Blakeslee, 1997; National Institutes of Health, 1997). A literacy-rich home promotes the child's development even further. The oral and literate home gives the child the foundation needed for success later on in school.

A prevailing attitude among some parents and even teachers is that in order for an ESL student to succeed in school where English is the means of communication and learning, it is preferable if much of the oral and literacy activity in the home occurs in English. However, it is now generally believed that it is the nature of the language interaction rather than the choice of language (that is, native language or English) that is critical to the child's development (Cummins, 1989). When parents communicate with children in their strongest language (often the native language), the conversation is likely to be more varied and complex in terms of language and thought. This exposes the child to language and ideas that will develop cognitive maturity. In addition, for later success in school, it is desirable to expose children early on to a wide range of oral and written uses of *any* language in a variety of contexts (Heath, 1992); parents can often expose children to more contexts if they use the native language. Brown, Hammond, and Onikama (1997) report that in several studies (Bhatnagar, 1980; Dolson, 1985; Cook, 1990) children whose parents communicated at home in their stronger language did better in schools.

If parents are advised to communicate mostly in English with their children with the intent of better preparing them for school, this may have a damaging cognitive (and emotional) effect; because the interaction takes place in the weaker language, it is likely to be of lower quality and quantity (Cummins, 1992). ESL teachers need to relay this important information to parents who may feel that they are harming their children by using the native language at home, when, in fact, they are helping them.

And now a cautionary word from Else:

GETTING LINGUISTICALLY AND CULTURALLY DIVERSE PARENTS to become involved in their children's education is a very delicate matter. Many parents of ESL students might feel inadequate for all sorts of reasons: They may be struggling to lead fulfilling lives in a foreign society, they may be underemployed, or they may be under financial stress. We do not want to add to their burden by expecting them to participate in their children's education in the same way that native English-speaking parents do, or in a way that adds to their feelings of inadequacy. Parents of ESL students may not be adept at school tasks that are typical for a U.S. American school, and even if they are comfortable with academics in their native language, their lack of proficiency in English puts them at a disadvantage. However, these parents also have a rich knowledge base that they can pass on to the next generation as well as to their children's native English-speaking friends, and we need to encourage them to do so.

As Helene states, using English is typically not part of ESL parents' knowledge base. When parents who are not fully proficient in English feel compelled to speak English at home, it can have damaging effects on the family. Helene discusses the detrimental linguistic consequences of this situation. However, we need to consider an additional emotional factor: Forcing the parents to use a nonproficient language with their children may aggravate already strained family dynamics. Speaking English puts the parent in the role of an unskilled adult. Children often surpass their parents in English proficiency, and taking away one area in which the parents are more proficient than their children—that is, using the native language—is not advisable. In many immigrant homes, parent-child roles are often disrupted so that parents end up relying on their children in areas where such reliance is not usual. For example, parents sometimes require their child's assistance in filling out an employment application form. Parents normally should not rely on their young children for obtaining employment. Neither should a young child be burdened with his or her parents' employment issues.

·Thus, by forcing parents to do things in which they are not well versed, we would be adding to an already existing strain. In previous chapters, Helene discussed the importance of designing student-centered instruction. Similarly, we need to design a parent-centered parental involvement program that capitalizes on what parents can do. We need to find out the funds of knowledge that parents have, and use those funds as a basis for the way they help their children at home (Moll, 1995).

CONTINUED INVOLVEMENT AT HOME AND AT SCHOOL

Once their children enter school, parents can help them succeed by continuing to provide a home environment rich in oral and literacy activities. When parents engage their children in conversation in the parents' stronger language, children continue to develop a higher level of vocabulary and thought processes. By reading to and with children in the native language, parents help their children develop an understanding of the relationship between oral and written language, which is the first step in learning to read. This understanding will help them grasp the oral-written correspondence in English as they learn to speak and read English in school.

If parents see themselves as co-educators of their children along with the school, the academic and linguistic growth of students is significantly increased (Cummins, 1994). In fact, as children bring home their assignments (in English) to practice and do at home, parents can be involved and have an impact even if they do not speak or read English. Cummins (1994) describes a two-year educational experiment that offers clear-cut evidence of the benefits to children of parents and schools working together. This experiment took place in a working-class area of London, England and was conducted by Tizard, Schofield, and Hewison (1982). Cummins explains:

The experiment consisted in having parents listen on a regular basis to their children read books sent home from school. These children's reading progress was compared to that of children who were given additional reading instruction in small groups several times a week by a trained reading specialist. Many parents in the district spoke little or no English and many were illiterate in both English and their first language (Greek and Bengali, for the most part). Despite these factors, parents almost without exception welcomed the project and agreed to listen to their children read as requested and to complete a record card showing what had been read.

It was found that children who read to their parents made significantly greater progress in reading than those who were given additional reading instruction, and this was particularly so for children who, at the beginning of the project, were experiencing difficulty learning to read. In addition, most parents expressed great satisfaction at being involved in this way by the schools, and teachers reported that the children showed an increased interest in school learning and were better behaved. Lack of literacy or English fluency did not detract from parents' willingness to collaborate with the school, nor did it prevent improvement in these children's reading (p. 43).

Other researchers report the same conclusion—parental involvement has a significant positive impact on student achievement. A recent study sponsored by the Center for Law and Education (conducted by Henderson and Berla, 1994) reviewed 66 studies, books, reports, and articles that all demonstrated the positive connection between involvement of families and improved student achievement. The studies suggest that the benefits for children when parents are involved in their education include better grades, more homework done, better attendance, fewer placements in special education classes, and more positive attitudes and behavior.

In addition to taking an active role in their children's education at home, parents can participate by attending functions and activities at school. Children sense from their parents' participation that school is important, and that their parents care about the place where their children spend a large portion of their day. This is especially significant for young children who are formulating their ideas and feelings about school, but it is also beneficial for secondary students to know that their parents are taking an interest in their education.

And now another caution from Else:

WE HAVE TO BE CAREFUL NOT TO CORRELATE physical presence of parents at school with interest in the education of their children. In many countries, parents are not expected to come to school for anything other than the annual parent-teacher meeting in which the child's progress is reviewed in very general terms. Many parents perceive the school administrators' plea for parents' involvement as a sign of professional weakness or as an indication that the school is in dire need of resources that should be in place. In some communities in other countries, school professionals are highly regarded and respected for their expertise, and when these experts turn to parents for advice about the education of their children, or when they turn to parents for help, parents are puzzled and reluctant to respond.

As Helene points out, what matters with parental involvement is the value that parents place on education and the support they give to their children at home. This support can come in different forms, beginning with making sure that homework is completed, or even making sure that the child has the time and a quiet place at home for completing homework. The support can also take the form of the parents systematically receiving information from the child about some school topic or issue, as was done, for example, in the London study described in this chapter. A routine: "Tell me what you did in class today," or a routine reading of a storybook, does not need to put the nonliterate or academically nonskilled parent in an uncomfortable position. Rather, it will help keep the parent updated on what goes on in the daily school lives of their children. Finally, that support comes in the form of the parent putting the child's education foremost in the family's daily life.

All this assumes an understanding on the part of the parents of what education in the United States is all about. If parents do not know how their child's school functions, what options they have, what the expectations are for their children and for themselves, it will be more difficult for them to participate in their children's education, let alone to support it. A curriculum such as the highly successful Parents as Educational Partners (Bercovitz and Porter, 1998) which teaches English as a second language to parents through the content of American schools and the American educational system, is an effective way of increasing parents' knowledge of how schools work while increasing their proficiency in English.

The evidence is clear—children have a better chance of success in school when their parents play an active role in their education. Consequently, ESL teachers need to find ways to help parents overcome any obstacles in the way of their becoming fully involved in their children's education.

WHY DO SOME PARENTS OF ESL STUDENTS SEEM RELUCTANT TO PARTICIPATE MORE FULLY IN THEIR CHILDREN'S EDUCATION?

AWARENESS

Some parents of ESL students may believe that talking and reading at home in the native language will somehow hamper their children's ability to learn English. Hence, they may not look for opportunities to interact extensively with their children in the native language. They may attempt to interact in English, no matter how minimal their own proficiency. Grade-level, content-area, and ESL teachers have been guilty of advising parents to speak more English and less of the native language at home so that their children will have more exposure to English (Scarcella, 1990). Although that advice seems logical, as explained in the previous section, using simple English in place of more highly developed utterances in the native language has been shown to be counterproductive to the child's cognitive development. Teachers need to encourage parents to foster frequent oral and literacy activities at home in the native language for the educational benefit of their children. Moreover, parents should be encouraged to take pride in their children's emerging ability to communicate in two languages, an asset for the children while in school, but even more important for them when they enter the work world as adults.

As Else discusses above, the apparent lack of parental participation in school meetings and functions can be a result of parents being unfamiliar with the way American schools function and with the expectation of their participation (Scarcella, 1990). In some cultures parents do not visit their children's school unless summoned because of a child's misbehavior; the idea of regular parental participation is new to them. They may believe that they should not interfere, question, or bother the teachers or the principal for any but the most serious reason. The school needs to indicate to parents by words and actions that parents are welcome at the school and that their participation is important.

LINGUISTIC/CULTURAL FACTORS

Although most parents of ESL students have high expectations for their children (Carrasquillo and Rodriguez, 1996), and have great interest in their education, many parents do not participate in school meetings and activities because of linguistic and cultural factors. For example, if a notice written in English is sent home asking parents to come to school for a meeting or an event, the parents may be unable to understand it. The children may be reluctant to explain the message in the native language because of the potential embarrassment of having their parents, who may look, act, and speak differently from American parents, come to school (Scarcella, 1990). Even if schools send home notices in the parents' native languages, some parents may not read enough of their native language to understand the message. If they somehow do get the message (by means of the native language or simplified English) about a school meeting or function, they may still be reluctant to attend, fearing that once they arrive, they will feel awkward because they may not be able to communicate. They may feel intimidated or embarrassed to visit a school where they anticipate entering a room where everyone is speaking English (Scarcella, 1990; Cummins, 1994). In fact, a few years ago at Kanoelani Elementary School in Waipahu, Hawaii, I attended a meeting where parents did want to participate, but felt uncomfortable at least initially, even though we had arranged for an interpreter. This is what transpired.

Helene Becker

> I was invited to be part of a team brought together to discuss concerns about a struggling sixth-grade ESL student who had been in our school for almost five years. Seven of us (teachers, counselors, and administrators) were gathered in a conference room in the school office, awaiting the arrival of the child's parents. After about 15 minutes, through a small window, someone noticed two people standing right outside the doorway. Evidently, the parents had been standing there for quite some time, but were too embarrassed to enter the room, not knowing what to say or do since they did not speak any English and had never attended a meeting at the school before. Once we realized that the parents were there, the bilingual

staff member at the meeting went out to greet them in their native language and welcome them to the school. She then escorted them into the room and we were able to have the meeting, with the bilingual staff member serving as an interpreter.

Even with our good intentions, unfortunately, we were unable to avoid some initial discomfort on the part of the parents. But schools that do not have bilingual personnel readily available or on call may find it next to impossible to involve parents; in fact, those schools may be conveying a message to students and parents about power relations in the school that may further alienate families (Cummins, 1994).

PRACTICAL MATTERS

Some parents may want to attend parent-teacher meetings and school functions but cannot because of work schedules, lack of transportation, or lack of a baby-sitter to care for a young child at home. They may not have adequate financial or people resources, such as nearby family members, to allow them to leave the home for a meeting or function at school. Schools need to help families solve these problems so that parents of ESL students can participate in more school activities. The next section describes ways that schools can help parents become true partners with schools in educating their children.

7.1 *INVESTIGATING PARENTAL INVOLVEMENT*

Interview a grade-level or content-area teacher who has ESL students in his or her class to find out about the degree of involvement of the ESL children's parents. Here are some questions you might want to ask:

1. Do the parents of your ESL students attend or participate in school meetings and events?

2. If not, what do you think are the reasons for this lack of participation?

3. Do the parents assist their children with schoolwork or engage them in literacy activities in the native language?

4. What steps, if any, has the school taken to encourage more parental involvement?

WHAT ROLE CAN ESL TEACHERS PLAY IN FACILITATING MORE PARENTAL INVOLVEMENT?

In light of the significant positive impact parents can have on their children's academic success, schools should "actively seek to establish a collaborative relationship with minority parents that encourages them to participate with the school in promoting their children's academic progress" (Cummins, 1994, p. 43). As advocates for ESL students, ESL teachers need to take steps to help promote parental involvement in all aspects of their children's education. ESL teachers should also work with school administrators to ensure that the linguistic, cultural, and practical needs of all parents are considered when school meetings and events are planned. The list below is a compilation of suggestions from my own experience and that of many others for promoting parental involvement. Schools may not be able to implement all of the suggestions, but incorporating as many as possible over time may have a significant impact on parental involvement and, in turn, on student achievement.

1. **Orientation Workshop**

   When their children enroll in school, parents should be provided with an orientation workshop about the school and community resources. Parents can also be informed about extracurricular activities such as clubs and sports groups that give ESL students the opportunity to learn and practice language in a relaxed social setting. Some parents are not aware of the value of such activities and may be reluctant to allow their children to participate, figuring that participation may interfere with study time. Schools need to promote ESL students' participation in these activities (Scarcella, 1990). It is advisable to make a videotape of the presentation so that parents who enroll their children later in the school year can view the tape. The tape can also include a "video tour" of various places in the school with explanations of their functions (such as the library, computer room, athletic field, etc.) Cassettes of the audio portion can be made in various languages, which can be played along with a soundless video portion for parents who do not understand much English.

2. **Oral and Literacy Activities**

   Parents should be informed (through oral and written communication) about the importance of extensive oral and literacy activities at home in the parents' stronger language. Teachers need to communicate to parents that reading and telling stories to their children in the first language will provide exposure to a variety of written and oral language forms that will make it easier to acquire a second language (Coelho, 1994).

3. **At-Home Reading Program**

   ESL teachers can work with grade-level teachers to set up a home reading program so that parents listen to their children read at home in English. Even if the parents do not understand or read English, involving parents in this way can play a vital role in their children's development of literacy, as shown in the study by Tizard, Schofield, and Hewison (1982) discussed earlier in this chapter.

4. **At-Home Discussions**

   Parents can be encouraged to keep abreast of their children's schoolwork by discussing with their children on a daily basis what they learned in school and checking up on homework assignments.

5. Parent-Teacher Communication

Teachers can ask parents to share their ideas regarding what teachers can do to help their children learn and how children learn best in that particular culture. Parents can have important insights to share with teachers regarding what works best for their children; parents need to feel that teachers want to hear their suggestions and that parent-teacher communication is a two-way encounter (not just teachers telling parents what to do)(Handscombe, 1994).

6. Translations

Schools should consider translating into other languages items used to communicate routinely with parents. These items include report cards, school handbooks, newsletters, field trip notices, and information about the school's ESL program (Coelho, 1994).

7. Personal Follow-Up

Notices sent home about meetings and school events should be available to parents in their native languages, as needed. After parents receive a notice, a native speaker, if available, should call parents to make sure they understood the information and to encourage them to attend. If a native speaker is not available, the ESL teacher can call and communicate as best as possible. Parents may be more likely to attend if they receive encouragement through a warm, personal phone call.

8. Interpreters

Schools should make an effort to provide interpreters for meetings and school events and parents should be informed beforehand of their availability (parents may be more likely to attend if they know there will be someone to interpret for them). Parents can also be invited to provide their own interpreters by bringing a bilingual relative or friend to meetings.

9. Useful Phrases

The school should provide classroom teachers with a list of useful phrases and sentences translated into several languages. This list can be used to write comments on student work and to communicate in writing with parents throughout the school year. The list can include items in the native language that teachers can copy onto student papers such as "Wonderful job!," "Good effort," or "Correct your mistakes," as well as requests such as "Please call me—I would like to meet with you."

10. Family Activities

The ESL teacher can plan activities for ESL families and advertise them in several languages in various places such as churches and neighborhood stores. Since parents enjoy seeing their own children perform, a good way of getting parents to attend is to have ESL students act in a play or participate in a cultural celebration (Scarcella, 1990). Other activities that have been successful in bringing parents into the school include potluck dinners and bingo/game nights. At the sign-in table for these events, it may be best to check off parent names from a list rather than having parents sign in, in case there are parents who are not literate. If parents feel welcomed and comfortable coming to the school for an ESL function, they may be more likely to attend other school functions.

11. Parent Seminars

Parents can be invited to the school to discuss specific topics of interest to them such as "Parenting in a New Culture" or "Helping Your Child Learn at Home." In organizing these meetings it may be welcoming to parents (and helpful to the facilitators) to ask parents from the same culture who have been in the community for a while to act as resource people (Coelho, 1994). A few years ago, after one of these parent meetings, the facilitators reported to me that, while discussing with parents the importance of developing the native language at home, they learned a useful piece of information. Many of the Hispanic parents at the meeting mentioned that they asked for household items by saying their function rather than their name. For example, they might say in Spanish, "Please bring me the *thing that cuts*" instead of "Please bring me the *knife*," or "I need the *thing for coffee*" instead of "I need the *cup*." Consequently, their children often did not know the names of these items in their own language. Parents at the seminar were happy to learn that they could help their children increase their vocabulary simply by referring to these items by name.

12. Transportation

The school can help families find transportation to parent functions by pairing up nearby families to facilitate carpooling. These nearby families can be encouraged to develop a network to support each other and to discuss common concerns.

13. Child Care

The school should try to arrange for child care at the school during parent functions, or allow small children to accompany their parents. Community volunteers may be willing to provide this child-care service.

14. Scheduling Events

When scheduling events for parents, teachers need to consider before and after work hours as well as the possibility of holding the same event two times, on different days and/or at different times. Giving busy parents options may increase their participation (Scarcella, 1990).

15. ESL Classes for Parents

ESL teachers can encourage the school to establish ESL classes for parents. Children will probably benefit from seeing their parents learning and studying English, too. It is to the children's and parents' advantage if the parents learn English; they are more likely to initiate or respond to interaction with the school than if they continue to rely on interpreters (Coelho, 1994).

16. Parents as Volunteers

ESL teachers can encourage grade-level teachers to consider recruiting parents of ESL students as volunteers in the classroom. They can assist students at classroom learning centers and with class projects. If there are several students from the same language group, the volunteer can read or tell stories to them in the native language. They can also talk to the class about aspects of their countries and culture. The other students in the class will learn that languages besides English and cultures besides American culture are valued in the classroom (Scarcella, 1990).

17. Multilingual Signs, Books

Schools can become more welcoming to parents by posting multilingual signs throughout the school and providing books in the native language(s) of the students in the school library.

18. Bilingual Staff

Schools should take steps to hire bilingual staff since, as Cummins (1994) states, "In general, successful parental involvement is likely to depend on the extent to which parents see the school as a welcoming environment rather than the intimidating environment it often is for many parents with limited knowledge of English. Clearly, the presence in the school of staff who speak the language of the parents will greatly facilitate parental involvement" (p. 43–44). Bilingual staff can perform many important unofficial functions in the school such as serving as role models for children and resource personnel for teachers who would like to learn more about the cultures of their students (Coelho, 1994).

THE COMMON ELEMENT IN ALL OF HELENE'S excellent suggestions is a genuine valuing of and respect for the parents of ESL students and the unique funds of knowledge they bring (Moll, 1995). Without this respect, the strategies that Helene suggests would have only a cursory effect, and might, in fact, backfire if they were perceived as insincere gestures. The underlying premise for all these strategies—in fact, for the whole of the educational milieu—should be that bilingualism and biculturalism are gifts that everyone should be lucky to receive.

Thus, when the importance of extensive oral and literacy activities at home in the parents' stronger language is stressed, as Helene suggests, the value of maintaining the native language and of developing bilingual proficiency should also be stressed. Any home reading program should include reciprocal reading where parents read to their children in the native language or, in the case of nonliterate parents, tell stories with wordless books or from traditional tales from their home culture. When translating information into the students' native languages, or providing teachers with a list of useful phrases in several languages, as Helene suggests, parents should be invited to give presentations to the whole staff about their language. Also, when parents are available to work as volunteers in the grade-level classroom, the grade-level classroom teacher should plan to have them present something to the whole class, or to have them tutor not only ESL children, but others as well. Our earlier discussions on equal status for all adults who work in the classroom are relevant for parents in the classroom as well.

Just as important as Helene's suggestion to offer ESL classes for parents is the idea of offering a language class for interested English-speaking teachers and parents in one or two of the most commonly used languages in the school. Schools that offer this opportunity to their English-speaking teaching staff have nothing but praise for it (Cloud, Genesee, and Hamayan, 2000).

Finally, a truly multicultural environment needs to be created in the school so that parents feel comfortable and feel as though they belong. This multiculturalism needs to go beyond the superficial indices of culture that typically focus on food, festivals, fashion, and folk heroes. True multiculturalism includes the different norms and values that make up a culture and is evident in every aspect of school life (Nieto, 1995).

In order to get a real-life perspective of how teachers have incorporated some of the suggestions listed above, I asked three practicing ESL teachers to discuss how they have promoted parental involvement in their respective schools. A bilingual/bicultural Spanish-speaking elementary ESL teacher in West Hartford, Connecticut had this to say:

> The key to parent involvement is trust. When ESL parents first bring their children to school, I make sure I'm available to greet them and help them communicate. They know that I am genuinely concerned about their children and I become the liaison between them and school. I try to make them feel that they are a part of our school community just like any other parents. They know that I respect their cultures and languages and that I do not expect them to fit the mold of parents in American culture.
>
> When someone at the school (principal, psychologist, nurse, secretary, etc.) asks me to contact a child's home, I make sure that I call at different times of the day and more than once. I don't give up. Some parents work several jobs and are very busy.
>
> Whenever we have a school activity, I ask teachers to give me the information ahead of time so that the parents have plenty of time to make arrangements. It's not easy for them to come to school on short notice because they usually need to make arrangements with their places of work and sometimes for transportation. We have volunteer parents calling and picking up parents and we've paired families. We also have a group of volunteers who maintain regular contact with ESL parents.

Teachers'
Voices

Irene Rodriguez,
Webster Hill
Elementary School,
West Hartford,
Connecticut

When parents call my voice mail at school, they hear my message in English and Spanish. This makes them more likely to call with a question or concern. I'm trying to get the classroom teachers to take more responsibility for contacting ESL parents. Some of the new teachers in the school speak a second language, so that's a help. We're also working on ways to get all students (not just ESL students) to talk to their parents every evening about what they learned in school that day, and I think this will get more ESL parents involved in school.

An elementary ESL teacher from a different school in West Hartford had this to offer:

Jean Hill, Whiting Lane Elementary School, West Hartford, Connecticut

We try to get our ESL parents involved from the very beginning of the school year by inviting them to a potluck dinner in the fall. At the dinner we share information about the school calendar, parent meetings, lunch payments, and so forth, all easier to do in person than in writing. We also have students share some of their work and we try to have a fun activity such as folk dancing.

We schedule at least two more parent activities for ESL parents during the school year. Our bingo night works quite well. We solicit prizes from merchants in the neighborhood beforehand. We have also had a breakfast before school for parents and grandparents. At the breakfast students read aloud some of their writing that we put together in a book beforehand.

We have found that if we want a good turnout at a parent function, we need to issue frequent reminders—in writing and by phone. We write invitations in very simple English and usually include a picture, so that parents get the general idea even if they don't understand all the details. For our potluck dinner, for example, we drew pictures of food so they knew it was a "food" event! All this takes a lot of time, but it's worth it.

Here is one more Teacher's Voice, this time from a secondary ESL administrator in Virginia.

Keith Buchanan, Fairfax County Public Schools, Virginia

Concerning parental involvement, I think of two major efforts: parent liaisons and a support group for Spanish-speaking parents.

As our county has gotten increasingly diverse, the school board recognized that non-English-speaking parents were disenfranchised from everything about their children's schooling. So we proposed a new position, parent liaison, for schools heavily affected by non-English-speaking students. A parent liaison is a part-time (up to 20 hours per week) paraprofessional who ideally has a foot in two cultural camps and can speak English and another language. Liaisons are hired from the community where the school is located, and there are 78 of them (out of 132 schools with ESL programs) in the district. They work to develop parent networks, plan programs for parents, and assist parents in understanding information about school and school programs. For example, when we saw that a kid was a very good soccer player, the liaison helped his parents to understand the workings of interscholastic sports, and arranged for him to have his qualifying physical. When the student found that the demands of the soccer program were interfering with his schoolwork, the liaison found tutors to help him.

Other liaisons have helped organize parent meetings concerning scholastic issues—credits, graduation requirements, college applications, etc. They work closely with ESL teachers, counselors, and social workers. They help families feel welcomed and empowered. Principals really love the liaisons because they help link a chunk of the school community to the school, and they help parents understand the school goals and programs.

Immigrant parents have so much on their plates; I came to realize that they could use some help in dealing with issues regarding their kids. Even though it seems that there is less need for parent involvement in school as the kids get older, I think of it as a different kind of need. That's how my support group got started. We began with benign topics such as high school credits, but we moved quickly on to issues such as disciplining kids in a new culture. We also talked about the parents' disdain for what they considered the overpermissiveness of American culture and we discussed ways for them to access social services.

The parents grew to help each other. By the third meeting, they formed their own phone network and they were able to elect a representative to the school PTA board. At last these immigrant parents' voices were being heard.

CHAPTER SUMMARY

Parental involvement in their children's education needs to occur in the home as well as at school. At home, parents can involve their children in oral and literacy activities in the parents' stronger language so that children develop a wide range of linguistic and cognitive skills. Once children enter school, parents can ask their children to read to them and discuss what they have learned in school. Some parents may also be able to assist their children with homework assignments.

Parents of ESL students may be reluctant to go to their children's school for meetings and functions, perhaps because the school environment is not "friendly" to parents who may not have a good command of English and may not understand how schools function. Since study after study has shown that parental involvement can have a significant positive effect on children's academic success, ESL teachers must strive to guide schools in finding ways to communicate with parents and to welcome them into the school community so that parents become true partners with schools in the education of their children.

7.2 *OUT IN THE FIELD...*

Facilitating the involvement of parents of ESL students in the school communi-ty is often a challenge for school districts. How are schools in your area meet-ing this challenge? With a colleague, imagine that you are a team of two auditors sent by the state to investigate what schools are doing to encourage such involve-ment. By referring back to the list of suggestions for parental involvement, devel-op a set of questions to ask an ESL teacher at a nearby school about steps the school has taken to foster this involvement. For example, looking at suggestion number one on page 175, the first question might be, "Has your school devel-oped an orientation program for parents of new ESL students at your school? If so, please describe the program." Ask an ESL teacher at the school to answer the questions and to discuss any other actions that his or her school has taken to encourage parental involvement. Also ask about any problems or obstacles the school has encountered while attempting to involve parents.

Discuss the answers with your teammate. How would you rate this school's attempts at involving parents? Excellent? Good? Fair? Poor?

Based on the answers, make at least three practical suggestions that the school could implement now to foster parental involvement. Also, devel-op one long-term goal that you believe will help the school achieve more parental involvement and, consequently, more overall student success. If possible, discuss your findings with another team; share your findings with the ESL teacher you interviewed, if he or she desires.

Suggested Readings

For school districts interested in making a sincere ongoing commitment to parental involvement, I recommend adopting the *Parents as Educational Partners Program* (Bercovitz and Porter, 1998) mentioned in Else's commentary on p. 172. This pro-gram provides ESL instruction to parents through a content-based curriculum revolving around school-related topics such as American schools and parent roles. Besides ESL classes, the program includes parent/child activities, parenting work-shops, and inservice training on parental involvement for teachers. The program has received high praise from parents, children, teachers, and administrators. To receive information about the program, contact the Adult Learning Resource Center, 1855 Mt. Prospect Road, Des Plaines, IL 60018, or call 708-803-3535.

8

PROMOTING EFFECTIVE SCHOOLWIDE INSTRUCTION

*In many, if not most, elementary and secondary school settings,
ESL students are taught by ESL teachers for only part of the school
day. During the remainder of the time, they are taught by grade-
level or content-area teachers who may have had extensive, some,
or no training at all in effective strategies for working with ESL
students. After doing a three-and-one-half-year study at a high
school in northern California, Harklau (1994) found that, "As
in many other U.S. public schools...Newcomers...are exited from
special programs quite rapidly. Thus, even though language minority students may take up to seven years to develop the level of
language proficiency necessary to compete on an equal footing
with native speakers of the school language (Collier, 1987),... they
are likely to be in mainstream classes long before then" (p. 242).
Because ESL students are typically enrolled in "mainstream" classes while they are still in the process of acquiring English, all teachers in a school must address the learning needs of second-language
learners by taking into account their different levels of English proficiency and different rates of learning (Cummins, 1994).*

Indeed, in some schools, the learning environment for ESL students is quite
bleak. When Harklau (1994) examined the learning environment for ESL students just entering the "mainstream," she found that, since "mainstream" teachers geared their lessons for native speakers, ESL students were almost ignored.
They were "seldom required to participate in classroom interactions, [so] L2
learners were able to tune out many mainstream instructional interactions
entirely. Students often sat, heads bent over desks, engrossed in their books and
papers, paying little attention to teacher or peer talk going on in the class...it
was an effort to understand spoken language used in a mainstream class...The
net result was that students were often withdrawn and noninteractive in mainstream classes. They were not even paying particular attention to the input,
much less engaging in interaction" (pp. 251–252).

This discouraging scenario is certainly not taking place in all grade-level and
content-area classes, as many teachers have already altered their instructional
practices to better suit the needs of ESL students. But it is probably not as rare
as one would wish it to be.

Although a few teacher education programs are recognizing the need to prepare *all* teachers to work with ESL students, many programs still do not offer

any courses at all to address this need (Kaufman and Brooks, 1996). Moreover, for many years to come, there will be veteran teachers in public school settings who received their university degrees long before the education of ESL students was even mentioned in teacher preparation courses. In order to promote optimal opportunities for ESL students to achieve academic success in elementary and secondary school settings, ESL teachers need to share with grade-level and content-area colleagues the knowledge, ideas, and experiences that may help them acquire the expertise necessary to be effective teachers of the ESL students in their classes.

At the same time, ESL teachers have much to learn from grade-level and content-area teachers. In order to prepare ESL students for content learning in the various academic subject areas, ESL teachers must work closely with their "mainstream" colleagues to gain an understanding of the content knowledge and skills necessary to be successful in those various subject areas (Harklau, 1994). Unfortunately, university programs that offer certification programs in teaching ESL require very little preparation in teaching the content areas (Kaufman and Brooks, 1996). Hence, professional sharing and cooperation are necessary in two directions so that grade-level and content-area teachers are learning from ESL teachers while ESL teachers find opportunities to learn from grade-level and content-area teachers. As Faltis and Hudelson (1994) point out, teachers should become "agents of change" (p. 459) working for better schools for all learners; members of the school community must work collaboratively to accomplish this.

◇ **Else's Perspective** ◇ HELENE KNOWS FROM EXPERIENCE that teachers working collaboratively with one another can benefit from each other significantly. By collaborating with the ESL teacher on the delivery of instruction for ESL students, grade-level/content-area classroom teachers become aware of the important role that they play in teaching language, and similarly, ESL teachers become aware of the importance of teaching content within the context of the ESL classroom. Each type of teacher also becomes aware of the content that the other teaches. However, the true professional development that occurs when two types of teachers collaborate is in learning the specialized strategies in which each teacher is skilled. By collaborating with one another, ESL and grade-level/content-area teachers can exchange ideas regarding the specialized methodology and techniques in each of their fields. ESL teachers can learn ways of introducing and developing new concepts, and grade-level/content-area teachers can learn ways of sheltering the content so that the language used in conveying new concepts does not interfere with comprehension.

By establishing a constant dialogue among all teachers involved in the education of ESL students, another very important goal is accomplished. Everyone in the school building who comes into contact with ESL students begins to take responsibility for these students (Cloud, Genesee, and Hamayan, 2000). To get to that stage of awareness, teachers and administrators first need to be cognizant of the type of instruction ESL students are receiving. They also need to know how the ESL curriculum correlates to the "mainstream" curriculum. They need to become familiar with the standards set for these students and to know what to expect of them. An effective learning environment can be created for ESL students only when non-ESL specialists take responsibility for the education of ESL students (Cummins, 1986). As Helene explains in the rest of this chapter, all school personnel must participate in staff development regarding the education of ESL students.

This chapter addresses the issue of promoting effective instruction of ESL students by all teachers in the school through professional sharing, cooperation, and collaboration. Various methods of working toward this goal are discussed in order to offer a repertoire of strategies to be reviewed and considered as potentially effective at a particular school.

WHAT ARE SOME EFFECTIVE PROFESSIONAL DEVELOPMENT STRATEGIES?

There are various means by which ESL and grade-level/content-area teachers can work together to promote better learning environments for ESL students. Some methods are designed to impart knowledge or demonstrate skills, whereas others are more open-ended and are meant to encourage dialogue between ESL and grade-level/content-area teachers in order to problem-solve together. Still others require teachers to observe one another and act as coaches. This section discusses the various options for professional development and what they are designed to accomplish.

PRESENTATIONS AND WORKSHOPS

Presentations and workshops in school settings often occur after school or on special days set aside for professional development purposes. They are usually conducted by one or more people who have expertise in a particular topic. They can be short (one or two hours) or can last all day or even several days.

The presentation/workshop format can be used effectively to disseminate information about the needs of ESL students and how to address those needs. Although some educators might argue that presentations are better conducted by local school district personnel (Jaramillo, 1998) who are familiar with the local ESL population, an effective presentation or workshop can be conducted by a presenter from outside the district as long as the person is familiar with the needs of the particular school and tailors the agenda to those needs.

An initial presentation or workshop for grade-level and/or content-area teachers aimed at introducing them to the needs of ESL students should include at least the following topics: second language acquisition (how students acquire a second language, the BICS/CALP distinction, length of time to acquire language); effective classroom strategies (repetition, pauses, reduction in speed and complexity of speech, frequent comprehension checks, use of realia, etc. [Harklau, 1994]); and cross-cultural awareness (culture shock, difficulties of living between two cultures old and new, the effect of former experiences [or lack thereof] on current educational functioning). Addressing these three core topics may increase the participants' awareness of the needs of ESL students and, ideally, set the stage for continued learning.

If possible, a presentation should also include a "shock language" experience where participants have the opportunity to see how it feels to be a student sitting in a classroom when one does not understand much of the language of instruction. One content-area teacher who participated in such an experience had this reaction:

> The lesson in Hebrew really opened my eyes. I understood nil! I never realized that students were mainstreamed without a solid base knowledge of the English language.
>
> I spend much time thinking about how I would work with a non-English-speaking student in my classroom…There is always time after class but I want the student to be involved in (what I hope to be) the pertinent dynamics of the lesson during the lesson (Kaufman and Brooks, 1996, p. 238).

When conducting a presentation or workshop, the presenter should attempt to engage participants in activities that offer opportunities for interaction and collaboration. In this way, teachers experience firsthand the kinds of activities they need to use in their own classrooms to foster academic success for ESL students. See Appendix B for two sample activities (designed for grade-level/content-area teachers new to the field of ESL) that have been used successfully in professional development workshops to impart some essential information while engaging participants in group interaction.

◆ Else's Perspective ◆ THE CONTENT OF PROFESSIONAL DEVELOPMENT that Helene suggests in this section is precisely where grade-level/content-area teachers need to begin in forming or expanding their knowledge about how best to teach ESL students. However, one of the biggest challenges of schoolwide or districtwide professional development is matching the content of presentations or workshops to the interest of the participants. Teachers may have no interest in what Helene or I think they need to know! In fact, if they have gone about the business of teaching without pursuing further knowledge in this area, it is likely that they do not see the field of ESL education as a need in their own professional development.

Thus, it is essential that teachers have some choice in the staff development in which they participate. Naturally, they will need some guidance in their choices, and the ESL teacher can help the grade-level/content-area teachers establish professional development goals in the area of ESL education, as well as helping them attain those goals. A skilled staff development guide can steer the novice teacher in a direction that will lead to the most relevant and pertinent topics for that teacher. An introductory session can simply describe the various areas in ESL that are likely to concern grade-level/content-area teachers, after which teachers can choose the specific areas they would like to specialize in. The list of general topics intro-

duced to teachers could include the following areas: second-language acquisition; ESL strategies; sheltering content-area instruction; assessment of
ESL students; the role of literacy in content-area achievement; the role of
culture in the grade-level/content-area classroom.

Discussion Sessions/Study Groups

A discussion or study group consists of a group of teachers who meet periodically
to discuss issues of interest and concern related to the education of the ESL students
in the school. A discussion or study group can be an effective way of opening the
lines of communication between ESL and grade-level/content-area teachers in the
spirit of helping one another become more effective in the classroom. Such groups
can provide a format for teachers to shape their own professional development
opportunities, thus allowing them to see themselves as important players in the
process (Clair, 1995). Participants can bring up general issues related to teaching
ESL students or particular issues about specific situations or students. Together,
participants can brainstorm solutions to problems or relate what has worked from
their own experiences. Teachers can meet by subject area or by teams, depending
on the way a particular school is organized. This type of forum can allow grade-
level/content-area and ESL teachers to solve problems together and learn from one
another in a supportive atmosphere.

Discussion or study groups can be a component or outgrowth of professional development presentations and workshops. Dwyer (1998) reports such a situation during the first year of a three-year-long professional development project for secondary content-area teachers in a small city school district in New
York State. After participants had participated in several large group workshops, they preferred to continue their learning by meeting in small study groups
by school level or discipline. In these study groups participants shared materials
they had developed and teaching strategies they had used successfully. "For
example, science teachers spent a session sharing strategies for structuring lab
assignments so that language minority students could participate fully and not
be dominated by native English-speaking lab partners. Math teachers spent a
session planning ways to support language minority students in units on prob-
ability with a heavy vocabulary load" (p. 8). Because teachers are likely to have
opportunities to focus on their individual issues and needs as well as to receive
periodic feedback and encouragement from one another as they test out new
strategies, perhaps discussion or study groups should be an integral component
of any professional development effort.

Articles/Handouts

Over the years I have distributed to grade-level/content-area teachers many articles on topics related to teaching ESL students as well as lists of teaching tips. I
have also received articles myself from colleagues on various topics of interest to
me. What I have learned from talking to teachers (and observing my own behavior) is that most teachers do not have time to read much of the literature and handouts they receive. Even though they may have good intentions, they are often too

For a sample handout for grade-level/ content-area teachers on ESL teaching strategies, see Appendix C, p. 218

busy with their day-to-day responsibilities to have the luxury of perusing everything placed in their school mailboxes. While I do believe that it is important to share information with colleagues, and I continue to distribute pertinent articles and useful handouts, I try to be discriminating and disseminate materials that are concise and immediately relevant, so that colleagues are more likely to read them.

A few years ago I attended a presentation at a conference during which the presenter, Judy Jameson, a teacher trainer from the Center for Applied Linguistics, discussed the futility of giving grade-level/content-area teachers long lists of principles and strategies to remember. Instead, she tells teachers to concentrate on three goals as they prepare lessons for classes that include ESL students: *increase comprehensibility, increase interaction* (among students and between teacher and students), and *promote higher-order thinking skills*. These are three "global" principles that promote appropriate and beneficial learning environments for ESL students. Of course, simply memorizing these principles is not a panacea for creating optimal learning environments for ESL students— it is one part of her 60-hour many-faceted professional development program! But ultimately, instead of asking grade-level/content-area teachers to study long lists of suggestions, it may be more effective (and realistic) to ask them to keep in mind a short list of basic principles that will help them plan more effective lessons for the ESL students in their classes (Jameson, 1999).

OBSERVATIONS

An observation involves either an ESL teacher watching a grade-level/content-area teacher's lesson or a grade-level/content-area teacher watching an ESL teacher's lesson. By observing what other teachers who work with ESL students do in their classrooms, the observer can learn from the observed teacher or can help the observed teacher become aware of ways to improve instruction. Since teachers typically work in their own classroom "worlds," often without knowing what other teachers do in their classrooms, it can be quite instructive to observe another teacher's lesson. In some cases, the teachers may decide to do ongoing periodic observations of one another's lessons so that a peer coaching relationship develops. Specifically, observations allow for the following to occur:

A grade-level/content-area teacher observing an ESL teacher can:
- see ESL teaching strategies in practice;
- observe ESL students in an ESL setting (to gain insight into their skills and abilities which may not be as apparent in the grade-level/content-area setting).

An ESL teacher observing a grade-level/content-area teacher can:
- observe the lesson with the intent of offering suggestions of ways to make the lesson more comprehensible/beneficial to the ESL students in the class;
- observe the ESL students in the class with the intent of seeing how they are managing with the content material;
- focus on the content of the lesson to see what knowledge and skills are needed to succeed in that particular class (with the intent of helping ESL students during ESL lessons to acquire the language and skills necessary to have access to the content material).

For ESL teachers who work in elementary schools and instruct ESL students through an inclusion or team-teaching model, observations occur informally on a daily basis. As the ESL or grade-level teacher instructs, the other teacher in the room has the opportunity to observe strategies and teacher-student interaction. Teachers can learn from one another and offer suggestions as appropriate. In order to demonstrate specific ESL teaching strategies, the ESL teacher can offer to teach a mini-lesson to the entire class and have the classroom teacher observe. The ESL teacher can model helpful strategies such as using visual aids, offering multiple clues to meaning, restating information several ways, checking often for comprehension, and so forth, so that the grade-level teacher can witness the effectiveness of using ESL teaching strategies with *all* students.

Inclusion and team-teaching program models are discussed in Chapter 3, pp. 52–66.

Else suggests a method for making observations even more effective.

Else's Perspective

HELENE IS RIGHT: OBSERVATIONS ARE AN EXCELLENT TOOL for professional development. However, their effectiveness is enhanced if teachers choose to focus on an aspect that they consider important. Just as teachers need to choose the specific topics they pursue in their professional development plan, observations must center around specific aspects of teaching or the classroom that are germane to teachers' daily responsibilities and tasks. The model that has been suggested by Showers (1985) for peer coaching can be very helpful here. Peer coaching was designed so that the teacher who wanted to learn would invite another teacher into his or her classroom to observe and give suggestions. The model that many schools use has the teacher who wishes to learn observing, rather than the other way around. Nonetheless, peer coaching can provide an effective model as it can help the transfer of knowledge and skills. Coached teachers generally practice new strategies more frequently and more appropriately than teachers who do not work closely with a fellow teacher (Baker and Showers, 1984). Coached teachers also continue to practice new strategies over the long term and change their teaching styles as a result of learning the new strategies.

According to peer coaching principles, observations should occur in the context of preconferences and postconferences between the two teachers that help define the focus of the observation. In the preconference, the two teachers determine the specific aspect of teaching that the observation will focus on. In the postconference, that specific aspect is picked up and serves as the central theme of the discussion. Any follow-up is also determined during the postconference. Peer coaching has been found to be extremely effective, and is worth the additional time and resources it requires (Baker and Showers, 1984). It allows teachers to learn from one another and to see, in a non-threatening environment, the similarities in what they do.

A few years ago while teaching in Hawaii, I was asked to observe an ESL student in a second-grade class to see if I could give the grade-level teacher some suggestions to help the student succeed better in the class. Robert, the ESL student, was behaving well in his pullout ESL class, but was displaying poor behavior and a lack of focus in the grade-level classroom. The time I was available to observe was during a math lesson.

Teachers' Voices

Helene Becker

When I arrived the lesson had already begun, so I moved quietly to the back of the room and sat right behind Robert. Immediately, I noticed that Robert was sitting too far away from the teacher. He was taking advantage of being near the back of the room and was fidgeting with play money that the teacher had distributed instead of paying careful attention to the teacher's directions. When the teacher told the students "Open your books to page 25," Robert either did not hear the instruction or did not understand it. The teacher called his name and repeated the instruction, at which point he looked at his neighbor's book to see the page number.

As the teacher was going over each of the homework problems, Robert, instead of checking his previously completed work as instructed, was continuing on in his math workbook, doing new work. After a few minutes, the teacher called on Robert for an answer and realized that he was not on task. She then asked the student sitting next to Robert to help him find his place in the workbook. He stayed on task for a few minutes, but then started amusing himself with the play money again.

A few days later I met with the grade-level teacher and offered her a few simple suggestions that I thought might help Robert stay on task and follow the lesson. For example, I asked her if she could move Robert's seat near the front of the room where she could more easily check that he was on task at all times. I also suggested that, when she asked students to turn to a certain page in their books, she should also write the page number on the chalkboard so that Robert could see the number as well as hear it.

From visiting this teacher's classroom I learned that Robert was behaving as any seven-year-old might behave if given the opportunity to fool around in the back of the room without being caught! I also learned that his lack of focus, at least in part, may have been due to his not understanding the oral directions; if the directions had been made comprehensible by expressing them through additional means (such as writing them on the chalkboard and thereby using a visual cue), he might have reacted appropriately. This teacher was grateful for the suggestions and asked me to come into her class during a language arts lesson to see if I could offer her some further suggestions.

If teachers are searching for ways to work more effectively with ESL students, observations can be extremely useful in zeroing in on the issues in a particular class setting and finding specific ways for making improvements. However, the observer must be sensitive to the manner in which he/she offers suggestions. Sensitivity is discussed later in this chapter (pp. 193–194).

TEAM-TEACHING/CO-TEACHING

A relatively new and promising professional development practice is one in which an ESL teacher team-teaches (or co-teaches) with a grade-level or content-area teacher. In this model, the two teachers share equally the responsibility for planning and teaching a content-area subject. Besides being beneficial for students, team-teaching is a valuable professional development opportunity for the teachers involved as it promotes on-the-job training and is immediately relevant. In fact, Kaufman and Brooks (1996) propose that team-teaching experiences be included in teacher preparation programs so that collaborative models such as team-teaching will be more likely to emerge in schools. An ESL administrator/teacher trainer in a large school district in Virginia had these comments about team-teaching as a professional development experience.

> We have found that the best professional development/training we have provided has been a co-teaching model, where, for example, an ESL teacher and a biology teacher together plan and teach a biology class where ESL kids are clustered. Besides sharing equally the responsibility for the class, they end up teaching each other their respective tricks of the trade. Veteran teachers seem to respond best to this form of professional development because it respects their prior experiences and they learn a tremendous amount from a colleague in a relatively nonthreatening manner.

UNIVERSITY COURSES

Another avenue for professional development is university courses, taken by teachers after school or during school breaks. The success of this route depends on the quality and quantity of courses available in a particular geographic area and the responsiveness of the local university to the particular needs of the surrounding school districts. Other factors affecting success are mandates set by the school district regarding taking such courses (that is, are they optional or mandatory for continued employment in the district?) and incentives (do teachers receive salary increments for accumulating credits?). The availability of university courses is a potential asset in an overall professional development plan.

SHARING TEACHING MATERIALS

When grade-level teachers have beginning-level ESL students in their classes, especially for the first time, it is often a challenge to ensure that these students are meaningfully occupied with appropriate learning activities and materials throughout the school day. Since the ESL teacher usually provides ESL instruction for only part of the school day, grade-level teachers often welcome suggestions regarding suitable learning activities and materials to use with the ESL students when the rest of the class is working on a lesson that is perhaps too language-dependent to be meaningful to the ESL students at that point. For example, if a beginning-level ESL student enrolls in a fourth-grade class in the middle of the school year, and the class is reading a novel written at the fourth-grade reading level, it may be more advantageous for the ESL student to do an alternative activity during those reading lessons. The ESL student could read a story with a similar theme written at an appropriate reading level for the student, and then perhaps illustrate scenes from the story. The ESL teacher could make suggestions such as these, as well as help locate appropriate reading materials.

See Chapters 3 and 4 for a discussions of the benefits to students when teachers team-teach.

Keith Buchanan, Fairfax County Public Schools, Virginia

For resource books on learning activities and materials for beginning-level ESL students, see Suggested Readings p. 198.

INFORMAL OPPORTUNITIES

In addition to planned professional development activities, there are many ongoing, informal opportunities for teachers to interact and learn from one another. Teachers often welcome tips and ideas that will help them be more successful in specific teaching situations with particular students in their classrooms. Here are some informal ways that ESL teachers can be of assistance to grade-level or content-area teachers:

- If meeting with a grade-level or content-area teacher to discuss the progress of individual students, the ESL teacher can offer some general suggestions of ways to help ESL students understand lessons, such as using visual aids and gestures, putting keywords on the board, and so forth.

- The ESL teacher can take a look at the content-area notebooks of the ESL students. By reading through their classwork and homework assignments, the ESL teacher may be able to suggest to grade-level/content-area teachers simple ways that they can modify assignments so that ESL students can complete them more successfully. For example, if a grade-level teacher requires students to learn the spelling and definition of 15 vocabulary words weekly, the ESL teacher may suggest that a beginning-level ESL student learn the 5 or 10 most important words, or even a different, more appropriate set of words furnished by the ESL teacher.

- During ESL lessons, the ESL teacher can ask ESL students to talk about the subjects or assignments that are particularly difficult for them. The ESL teacher can then meet with individual grade-level/content-area teachers to offer suggestions for making lessons and assignments more accessible to ESL students.

Else offers a valuable resource for schools committed to improving student learning through quality professional development.

Else's Perspective IT MIGHT BE HELPFUL FOR TEACHERS OR ADMINISTRATORS planning for professional development, either for themselves or for colleagues, to consult the standards developed by the National Staff Development Council. These can be obtained from the Council's web site at *www.nsdc.org* or in print (National Staff Development Council, 1994). The standards are divided into three categories:

- **Context**: for example, the need for continuous improvement
- **Process**: for example, using as a basis knowledge about human learning and development, using multiple sources of information, and providing the follow-up necessary to ensure improvement
- **Content**: for example, creating the environment that maximizes student learning, using research-based teaching strategies, and using various types of performance assessment in the classroom

WHAT ARE SOME ISSUES ASSOCIATED WITH PROFESSIONAL DEVELOPMENT?

FOSTERING GOOD PROFESSIONAL RELATIONSHIPS

Whatever combination of professional development methods is used to promote effective schoolwide instruction for ESL students, the knowledge and skills that teachers already possess should be recognized, respected, and then augmented. It is helpful for ESL and grade-level/content-area teachers to maintain an ongoing dialogue with one another so that they can truly understand the challenges they face in their respective roles as teachers of ESL students. These challenges should be kept in mind as teachers attempt to help one another to be more effective in the classroom. This understanding is essential in fostering harmony among the many different teachers in a school, all of whom have different backgrounds and experiences, but who also have the common goal of providing a quality education for all students in the school. As Stevick (1998) states with respect to the language classroom (but which applies to any learning situation), "...success depends less on materials, techniques,...and more on what goes on inside and between the people...The most important aspect of 'what goes on' is the presence or absence of harmony..." (p. 4).

Even when teachers have the best intentions in attempting to improve instruction for students, insensitivity to one another's affective needs can cause the opposite result. A few years ago, an ESL teacher at an elementary school related the following incident to me, which illustrates the importance of using a sensitive approach when trying to encourage change in teacher behavior. The incident involved a special education teacher, but it could easily have been an ESL teacher.

> The other day a memo was circulated among the teachers in my "group"—the special education, speech, and ESL teachers—to ask for input for an upcoming monthly group leaders' meeting. At these meetings, the group leaders discuss issues brought up by teachers in their respective groups. Teachers write their concerns on a form that circulates among us so that we can each read the comments of others before the sheet is returned to the group leader in preparation for the meeting.

> I did not have any particular issues to enter on this month's sheet, but as usual I read what others had written. One of the entries by a special education teacher caught my attention. She wanted our group leader to bring up the following concern at the meeting:

> "Classroom teachers must realize that they cannot continue to 'dump' their problems onto the special education teachers. They need to ask themselves, 'What am I doing in the class to help this student?' They are too quick to refer a child to special education—many of these children might just be slower learners than the others, or they may have learning styles that are not being addressed. Special education is not a *place*—it's a *service*!"

> I read this entry with great interest because there have been times when I have wanted to say the exact same thing to teachers with respect to their attitudes toward ESL students! Some teachers just

want the ESL teacher to take care of the "problem" and are annoyed that the ESL child is in their class in the first place. Perhaps they are not thoroughly examining whether or not they are making the proper accommodations to help the child succeed. However, I do not believe that this special education teacher took the most expedient approach to persuading teachers to change. I overheard several angry teachers in the staff lounge reacting to the comments made by the special education teacher. (I guess the word had spread.) One said, "She never had big classes, so she doesn't understand what it's like to have 28 kids in the room, each with different needs!" Another called the special education teacher "arrogant." For grade-level and content-area teachers to make real, permanent changes in their teaching, they must be motivated by something other than criticism. Now they are just going to dig their heels in.

Criticism only serves to alienate teachers from one another and make it less likely that they will work together to meet common challenges. Perhaps a better approach for this special education teacher to have taken would have been to ask a question such as, "Are we doing all we can to keep students in the classroom rather than sending them out for special services?" This might have initiated a productive dialogue rather than preventing a dialogue from even beginning.

LONG-TERM EFFECTS

When professional development initiatives are undertaken, it is wise for schools to consider ways to ensure that positive changes that result from the initiatives endure from year to year. Since staff turnover is inevitable as teachers, counselors, and administrators change schools or school districts, retire, or leave the profession for other endeavors, schools must plan for the continuation of improvements despite staff changes.

As a result of conducting a federally funded three-year professional development project for math and science secondary teachers in a small city school district in New York State, Dwyer (1998) proposes that educators who are planning a professional development program "spread the ownership base beyond immediate participants—in our case, teachers—to include administrators and community members..." (p. 9). Although her program was successful in altering the behavior and attitudes of the teachers who volunteered for the program, Dwyer reports that once the federal grant money for the project had been spent, there was not enough local support to continue the program with the school district's own budget. Continual local funding could have been used to offer the program in subsequent years to teachers of other disciplines and to new teachers in the school. She also regrets that those running the project did not foresee the need to institutionalize positive changes so that they would continue despite staff turnover. For example, during the three-year program, ESL students were clustered into the classes of the math and science teachers who had volunteered for the training. Later on, the system began to break down. "We did not institutionalize crucial changes at every level in the school, especially in guidance, scheduling, and departmental procedures. If we had, perhaps the guidance department head would have understood the need to cluster language minority students in the classes of cadre members consistently" (p. 10).

The ESL administrator who spoke earlier about team-teaching as a means of professional development now discusses the successes of extensive professional development initiatives as well as the difficulties involved in sustaining the positive results.

> In our district we have worked intensively with grade-level/content-area teachers over the past five or six years to help them provide appropriate instruction for ESL students in their regular classes. We have also trained them to teach their subject matter to entire sections of ESL students (i.e., "sheltered" classes).
>
> For three years we had a special grant to train math teachers to teach not just ESL kids, but entire sections of high-schoolers who had limited formal schooling. The first year we developed curriculum and did training in five schools. That program has now expanded to over 35 schools with a cadre of veteran teachers now doing the training.
>
> Science and social studies teachers have also received lots of training, but the reality is that our school system is so large that there is always substantial teacher turnover. Another problem is that the same teacher may not be teaching the same courses year after year. Therefore, a teacher who has been trained to teach an ESL section of social studies may only teach it for one or two years, and then we have to train someone else. Some principals consistently assign only the new teachers to teach the ESL sections of courses because other faculty members don't want to be bothered getting trained to teach them. Obviously, we still have work to do!

Keith Buchanan, Fairfax County Public Schools, Virginia

The situation above underscores the need to involve all staff, including administrators, in professional development programs so that there is a deeper and more widespread understanding of practices that help ESL students to be successful. Perhaps then these practices will become permanent policies, and ESL students for years to come can reap the benefits.

Else's Perspective

ALL THE GOOD PROFESSIONAL DEVELOPMENT PRACTICES and strategies that Helene discusses in this chapter point in the direction of making teachers more reflective and more aware of the conditions of their classroom and of learning (Freeman, 1996). Reflective teachers ask questions about their teaching and about how their students learn, and they modify their instruction accordingly. They observe patterns in learning and performance and try to make sense of how what they do in the classroom affects student behavior. In other words, reflective teachers are constantly conducting small-scale classroom research projects.

Some people have even argued that teaching behaviors are affected primarily by apprenticeship, observation, and reflection rather than by the content of teacher education programs and teachers' experiences in those programs (Kagan, 1992). Teachers need to develop what some have called "robust reasoning" (Johnson, 1999), a process in which teachers ask guiding questions to help them improve teaching practices. They need to ask questions such as the following: Who am I as a teacher? Who are my students, and how do they experience my teaching? What do I know about my teaching context? What do I know about the subject-matter content that I teach? Why do I teach the way I do? What are the consequences of my teaching practices for my students? How do I make sense of theoretical knowledge? Who is my professional community? What sort of change do I see as fit for my own teaching?

By constantly asking questions such as these, teachers can continually expand their understanding of their classrooms and of the learning they are helping students accomplish.

CHAPTER SUMMARY

This chapter has proposed various ways for ESL and grade-level/content-area teachers to work together to effect positive changes in instructional environments for ESL students. As teachers are attempting more and more to blend ESL and content-area instruction (in the form of sheltered instruction, for example), it makes sense that the ESL and grade-level/content-area teachers blend their respective talents to collaborate on instructional practices. Depending on factors such as teachers' attitudes and needs, prior training experiences, years of teaching experience, and years of working with ESL students, as well as a school district's built-in conventions for professional development, some methods of professional development may be more appropriate in a particular school than other methods. In most cases, a combination of methods may work best.

As Dwyer (1998) states, "The stakes are very high for language minority learners in our schools. Without planned, systemic change, it is likely that they will continue to be served poorly in mainstream classes...It is in the best interest of our students that we learn to be as strategic and savvy as possible in our efforts to create and maintain change for their benefit" (p. 10).

ESL teachers must remain hopeful yet realistic when attempting to encourage improvements in learning environments for ESL students. As Pennington (1995) states, "Because it means challenging,...and then reconstructing ingrained practice and long-held beliefs, lasting change in teaching practice is not easy to accomplish" (p. 705). Freeman (1989) underscores the reality when he draws a parallel between getting teachers to change their practices in the classroom and getting people to change their health habits. In both cases, the information for positive changes may be available, but effective ways of getting people to make those changes remain elusive. Perhaps the best route is to have ESL and grade-level/content-area teachers work together from the start in teacher preparation programs (Kaufman and Brooks, 1996) so that collaboration becomes routine. But ESL teachers who are already employed in schools must make attempts through various avenues and hope for the best. As Harklau (1994) concludes, changes in schools often begin with individual educators who examine their situations and begin talking to other teachers. For the sake of ESL students, ESL teachers need to keep talking.

8.1 *PROFESSIONAL DEVELOPMENT FOR GRADE-LEVEL/*
CONTENT-AREA TEACHERS

What steps has your local school district taken to promote effective schoolwide instruction for ESL students? In order to find out, interview a grade-level or content-area teacher. You might want to ask the following questions:

1. Does your school provide any training, formal or informal, in effective teaching strategies for ESL students in your classes? If so, please explain.
2. What types of training experiences have been most helpful, and why?
3. What types of training experiences have been least helpful, and why?
4. What kind of training/assistance would you like to have in the future?

8.2 *INTERACTIONS BETWEEN ESL AND GRADE-LEVEL/*
CONTENT-AREA TEACHERS

What kinds of interactions take place between ESL and grade-level/content-area teachers in your local school district? Interview an ESL teacher to find out. Here are some suggested questions:

1. Do you interact with grade-level/content-area teachers in your school with the intent of improving instruction for ESL students? Please describe this interaction.
2. What kinds of interaction/collaboration would you like to see in the future?

8.3 *OBSERVING A GRADE-LEVEL OR CONTENT-AREA CLASS*

If possible, observe a grade-level or content-area class that contains some ESL students. In your view, has this teacher created an appropriate learning environment for ESL students? While observing, see if you can jot down notes in the appropriate column of a chart like the one below. Afterwards, discuss your observations with a colleague.

Techniques/materials/attitudes, etc. that are helping ESL students learn in this classroom:	Techniques/materials/attitudes, etc. that could be improved to help ESL students learn in this classroom:
Evidence that these factors are working:	Evidence that these factors need improvement:

8.4 DESIGNING A QUESTIONNAIRE FOR ESL STUDENTS

Investigate the perceptions of ESL students in your local school district regarding how well their ESL classes, as well as their grade-level/content-area classes, are meeting their educational needs. What changes could they suggest that might help them learn better? With a colleague, design a questionnaire for ESL students in order to find out their perspective.

Perhaps you can find an ESL teacher who would be willing to give the questionnaire to his or her students. If so, after reading the responses, discuss with your colleague your ideas for a professional development program in that particular school—that is, what kinds of professional development activities might help teachers in that school be more successful in meeting the learning needs of the ESL students?

Suggested Readings

Judy Jameson of the Center for Applied Linguistics has published valuable materials for conducting professional development sessions for secondary content-area teachers. The program, *Enriching Content Classes for Secondary ESOL Students* (1998), consists of an extensive step-by-step manual for the trainer and a study guide for participants.

Elizabeth Claire and Judie Haynes have co-authored several books that include alternative learning activities for beginning-level elementary ESL students. ESL teachers can suggest that grade-level teachers use these resources when ESL students cannot participate meaningfully in particular classroom activities. I especially recommend the *Classroom Teacher's ESL Survival Kit #1* (1994) and *#2* (1995). A good resource book for suggestions of alternative reading material for ESL students is *The Literature Connection: A Read-Aloud Guide for Multicultural Classrooms* by Betty Ansin Smallwood (1991). At the secondary level, if ESL students are not able to understand their textbooks, you can suggest to content-area teachers that ESL students be provided with textbooks written in simplified English, as a supplement to their regular textbook. These helpful textbooks are published by Ballard and Tighe, Globe Fearon, and Steck-Vaughn among others.

Other resources for professional development are *Doing Teacher Research: From Inquiry to Understanding* by Donald Freeman (1998) and *Training Others to Use the ESL Standards: A Professional Development Manual* edited by D. J. Short, E. L. Gomez, N. Cloud, A. Katz, M. Gottlieb, and M. Malone (2000).

9

LESSONS FROM MY STUDENTS

When a highly skilled teacher is observed conducting a class, teaching appears to be a simple and effortless activity. The lesson flows gracefully and logically—almost automatically. The students are enthusiastic and involved in learning activities that present just the right amount of challenge—not too much, not too little—for each student in the class.

I remember being a student teacher in 1974, sitting for two weeks in the back of my cooperating teacher's classroom, observing her teach before I had my chance to try. Her lessons flowed steadily from beginning to end, leading me to believe that teaching would be easy. I remember how surprised I was the first time I stood in front of 25 ninth-graders and attempted to teach them Spanish. My lesson wasn't awful (at least I don't *think* it was), but it was far from graceful and effortless! Teaching is a highly complex activity, and only the teacher who is very skilled can make it appear so simple.

How do effective teachers develop the skills that make their lessons appear easy to orchestrate and appropriate for all students in the class? Obviously, a lot can be learned from attending university classes, participating in conferences and workshops, reading professional literature, observing experienced teachers, discussing issues and ideas with others and, of course, reflecting upon one's own teaching. However, some of the most important lessons that teachers learn do not come from these standard sources—they come from the students themselves.

Most students are probably not aware of the important role they play in the training of teachers. However, to the wise teacher, the classroom is a laboratory in which various approaches and strategies are tested and refined, and in which students communicate, in blatant as well as subtle ways, whether a lesson was a success, a failure, or somewhere in between.

This final chapter describes some powerful lessons I have learned in various K–12 settings, from students who stand out in my mind because of the impact they have had on my teaching. Although I continue to learn through courses, conferences, workshops, books, and other teachers, my students still play a critical role in my ongoing development as an ESL teacher as I strive to make the highly complex act of teaching appear simple and effortless.

JESSICA: A LESSON IN ADDRESSING THE NEEDS OF ALL STUDENTS

Sometime back in the early 1980s when I first started teaching ESL in a public school setting, Jessica entered my ESL Level I class in December. She had just arrived from Peru speaking almost no English. I wasn't particularly happy to have another new student entering my

Helene Becker

class a few months after the start of the school year (she was the fourth); I found it frustrating because the other students already knew the class routines and were well along in the textbook.

I decided to have Jessica work with the class during some portions of the lesson, and then have her work on her own in the textbook for the rest of the class time until she caught up. This way I wouldn't have to worry about whether she understood the more difficult parts of my lessons—that would be her time for independent work.

This plan worked well for a few days, but then Jessica began to display playful and disruptive behavior. She would start to do her independent work in the textbook, but after about two minutes, she would try to talk to others (usually in Spanish), or she would make faces while I was talking to the class. She would even get out of her seat without permission to go sit near a friend. After a week or so of trying to get her under control, I realized that Jessica was not the kind of student whom I could expect to work independently.

I looked at her previous school records and discovered that she had had some interruptions in her education in Peru and that she had poor grades. After looking at the written work she was handing in, I could tell that her writing skills even in Spanish were probably quite low—her letter formation and use of punctuation were like those of an early elementary school student. Obviously, I was not meeting Jessica's needs in my ESL classroom. I had to come up with a better solution than having her do "independent study" to catch up.

As a result of having Jessica in the class (and many other "Jessicas" since then), I realized that I could not expect all the students in a class to be at the same proficiency level and to have the same learning styles. I needed to accept and expect a wide range of levels and styles within each class and to plan my lessons accordingly. In fact, I eventually came to realize that no two students in *any* of my classes were truly at the same level in all areas. For example, some were comfortable and skilled at speaking but poor at reading, whereas others had strong reading skills but could not communicate well orally. I realized that I needed to do more activities in my classes that allowed for and addressed the many different needs that I would always encounter in ESL classes even when the classes were comprised of students at the same so-called level of proficiency.

WHAT I LEARNED FROM THE MANY JESSICAS I HAVE TAUGHT

- K–12 teachers should expect and be prepared for new students to arrive at any time during the school year. Because of bureaucratic red tape, political conflicts, economic issues, school calendars in other countries, and so forth, families often have little control over the time of year they arrive in their new country and, as a result, when their children can start school. Once in their new country, a family may move often until their situation stabilizes, causing their children to change schools frequently.

- Teachers should conduct lesson activities and use techniques that accommodate the many different language proficiency levels, academic proficiency levels, and learning styles found in almost every class. Over the years, students have "taught" me to use the following guidelines in planning lessons:

1. Pair and small group work allow students at different levels to learn from one another in a relatively nonthreatening manner (that is, they can test out language and ideas in the presence of only a few students instead of the entire class). Working in small groups also gives students much more opportunity to practice using language than trying to participate in a large group discussion.

2. Teachers need to build redundancy into lessons so that students who do not understand a direction, vocabulary word, or lesson concept have multiple opportunities to "get it." It is best to present information through a variety of learning channels (auditory, visual, kinesthetic, etc.).

3. Teachers need to use a variety of question types in order to allow students at different proficiency levels to participate and to give all students the opportunity to answer lower-order as well as higher-order questions. Students who are at a Level I speaking stage may be able to answer questions by saying a simple "yes" or "no," or pointing to an object, word, or place. Students at Level II may be able to answer questions with a one- or two-word phrase. Students at Level III, IV, or V can be expected to answer questions that require more complete phrases or full sentences. But students at all proficiency levels can be challenged to think critically even if they may only be able to express their answers in simple English.

Levels of language acquisition are described in Appendix A, p. 207

4. When teaching something new, teachers need to assist struggling students by offering many examples. For example, if students are going to do a grammar exercise, the teacher should do the first few items with the students. If students are going to work in groups to complete a project, they should be shown beforehand a sample of a finished product so that they can more easily understand the assignment.

5. Teachers need to make sure all students are learning by checking frequently for comprehension. It is best to assume that students do not understand until there is evidence that they do. Depending on the lesson, students can show comprehension by explaining the material orally or in writing, drawing a picture, doing an action, or completing an example on their own. Through experience I have come to understand that just because I have *taught* something does not necessarily mean that students have *learned* something! The only way to know for sure what students have learned is for them to demonstrate their knowledge in some way.

RUSSELL AND KAREN: A LESSON IN CLASSROOM DISCIPLINE

Teachers'
Voices

Helene Becker

My first teaching job right out of college was in a parochial school in the Bronx, New York. I was only 20 years old and petite, and the high school students sitting in front of me were almost my age and seemed very big. "No problem," I thought. "Since I'm close in age to these students, I'll just show them that I'm their 'friend.'" I figured that as long as I was nice, fair, and reasonable, the students would like me and I would not have discipline problems. I quickly discovered I was wrong.

Russell, a tenth-grader in my Spanish II class, had been late to class several times, and I informed him that the next time he was late I would have to give him an after-school detention (this rule had been previously discussed with the class, so I was being "fair and reasonable"). The following day, as the late bell rang, I could hear Russell running down the hallway. He did not arrive on time, so I handed him a detention slip. I resumed teaching the lesson, and when the class ended, Russell came up to my desk looking forlorn. "Miss Becker, if you give me this detention, I will be over the limit and I won't be allowed to play basketball in Friday's game. The team needs me. Can't you just give me one more chance? I promise I won't be late again." Russell sounded sincere, and I was naive about the predicament that would follow. "OK, but no more coming late."

A few days later, another student, Karen, exceeded the lateness limit, so I handed her a detention slip. At the end of the lesson she approached my desk—she was livid. "You're unfair! You didn't give Russell a detention and now you're giving me one. You're playing favorites. I hate this class!" Needless to say, Russell and Karen taught me more about student discipline than any textbook could.

WHAT I LEARNED FROM THE MANY RUSSELLS AND KARENS THAT I HAVE TAUGHT:

Frameworks

- Regarding discipline, teachers need to formulate rules and then stick to them. Students are more likely to follow the rules if they know that there are always consequences if the rules are broken.
- Students should be treated equally; the same rules apply to all.
- Teachers are not the students' "friends"; teachers need to be fair but firm authority figures in an elementary or secondary classroom.

VITALY: A LESSON IN HAVING HIGH EXPECTATIONS

Teachers'
Voices

Helene Becker

Vitaly was a student from Russia whom I met back in 1982 when I was teaching ESL in an elementary school in West Hartford, Connecticut. He arrived in the United States as a sixth-grader speaking some English; I decided to have him join a small group of intermediate-level sixth-graders whom I saw for ESL pullout instruction three times per week.

From the beginning it was evident that Vitaly was going to be a challenge. He participated somewhat in class discussions, but put little effort into his written work and did almost no homework. I tried all sorts of ways to encourage Vitaly to work harder— reasoning with him, rewarding him, punishing him, calling his parents—but nothing worked. I could not motivate him to put effort into his schoolwork. His grade-level teacher found him to be unmotivated in her classroom, as well.

Even though I was not succeeding in motivating Vitaly, I never gave up! Each time I saw him, I gave him the benefit of the doubt and assumed that he had done his homework and was going to do a good job in class that day. This way I could be freshly disappointed each time he let me down. In other words, I held him to the same expectations daily as I held everyone else; I continued to expect him to do his best, no matter how discouraged I got.

Vitaly went on to middle school, and shortly thereafter, moved to another town. After that, I didn't hear much about him, but I always wondered if he had ever changed his attitude about school. I considered him to be one of my personal failures in that I was not able to motivate him to succeed in school.

Several years later, I was in the midst of teaching a lesson at the local high school when I looked up to see Vitaly standing at the door with a red rose in his hand. Shocked, I told him to come in, and he proceeded to hand me the rose. He said, "Miss Becker, I just wanted to say I'm sorry for all the trouble I gave you. Now I see how important school was and I wish I had listened to you earlier and had tried harder. Thank you for everything."

Apparently, Vitaly had dropped out of school in eleventh grade and was now trying to get his high school equivalency diploma. After working at some minimum-wage jobs, he finally realized that he was going to be stuck in those kinds of jobs unless he acquired more education. He now wanted to get his high school diploma and go on to college. It took many years, but Vitaly finally developed some motivation!

WHAT I LEARNED FROM THE MANY VITALYS I HAVE TAUGHT:

- Teachers need to have high expectations for all students. Elementary as well as secondary students should be expected to make school a high priority in their lives and should be encouraged to do their very best. Some students understand this message right away and work hard. Other students, such as Vitaly, take many years to realize that education (or the lack of it) can have a profound impact on their futures. But teachers should never give up trying to motivate students to learn.

9.1 AN INFLUENTIAL TEACHER

Think back to your teachers in elementary and secondary school. Was there a teacher who had a positive impact on you in some way? Was this impact related to having high expectations for you in some aspect of your life? Did you realize the impact at the time, or some time later? Take a few minutes to write down your thoughts about this teacher and the impact he or she had on you. If possible, share your response with a colleague.

Teachers'
Voices

Helene Becker

JOSEPH: A LESSON IN ADDRESSING EMOTIONAL NEEDS

Joseph was a fifth-grade ESL student of mine a few years ago. He came to Hawaii from the Philippines where he had studied English in school but had never actually used it. Hence, when he started fifth grade in Hawaii, he could not communicate much in his grade-level classroom. His teacher and I decided that I would pull him out of his fifth-grade classroom three times a week so that I could help him learn some basic conversational skills. He learned quickly; within two months he was able to communicate quite well. He had a good attitude about school and seemed to be adjusting well, although he was a shy child and did not socialize much with the other students.

Within a few more months, however, Joseph began to appear unhappy and withdrawn. He complained of headaches and even asked to go home a few times. His grade-level teacher reported that, despite his change in demeanor, Joseph was keeping up with his academics. When I asked Joseph if he was having some problems, he said only that he had a history of getting bad headaches and that nothing else was wrong. But a few weeks later, I received the following letter from him by means of his dialogue journal:

Figure 9.1: Joseph's Dialogue Journal Entry

> Dear Mrs. Becker,
>   Mrs. Becker, may I tell you something, can you help me with my problems. I have a hard time with my homework and maybe it will end to F and I am very tired and everynight I can't sleep because for thinkiing of my homework, sometimes the other one I can't finish because of the another homework and I am thinking about my grade that will be a F please help me Mrs. Becker.
>
>   Sincerely, Joseph

Naturally, Joseph's journal entry saddened and worried me, and I immediately went to his grade-level teacher to discuss ways of lightening up the workload for Joseph. She reported that she had had no idea that the work she was assigning the class had been so time-consuming and distressing for Joseph.

After the grade-level teacher assigned Joseph less homework, he continued to be somewhat subdued and melancholy for a while, but over time he had fewer headaches and seemed better adjusted. Fortunately, he had been astute enough to write about his problem in his dialogue journal so that teachers could make adjustments for him. However, I don't think the workload was the only thing bothering him; I believe Joseph was also suffering from sadness and loneliness due to leaving his friends and his life in the Philippines. In fact, after a while, he began to talk about how much he missed the Philippines. I tried to help him see that it takes a period of time to adjust to a new place and culture and that he would probably feel much better in his new environment soon.

WHAT I LEARNED FROM THE MANY JOSEPHS I HAVE TAUGHT:

- Teachers need to pay close attention to students' emotional well-being, especially when students are newly arrived in our schools and our culture.
- Students need an outlet for discussing their problems, concerns, and difficulties. Dialogue journals are well-suited for this purpose because they are private and in written form; some students may find that they can express their feelings more easily in writing than face-to-face.
- Schools need to be proactive in making ESL students feel comfortable and welcomed into their new school community. Teachers and students alike should make a special effort to invite ESL students to participate in academic, social, and sports activities. This interaction benefits the ESL as well as the non-ESL students as it allows everyone the opportunity to mingle with and learn from one another.

Frameworks

For a discussion of dialogue journals, see Chapter 5, pp. 136–137.

9.2 *LEARNING FROM STUDENTS*

Investigations

If you are currently teaching or have taught, do any of your students stand out as having taught you a powerful lesson? If so, write about it or discuss it with a colleague. If not, ask a colleague to tell you about students who have had a considerable impact on his or her teaching. What lessons did your colleague learn from the students?

CHAPTER SUMMARY

Learning to teach English as a second language in a K–12 setting is a complex, but highly rewarding, undertaking. Although much can be learned from traditional sources, powerful lessons can be learned from the students themselves. When close attention is paid to the signals received from students, teachers may find that, over time, their teaching becomes more and more deceptively simple to the observer. In actuality, however, experienced teachers' actions in the classroom are far from simple—they reflect many years of experimenting, evaluating, and refining. This process is ongoing as teachers teach their students while, at the same time, students continue to teach their teachers.

Else's Perspective UNLIKE HELENE, WHOSE STUDENTS HAVE BEEN CHILDREN or adolescents, in the last decade or so, my students have been mostly teachers. Like Helene, I have learned much from these students. Teachers have taught me specific aspects of teaching—such as teaching strategies and tricks of the trade—that I have subsequently passed on to other teachers. They have also prompted me to contemplate general issues in teaching ESL students that define who we are as educators—issues such as the importance of advocacy on behalf of students, and the possible conflicts that may arise when our role as advocates of ESL students clashes with our role as agents of the system within which we teach. The numerous discussions I have had with teachers regarding moral and philosophical issues such as this have shown me the commitment and passion with which most teachers practice their profession.

I have also seen the dire conditions in which many ESL teachers work. Possibly as a result of lack of support, many ESL teachers develop a sense of powerlessness within their profession. They feel that they do not control their own classroom and that many of the vital decisions in teaching have been taken away from them. "Teacher-proof" curricula and materials and requirements for unnecessarily rigid adherence to standards are some outrageous examples of teaching power being stripped away from the teachers who know best how to guide students to learn. Despite tendencies in many districts to devalue what the teacher knows, you must remember that you, the teacher, know what I, or other teacher trainers or administrators, cannot fathom. In this regard, it is important to heed one of Helene's most important messages in this chapter: that she has learned most from her students—not from university courses or workshops led by educational consultants, experts, or teacher trainers.

Teachers do learn most of what they know from observing and listening to their students. This statement is sobering for people like me, who need to remind ourselves and the teachers with whom we work that educational consultants and teacher trainers can simply give teachers a historical, political, and theoretical context for what they do. We can share with them what other teachers have discovered in their classrooms. But ultimately, it is the teacher who must continue to discover what works in the classroom. It is for this reason that this book was written by a teacher and the main text was narrated by a teacher. It was my hope, as a teacher trainer, to simply provide the musical score that enriches the text and makes your discoveries more resonant. As I often tell my workshop participants: Please question everything I have said, and teach me what you have learned.

Appendix A

ORAL PROFICIENCY LEVELS (1–5):
Student Behaviors

Level 1 (pre-production)
At Level 1 students have **minimal comprehension** and **no verbal production**. They will:

- try to make sense out of messages
- gain familiarity with the sounds, rhythm, and patterns of English
- attend to shared reading, but rely on picture clues for understanding

Level 2 (early production)
At Level 2 students have **limited comprehension** and produce **one- or two-word responses**. They will:

- demonstrate increased confidence
- listen with greater understanding
- identify people, places, and objects
- use routine expressions independently
- repeat, recite memorable language

Level 3 (speech emergence)
At Level 3 students have **increased comprehension** and produce **simple sentences**, but with errors. They will:

- speak with less hesitation and demonstrate increasing understanding
- produce longer phrases or sentences (with grammatical inaccuracy)
- participate more fully in discussions, including those with academic content
- explain, describe, compare, and retell in response to literature
- engage in independent reading
- use writing for a variety of purposes

Level 4 (intermediate fluency)
At Level 4 students have **very good comprehension**, produce **more complex sentences**, and have fewer errors in production. They will:

- produce connected discourse and narrative
- use more extensive vocabulary
- demonstrate increased levels of accuracy
- demonstrate use of higher-order language (persuade, evaluate, criticize, etc.)
- read a wider range of texts with increased comprehension
- explore content concepts in greater depth
- write with greater accuracy
- conduct research projects

Level 5 (advanced fluency)
At Level 5 students have **comprehension and production skills comparable to native speakers of the same age.**

(Adapted from Cloud, Genesee, and Hamayan, 2000, p. 126, and Tinajero and Schifini, 1997, p. T25)

Appendix B

PROFESSIONAL DEVELOPMENT WORKSHOPS FOR GRADE-LEVEL AND/OR CONTENT-AREA TEACHERS:
Sample Activities and Handouts

SAMPLE ACTIVITY I:
Introduction to ESL
This activity serves as an introduction to the field of ESL and to the needs of ESL students. It is a good way to start a workshop because participants are immediately engaged in a group task designed to furnish them with essential information in a short amount of time.

PURPOSE AND OVERVIEW:

To present to participants some basic ESL principles and to impart information about the ESL students in their school district. Participants are asked to answer a set of questions which introduce important issues and provoke discussion.

MATERIALS AND PREPARATION NEEDED:

1. Prepare a "test" similar to the sample on p. 209. Make one copy for each participant.

2. Prepare an answer sheet for your use (see sample on pp. 210–212).

PROCEDURE:

1. Announce to participants that you will start the workshop with a "test." Emphasize that this is a fun test with no pressure or grades.

2. Have participants form groups of 3–4 people.

3. Distribute the test (see following sample). Participants should work together, discussing each item.

4. When most groups are finished (in about 15–20 minutes), read each question aloud, asking participants to volunteer their answers. Discuss each answer thoroughly and answer any questions that arise.

(**Note**: These are sample questions—you may want to add, delete, or alter questions to suit your needs.)

TEST YOUR ESL KNOWLEDGE!

Part I—Fill in the blanks.

1. The average non-English-speaking student acquires enough English language skills to communicate socially in _____ year(s).

2. The average non-English-speaking student acquires enough English language skills to participate effectively in grade-level/content-area classes in _____ year(s).

3. Approximately _____% of students in this school district speak a language other than English at home.

4. The three languages (other than English) spoken most at home by students in this school district are _____ , _____ , and _____.

5. The school in this district that has the most students currently receiving ESL instruction is _____.

6. The school in this district that has the fewest students currently receiving ESL instruction is _____.

Part II—True or False? (*If you choose "false," think about why the statement is false.*)

_____ 1. The more English the ESL students hear, the more English they will learn.

_____ 2. Providing special considerations for teaching ESL students is not needed, since historically immigrants learned English without special assistance and participated effectively in society.

_____ 3. ESL students need little extra assistance in math because math does not require English skills.

_____ 4. Because ESL students need to acquire oral language, the lecture approach is an effective method for teaching them basic language skills.

_____ 5. In most cases it is better for ESL students to speak their first language at home.

_____ 6. Students need to make a choice about which language and culture they wish to embrace. Otherwise, they will have difficulty with identity and self-esteem.

_____ 7. If a student's pronunciation in English is good, we can assume that the student has acquired the skills necessary to be successful in academic work.

_____ 8. Students should be corrected as much as possible when they make mistakes because this is how they will acquire language skills.

(This "test" was adapted from a presentation given by John Mundahl, 1994.)

TEST YOUR ESL KNOWLEDGE!

ANSWERS AND EXPLANATIONS

Part I—Fill in the blanks:

1. The average non-English-speaking student acquires enough English language skills to communicate socially in __**1 to 3**__ year(s).

Research has shown that "social language" is acquired by many students relatively quickly (although there is great variation).

2. The average non-English-speaking student acquires enough English language skills to participate effectively in grade-level/content-area classes in __**5 to 7**__ year(s) (7 to 10 years if students have had little prior schooling).

Research has shown that "academic language" takes much longer to acquire than social language for most students. Academic language includes language specific to each of the content areas as well as the language used to learn content such as the structures and vocabulary found in textbooks. This language is very different from the social language students use to communicate with friends. Reading and writing skills are also part of academic language.

(The answers to the following four questions should be available by contacting the ESL program coordinator in your school district.)

3. Approximately _____% of students in this school district speak a language other than English at home.

4. The three languages (other than English) spoken most at home by students in this school district are _____, _____, and _____.

5. The school in this district that has the most students currently receiving ESL services is _____.

6. The school in this district that has the fewest students currently receiving ESL services is _____.

Part II—True or False? (If you choose "false," think about why the statement is false.)

__False__ 1. The more English the ESL students hear, the more English they will learn.

It is not enough simply to hear English; the meaning must be made comprehensible in order for students to learn the language. Participants should think about the experience of sitting in a church or synagogue year after year, listening to Latin or Hebrew. Will they ever learn the language just by sitting there and listening? Probably not. Participants can also think about listening to a foreign language station on the radio. Will they ever learn the language just by listening without any instruction or interaction? Most likely not. This is precisely why the "lecture approach" does not help ESL students learn. If there is no interaction with the language in order to make it comprehensible, language will not be learned.

 False 2. Providing special considerations for teaching ESL students is not needed since historically immigrants learned English without special assistance and participated effectively in society.

Many immigrants who came to this country at the beginning of the 20th century did not learn English well and dropped out of school. However, in those days you could obtain many kinds of jobs (for example, farm work, factory work, even running your own business) without a high level of academic skills. Society is much more complex now; many of the jobs that did not require academic skills have disappeared, and running a business or working in many other fields requires a high level of skill in reading, writing, and computers.

 False 3. ESL students need little extra assistance in math because math does not require English skills.

Learning math requires English skills in order to understand the teacher and the textbook. Word problems can be especially difficult because they often describe contrived situations outside of a larger context and also contain specific math terminology.

 False 4. Because ESL students need to acquire oral language, the lecture approach is an effective method for teaching them basic language skills.

See Part II, item #1 above.

 True 5. In most cases it is better for ESL students to speak their first language at home.

This is "true" for the following reasons:

A) The student's first language is most likely the language in which the child and parents communicate most easily. Therefore, the parent can challenge the child to think and reason at a higher level than if the communication took place in English. This higher level of thinking helps develop the child's cognitive skills. If parents and children communicate at home in their second language, i.e, English, the communication is likely to be less complex, and therefore, less beneficial to the child's cognitive development.

B) Parents need to "parent" their children by guiding and disciplining them, as well as by showing them love and affection. These parent responsibilities and emotions are most effectively expressed through the native language.

C) After an entire school day of speaking English, a child needs some "downtime" at home where he/she can relax and speak the native language.

D) Practicing and preserving the native language at home will most likely benefit the child when he/she is an adult and enters the employment market.

E) It is unnatural for speakers of the same first language to communicate in a second language (unless another person is present who does not speak that first language). Speakers will communicate in the language that is most natural for them. It is usually fruitless to insist they do otherwise.

False 6. Students need to make a choice about which language and culture they wish to embrace. Otherwise, they will have difficulty with identity and self-esteem.

Americans historically have embraced both their American identity and their ethnic origins without having to make any exclusionary choices. In other areas of the world, such as Europe, it is quite common for people to operate well in two or more languages and cultures.

False 7. If a student's pronunciation in English is good, we can assume that the student has acquired the skills necessary to be successful in academic work.

See Part I, item #2 above.

False 8. Students should be corrected as much as possible when they make mistakes because this is how they will acquire language skills.

When learning a language, it is natural to make mistakes when attempting to speak or write. However, it is critical in the language acquisition process for students to speak and write as much as possible. If every mistake is corrected, students are likely to be inhibited about communicating and will not acquire language as quickly as if they felt comfortable and free to make mistakes. A good way to help students learn correct language is to model it for them. For example, if a student says, "John need pencil," the teacher can say, "Oh, I see. John needs a pencil."

SAMPLE ACTIVITY II:

Strategies Demonstration

This activity is an eye-opener for grade-level and content-area teachers, especially for those who have never taught or studied a second language. They learn that it is possible to derive meaning from a language that they do not understand when strategies are used to make the language comprehensible.

PURPOSE AND OVERVIEW:

To demonstrate to participants some effective strategies for making language comprehensible. Using a language other than English, the presenter tells a brief story, without giving any clues to meaning. The presenter then retells the story, this time giving clues to meaning to make the language comprehensible to participants. The contrast demonstrates the value of teaching with ESL strategies.

MATERIALS AND PREPARATION NEEDED:

1. Select a brief story which you are able to read aloud (or tell from memory) in a language other than English (see sample story on p. 215). Or, instead, you can use the story line from a children's "big book" translated into a language other than English.

2. Draw some simple pictures, large enough for participants to see, which illustrate the story line (see sample pictures on p. 216). If a "big book" is used for this demonstration, the pictures in the book can serve this purpose. The English text can be pasted over with the text in the foreign language.

3. Prepare a sheet of newsprint with the heading, "Strategies that Help ESL Students Learn the Lesson Material" (see sample on p. 217).

4. Photocopy for participants, the handout entitled, "Strategies for Teaching ESL Students in the Content Areas" (see Appendix C, pp. 218–221).

5. Check that in the presentation room, there is a board on which to write and to place/tape pictures.

PROCEDURE:

1. Ask participants if they understand _____ (the language you have chosen for the demonstration). If so, ask them to pretend that they do not. (For this demonstration to be effective, most of the audience should not understand the language you have chosen for the demonstration.)

2. Say to the audience, "I'm going to read you a story in _____. Try to understand as much as you can. Think of yourself as a beginning-level ESL student struggling to understand a teacher who is speaking English. But don't worry—I will not call on you to answer any questions, so you can relax."

3. Read the story straight through, without giving any clues to meaning such as gestures, voice intonation, visual cues, etc.

4. When you are finished, ask participants if they understood anything, and how they felt while they were listening. Do not allow someone in the audience who understands the foreign language to give away the story line.

5. Tell participants that you will read the story again, this time using some ESL strategies to help them understand the story line, even if they don't understand much _____.

6. Read the story again, this time using as many ESL strategies as you can. For example, use the pictures you prepared (or the pictures in the "big book") to point to items that illustrate the meaning of key words. Draw additional quick pictures on the board, if necessary. Use

gestures, intonation, write key words on the board—do anything to get the meaning across. (Practice beforehand on a friend or colleague to make sure you are successful in making the language comprehensible.)

7. In small groups, have participants tell each other what they understood of the story. At this point, participants are usually amazed that with a little help from each other, they can piece together the entire story even though they do not understand any _____ . This also illustrates the value of working together in a small group.

8. Have a volunteer(s) tell the story to the large group. Address any misunderstandings about the story line.

9. Post the newsprint entitled, "Strategies that Help ESL Students Learn the Lesson Material." Have participants call out all the strategies that helped them understand the story. List them on the newsprint. Add any other strategies you may have used that the participants did not mention (see list on p. 217).

10. Ask participants to look at the list of strategies and think about their own lessons. Which strategy(ies) do they plan to use this week and how? Ask participants to share their answers in small groups (or in the large group).

11. Distribute the handout, "Strategies for Teaching ESL Students in the Content Areas." This handout contains a more extensive list of useful strategies than could be illustrated in this type of demonstration lesson.

(This activity was adapted from a presentation given by Sue Goldstein, 1994.)

SAMPLE ACTIVITY II:

Strategies Demonstration Story
"En el consultorio del doctor"—Spanish Version

Hace tres días que la hija de la señora Mendoza no asiste a la escuela. La hija, Carolina, dice que está enferma. Señora Mendoza decide llevarla al doctor.

Dr. Chávez:	¿Cómo se siente su hija, Señora Mendoza?
Sra. Mendoza:	Dice que está muy mal y que no puede asistir a la escuela. Lleva tres días en cama mirando la tele.
Dr. Chávez:	Hmmm… Carolina, ¿te duele el estómago?
Carolina:	¡Ayyy! Sí, me duele mucho el estómago.
Dr. Chávez:	¿Tienes fiebre?
Sra. Mendoza:	Dice que sí, pero cuando le tomo la temperatura tiene 37 grados, o sea, normal.
Dr. Chávez:	Vamos a ver… ¿Tienes dolor de cabeza?
Carolina:	¡Sí! Y tengo tos, y estoy mareada y…y…
Dr. Chávez:	Parece que estás muy grave, Carolina. Tenemos que operarte immediatamente. Creo que tienes la *escuelacitis*. Es una condición del cerebro.
Carolina:	¿Una operación? ¿El cerebro? Pues…la verdad es que ahora me encuentro un poco mejor.

SAMPLE ACTIVITY II:

Strategies Demonstration Story
"At the Doctor's"—English Version

Mrs. Mendoza's daughter, Carolina, has not gone to school for three days. She says she's sick. Mrs. Mendoza decides to take her to the doctor.

Dr. Chávez:	How is your daughter feeling, Mrs. Mendoza?
Mrs. Mendoza:	She says that she is very bad and that she can't go to school. She spent three days in bed watching TV.
Dr. Chávez:	Hmmm…Carolina, does your stomach hurt?
Carolina:	Ohhh! Yes, my stomach hurts a lot.
Dr. Chávez:	Do you have a fever?
Mrs. Mendoza:	She says yes, but when I take it, the temperature is 37 degrees, that is to say, normal.
Dr. Chávez:	Let's see… Do you have a headache?
Carolina:	Yes! And I have a cough and I'm dizzy and…and…
Dr. Chávez:	It appears that this is very serious, Carolina. We must operate immediately. I believe that you have *schoolitis*. This is a condition of the brain.
Carolina:	An operation? The brain? Well…the truth is that I'm feeling a little better now.

(Adapted from Hershberger, R., M.G. Fast, G. Lopéz-Cox, S. Navey-Davis, and L. Nalbone. 2001.
Plazas: Lugar de encuentro para la hispanidad. *Boston: Heinle & Heinle.)*

LIST OF STRATEGIES GENERATED BY PARTICIPANTS DURING SAMPLE ACTIVITY II:

Strategies that Help ESL Students Learn the Lesson Material

pictures

gestures; actions; drama

pointing

repetition

clear pronunciation

key words on the board

slower rate of speech

simplified language

elimination of distractions

energy; enthusiasm

discussion with a partner or small group

emphasis on key words or points

pauses

facial expressions

verification of student understanding

clear printing on board

vocal expression; intonation

Appendix C

Strategies for Teaching ESL Students in the Content Areas

STRATEGY 1—*Analyze the textbook material from the perspective of the ESL student.*

A student who is learning English and may have a limited educational background will probably not be able to cover all the material of a lesson, so objectives should be prioritized and kept to a reasonable number. Determine at the outset what it is that the student must know at the end of the lesson and share that information with the student.

STRATEGY 2—*Determine what the student already knows and provide needed background information.*

ESL students come to the classroom with a wide range of background experiences and educational preparation. Through organizational activities such as semantic mapping, feature matrices, time lines, flow charts, KWL, etc., the teacher can get an idea of where to begin with a lesson. These activities also serve to let the students know where they stand in relation to the content of the upcoming lesson. Oftentimes, they know more than they think they know, but less than what the teacher expects them to know.

STRATEGY 3—*Identify and teach essential vocabulary.*

Make a list of 12 or so words necessary to understand the lesson. Have the student select any additional words that are not known and develop a word bank or glossary. For each word, supply the students with a paraphrase or simpler word which they might know. Be conscious of the kinds of words and patterns that often cause difficulty for ESL students, such as inverted word order, homonyms, words with multiple meanings, etc. Where possible, supply an equivalent word in the student's primary language.

STRATEGY 4—*Present the lesson orally and provide sufficient time for discussion.*

ESL students are often asked to read text material and complete assignments without sufficient preparation. Since many students have stronger oral skills than literacy skills, oral pre-reading activities are essential so that the students understand what they are supposed to do and have the needed background information and linguistic skills to accomplish the tasks. Without pre-reading assistance, students will focus on individual words in the text, and the linguistic difficulties will prevent comprehension of text meaning.

The use of certain routines in lesson presentation will provide students with security and enhance self-confidence.

Strategy 5—*Personalize the lesson to the extent possible.*

Textual material may rely on cultural assumptions and information that native speakers of English might easily have, but those new to this country might not. Many concepts may be abstract and difficult for students to translate into their own realm of experience. Provide as much interpretive and explanatory information as possible for the concepts and ideas that the text introduces. Use personalized and culturally relevant examples to get the point across. The object is not only to help the students understand the concepts of the lesson, but also to see how these ideas relate to their own lives.

Strategy 6—*Use a variety of visual aids.*

ESL students need as many visual clues as possible to help them derive meaning from textual material which tends to be "context-reduced." Visual clues may include facial expressions, gestures, objects, pictures, words written on the board, charts, graphs, maps, etc. They also need to develop the skills necessary to interpret these visual aids in order to derive maximum meaning.

Strategy 7—*Lighten the linguistic load by simplifying grammatical structures and paraphrasing.*

Academic writing, even at the elementary level, often uses abstract and complex grammatical structures. In presenting the lesson, simplify these structures so that students will understand the meaning of the content.

To lighten the linguistic load:

   a. avoid polysyllabic words.

   b. limit sentences to one concept.

   c. use familiar vocabulary and personal references.

   d. use concrete examples and contextualize.

   e. write a summary of the lesson in a simpler form of English.

   f. create titles, subtitles, margin notes, and captions.

   g. record difficult sections of the lesson on a cassette.

   h. use the primary language of the student, when possible, to clarify, reinforce, or introduce new concepts.

Strategy 8—*Assist the language learning process along with teaching the content.*

"Mainstream" teachers must also be language teachers for the ESL students. Language acquisition is developmental and takes time. Language is acquired most effectively in a non-threatening atmosphere where the emphasis is on meaningful communication and authentic language activities and materials. While teaching content, classroom teachers can help students increase their proficiency in English by:

   a. modeling the pronunciation of difficult words in the lesson.

   b. helping students correctly pronounce difficult words in subject matter vocabulary.

c. helping students learn and practice verb patterns.

d. explaining word meanings and idiomatic expressions.

e. emphasizing basic grammatical structures that are necessary to understand concepts in the content areas.

f. creating a classroom climate where students feel comfortable taking risks and making mistakes.

STRATEGY 9—*Teach study skills and the use of textbook aids.*

Students need to develop skills that will allow them to assume more of the responsibility for their own learning. They need to recognize that textbooks are organized differently from literature books or basal readers. Science texts, math books, and social studies materials all have their own look. When presenting textual material:

a. have students pay attention to the organizational features of the text so that they can learn to anticipate the development of ideas.

b. help students take time to read captions and other visual information before they try to read the text.

c. direct students to look at titles, subtitles, and summaries, and to guess what the textbook chapter will be about.

d. make students aware of all the aids within the textbook, such as the glossary, index, study questions, table of contents, marginal notes and footnotes, use of italics, etc.

STRATEGY 10—*Use hands-on activities.*

For students who are not proficient in the language of instruction, experiential activities are of great importance. Students have different learning styles and need to have the opportunity to acquire content knowledge through the use of all their senses. Present information both verbally and visually. Prepare activities that require students to be actively involved; e.g., experimenting, measuring, building something, making charts or maps, cooking, etc.

STRATEGY 11—*Monitor the student's progress.*

Formal and informal types of evaluation are necessary to decide whether a student is ready to continue with more difficult material. To monitor student progress:

a. ask questions at a variety of levels during the presentation to check students' comprehension. Allow for both oral and written responses.

b. observe students performing tasks that you have assigned.

c. provide opportunities for students to demonstrate skills and knowledge in a variety of ways.

d. ask the students how they feel about their own progress and current achievement level.

STRATEGY 12—*Encourage the use of more advanced reading strategies.*

Second language students often spend hours looking up every word they don't know in the dictionary, and by doing so they lose the meaning of the text. Teach students to first scan the text and select a limited number of frequent words they do not know. Have them look up *these* words and write a simple definition. Next, have them read the text and state the main idea for each section. Writing down the main idea in *one* sentence for each section is a good way to have them synthesize what they have understood.

Make sure that students can recognize and use various literary devices that carry the meaning of the text; e.g., words that denote sequence, comparison and contrast, cause and effect, description, etc.

STRATEGY 13— *Select literature to which students can relate.*

Try to find reading material that is relevant to the experiences and interests of the ESL students. Legends and stories from their particular cultural backgrounds will help to bridge the gap between home and school. Literature that shows pictures of people similar to themselves will be of greater interest to them, and story themes with which they can identify will be easier to understand. Give them opportunities to tell or write stories about themselves, their experiences, their culture, and share these with classmates.

STRATEGY 14—*Use learner-centered activities in small, cooperative groups.*

The social dynamics of the classroom are critical elements for ESL students. Small-group activities can offer these students the opportunity to explore concepts and experiment with language in a low-anxiety setting. Cooperative heterogeneous groups provide the best way to give ESL students both the support they need and the opportunity to contribute in a meaningful way to class endeavors. A "buddy system" can also be implemented to give the ESL students someone other than the teacher to call upon for help. Utilizing the other students in the class in these ways can make the teacher's task easier and can create a feeling of camaraderie in the classroom.

STRATEGY 15—*Utilize the unique identity of each student.*

ESL students bring their own set of cultural values and linguistic systems with them. These students provide a marvelous opportunity for "mainstream" classes to get to know a new country, history, language, and way of living. Identifying the unique aspects that each student brings can help the teacher provide learning experiences that are multicultural in nature for all students and teach respect for people and things that are different from one's own. Honoring the culture and language of ESL students in the classroom will enhance self-esteem and often results in a more positive attitude toward school and a higher level of academic achievement.

(This is adapted from a handout by Joyce Biagini, Minnesota State Department of Education, St. Paul, Minnesota.)

References

Agor, B. 2000. *Integrating the ESL standards into classroom practice, grades 9–12.* Alexandria, VA: Teachers of English to Speakers of Other Languages.

Atwell, N. 1987. *In the middle: Writing, reading and learning with adolescents.* Portsmouth, NH: Heinemann.

August, D., and K. Hakuta (eds.). 1997. *Improving schooling for language minority children: A research agenda.* Washington, DC: National Academy Press.

Bailey, K. M. 1998. *Learning about language assessment: Dilemmas, decisions, and directions.* Boston: Heinle & Heinle.

Baker, R.G., and B. Showers. 1984. "The effects of a coaching strategy on teachers' transfer of training to classroom practice: A six-month follow-up study." Paper presented at the annual meeting of the American Educational Research Association, New Orleans, LA.

Bercovitz, L., and C. Porter. 1998. *Parents as educational partners.* Des Plaines, IL: The Center, Adult Learning Resource Center.

Bhatnagar, J. 1980. Linguistic behavior and adjustment of immigrant children in French and English schools in Montreal. *International Journal of Applied Psychology* 29: 141–158.

Birdsall, H. 1996. Helping Rosa learn to read: An informal partnership between ESOL and special education. *Newsletter of Connecticut Teachers of English to Speakers of Other Languages* 23 (4): 1, 4–6.

Blakeslee, S. 1997. Studies show talking with infants shapes basis of ability to think. *The New York Times* (April 17, 1997) A14.

Brinton, D., and P. Master (eds.). 1997. *New ways in content-based instruction.* Alexandria, VA: Teachers of English to Speakers of Other Languages.

Brinton, D., L. Sasser, and B. Winningham. 1992. In Richard-Amato, P. A. and M. A. Snow (eds.), *The multicultural classroom: Readings for content-area teachers.* White Plains, NY: Longman. 5–15.

Brown, H.D. 1994. *Teaching by principles: An interactive approach to language pedagogy.* Englewood Cliffs, NJ: Prentice Hall Regents.

Brown, J. D. 1996. *Testing in language programs.* Upper Saddle River, NJ: Prentice Hall Regents.

Brown, Z. A., O. W. Hammond, and D. L. Onikama. 1997. *Language use at home and school: A synthesis of research for Pacific educators.* Honolulu, HI: Pacific Resources for Education and Learning.

Carrasquillo, A.L., and V. Rodriguez. 1996. *Language minority students in the mainstream classroom.* Bristol, PA: Multilingual Matters.

Cazabon, M. 2000. Voices from the field: How is program success evaluated? In N. Cloud, F. Genesee, and E. Hamayan (eds.), *Dual language instruction: A handbook for enriched education.* Boston: Heinle & Heinle.

Cazabon, M., Lambert, W. and G. Hall. 1993. *Two-way bilingual education: A progress report on the amigos program.* Santa Cruz, CA: National Center for Research on Cultural Diversity and Second Language Learning.

Celce-Murcia, M. 1991. Language teaching approaches: An overview. In Celce-Murcia, M. (ed.), *Teaching English as a second or foreign language* (2nd ed.) Boston: Heinle & Heinle. 3–11.

Chall, J. 1983. *Learning to read: The great debate.* New York: McGraw-Hill.

Chamot, A., and J. M. O'Malley. 1987. The cognitive academic language learning approach: A bridge to the mainstream. *TESOL Quarterly* 21(2): 227–249.

Chamot, A., J. M. O'Malley and L. Kupper. 1992. *Building bridges: Levels I, II and III.* Boston: Heinle & Heinle.

Chicago Public Schools. 1998. *Chicago public schools' language and cultural education initiatives: A framework for success.* Chicago, IL: Chicago Public Schools, Office of Language and Cultural Education.

Clair, E., and J. Haynes. 1994. *Classroom teacher's ESL survival kit #1.* Englewood Cliffs, NJ: Alemany Press: Prentice Hall Regents.

Clair, E., and J. Haynes. 1995. *Classroom teacher's ESL survival kit #2.* Englewood Cliffs, NJ: Alemany Press: Prentice Hall Regents.

Clair, N. 1995. Mainstream classroom teachers and ESL students. *TESOL Quarterly* 29(1): 189–196.

Cloud, N. 1994. Special education needs of second language students. In Fred Genesee (ed.), *Educating second language children: The whole child, the whole curriculum, the whole community.* New York: Cambridge University Press. 243–277.

Cloud, N., F. Genesee, and E. Hamayan. 2000. *Dual language instruction: A handbook for enriched education.* Boston: Heinle & Heinle.

Coelho, E. 1994. Social integration of immigrant and refugee children. In Fred Genesee (ed.), *Educating second language children: The whole child, the whole curriculum, the whole community.* New York: Cambridge University Press. 301–327.

Collier, V. 1987. Age and rate of acquisition of second language for academic purposes. *TESOL Quarterly* 21: 617–641.

Collier, V. 1989. How long? A synthesis of research on academic achievement in a second language. *TESOL Quarterly* 23: 509–531.

Collier, V. 1995. *Promoting academic success for ESL students: Understanding second language acquisition for school.* Elizabeth, NJ: New Jersey Teachers of English to Speakers of Other Languages—Bilingual Educators.

Cook, J. P. 1990. "Does fathertalk or first language literacy predict academic success?" Paper presented at the Annual Meeting of the Teachers of English to Speakers of Other Languages (March 1990), San Francisco, CA. (ERIC Document Reproduction Service No. ED 368213.)

Crawford, J. 1992. *Hold your tongue: Bilingualism and the politics of "English only."* Reading, MA: Addison-Wesley.

Cummins, J. 1979. Cognitive/academic language proficiency, linguistic interdependence, the optimum age question and some other matters. *Working Papers on Bilingualism,* 19: 121–129.

Cummins, J. 1981a. Age on arrival and immigrant second language learning in Canada: A reassessment. *Applied Linguistics* 2: 132–149.

Cummins, J. 1981b. The role of primary language development in promoting academic success for language minority students. In *Schooling and language minority students: A theoretical framework*. Sacramento, CA: California State Department of Education. 3–49.

Cummins, J. 1982. *Tests, achievement, and bilingual students* (Focus, No. 9) Wheaton, MD: National Clearinghouse for Bilingual Education.

Cummins, J. 1984. *Bilingualism and special education: Issues in assessment and pedagogy*. San Diego, CA: College-Hill Press.

Cummins, J. 1986. Empowering minority students: A framework for intervention. *Harvard Education Review,* 56(1): 18–36.

Cummins, J. 1989. *Empowering minority students*. Sacramento, CA: California Association for Bilingual Education.

Cummins, J. 1992. Language proficiency, bilingualism, and academic achievement. In P. A. Richard-Amato, and M. A. Snow (eds.), *The multicultural classroom: Readings for content-area teachers*. White Plains, NY: Longman. 16–26.

Cummins, J. 1994. Knowledge, power, and identity in teaching English as a second language. In Fred Genesee (ed.), *Educating second language children: The whole child, the whole curriculum, the whole community*. New York: Cambridge University Press. 33–58.

Dolson, D. 1985. The effects of Spanish home language use on scholastic performance of Hispanic pupils. *Journal of Multilingual and Multicultural Development* 6: 135–155.

Dwyer, M. 1998. Creating and sustaining change for immigrant learners in secondary schools. *TESOL Journal* 7(5): 6–10.

Echevarria, J., and A. Graves. 1998. *Sheltered content instruction: Teaching English-language learners with diverse abilities*. Needham Heights, MA: Allyn and Bacon.

Echevarria, J., M. Vogt, D. Short, and C. Montone. 1988. *The sheltered instruction observation protocol*. Santa Cruz, CA: Center for Research on Excellence and Diversity in Education.

Eskey, D. 1983. Meanwhile, back in the real world...: Accuracy and fluency in second language teaching. *TESOL Quarterly* 17(2): 315–323.

Faltis, C., and S. Hudelson. 1994. Learning English as an additional language in K–12 schools. *TESOL Quarterly* 28(3): 457–468.

Freeman, D. 1989. Teacher training, development, and decision making: A model of teaching and related strategies for language teacher education. *TESOL Quarterly* 23(1): 27–45.

Freeman, D. 1996. Redefining the relationship between research and what teachers know. In K. Bailey and D. Nunan (eds.), *Voices from the Language Classroom*. New York: Cambridge University Press. 88–115.

Freeman, D. 1998. *Doing teacher research: From inquiry to understanding*. Boston: Heinle & Heinle.

Freeman, Y. S. and D. E. Freeman. 1992. *Whole language for second language learners*. Portsmouth, NH: Heinemann.

Garcia, S. B. and A. A. Ortiz. 1988. Preventing inappropriate referrals of language minority students to special education. *Occasional Papers in Bilingual Education*. Washington, DC: National Clearinghouse for Bilingual Education.

Genesee, F. and E. V. Hamayan. 1994. Classroom-based assessment. In Fred Genesee (ed.), *Educating second language children: The whole child, the whole curriculum, the whole community*. New York: Cambridge University Press. 212–239.

Genesee, F. 1994. Introduction. In Fred Genesse (ed.), *Educating second language children: The whole child, the whole curriculum, the whole community*. New York: Cambridge University Press. 1–12.

Genesee, F., and J. Upshur. 1996. *Classroom-based evaluation in second language education*. New York: Cambridge University Press.

Goldstein, S. 1994. "Training staff to teach students acquiring English in addition to their primary languages." Presentation given at the Connecticut Institute for Teaching and Learning.

Gomez, M.L., M.E. Graue, and M.N. Bloch. 1991. Reassessing portfolio assessment: Rhetoric and reality. *Language Arts*, 68: 620–628.

Goodman, K. 1986. *What's whole about whole language*. Portsmouth, NH: Heinemann.

Gordon, J. 1997. *The multidimensional learning web*. Des Plaines, IL: Illinois Resource Center.

Gould, S.J. 1981. *The mismeasure of man*. New York: W. W. Norton.

Graves, K. 2000. *Designing language courses: A guide for teachers*. Boston: Heinle & Heinle.

Hakuta, K. 1986. *Mirror of language*. New York: Basic Books.

Hamayan, E. 1994. Language development of low-literacy students. In Fred Genesee (ed.), *Educating second language children: The whole child, the whole curriculum, the whole community*. New York: Cambridge University Press. 278–300.

Hamayan, E. 1995. Approaches to alternative assessment. *Annual Review of Applied Linguistics* 15: 212–226.

Hamayan, E., and J. Damico. 1991. *Limiting bias in the assessment of bilingual students*. Austin, TX: Pro-Ed.

Handscombe, Jean. 1994. Putting it all together. In Fred Genesee (ed.), *Educating second language children: The whole child, the whole curriculum, the whole community*. New York: Cambridge University Press. 331–356.

Harklau, L. 1994. ESL versus mainstream classes: Contrasting L2 learning environments. *TESOL Quarterly* 28(2): 241–272.

Hawkins, B. 1988. *Scaffolded classroom interaction and its relation to second language acquisition for minority language children*. Unpublished doctoral dissertation, University of California, Los Angeles.

Heath, S. B., and L. Mangiola. 1991. *Children of promise*. Berkeley, CA: National Writing Project, National Center for the Study of Writing and Literacy.

Heath, S. B. 1992. Sociocultural contexts of language development: Implications for the classroom. In P. A. Richard-Amato, and M. A. Snow (eds.), *The multicultural classroom: Readings for content-area teachers*. White Plains, NY: Longman. 102–125.

Henderson, A., and N. Berla. 1994. *A new generation of evidence: The family is critical to student achievement*. Washington, DC: The Center for Law and Education.

Hershberger, R., M.G. Fast, G. Lopéz-Cox, S. Navey-Davis, and L. Nalbone. 2001. *Plazas: Lugar de encuentro para la hispanidad*. Boston: Heinle & Heinle.

Irujo, S. 1998. *Teaching bilingual children: Beliefs and behaviors.* Boston: Heinle & Heinle.

Irujo, S. 2000. *Integrating the ESL standards into classroom practice, grades 6–8.* Alexandria, VA. Teachers of English to Speakers of Other Languages.

Jameson, J. 1999. "In-service in three principles guiding lesson planning." Demonstration given at the TESOL conference in New York.

Jaramillo, A. 1998. Professional development from the inside out. *TESOL Journal* 7(5): 12–18.

Johnson, K. 1999. *Understanding language teaching: Reasoning in action.* Boston: Heinle & Heinle.

Kagan, D. 1992. Professional growth among pre-service and beginning teachers. *Review of Educational Research* 62(2), 129–169.

Kaufman, D., and J. Brooks. 1996. Interdisciplinary collaboration in teacher education: A constructivist approach. *TESOL Quarterly* 30(2): 231–248.

Kessler, C., L. Lee, M. L. McCloskey, M. E. Quinn, and L. Stack. 1996. *Making Connections.* Boston: Heinle & Heinle.

Kozol, J. 1991. *Savage inequalities: Children in America's schools.* New York: Harper Collins.

Krashen, S. 1981. *Second language acquisition and second language learning.* Oxford, England: Pergamon Press.

Krashen, S. 1982. *Principles and practice in second language acquisition.* Oxford, England: Pergamon Press.

Larsen-Freeman, D. 1991. Teaching grammar. In M. Celce-Murcia (ed.), *Teaching English as a second or foreign language.* (2nd ed.). Boston: Heinle & Heinle. 279–296.

Los Angeles Unified School District, Office of Communications. 1998. *This is the Los Angeles unified school district.* Los Angeles, CA: Board of Education, Los Angeles Unified School District.

Lucas, T. 1997. *Into, through and beyond secondary schools: Critical transitions for immigrant youths.* Washington, DC: Center for Applied Linguistics.

Mace-Matluck, B., R. Alexander-Kasparik, and R. Queen. 1998. *Through the golden door: Educational approaches for immigrant adolescents with limited schooling.* Washington, DC: Center for Applied Linguistics.

Martinez, P. E. 1981. "Home environment and academic achievement: There is a correlation." Paper presented at the National Association for Bilingual Education Conference, Boston, MA.

Maslow, A. 1970. *Motivation and personality.* 2nd ed. New York: Harper and Row.

McCloskey, M. L., and L. Stack. 1996. *Voices in literature.* Boston: Heinle & Heinle.

McDonald, J.P. 1993. Three pictures of an exhibition: Warm, cool, and hard. *Phi Delta Kappan* 74: 480–485.

McLaughlin, B. 1995. *Fostering second language development in young children: Principles and practices.* Washington, DC: Center for Applied Linguistics.

Met, M. 1994. Teaching content through a second language. In Fred Genesee (ed.), *Educating second language children: The whole child, the whole curriculum, the whole community.* New York: Cambridge University Press. 159–182.

Meyer, D. 1996. Teaching expository text structures: Critical components for content and literacy development. *Linguathon* 11(2): 7–8.

Miramontes, O., A. Nadeau and N. Commins. 1997. *Restructuring schools for linguistic diversity: Linking decision making to effective programs.* New York: Teachers College Press.

Molinsky, S., and B. Bliss. 1996. *Classmates.* Upper Saddle River, NJ: Prentice Hall Regents.

Moll, L.C. and Greenberg, J. 1990. Creating zones of possibilities: Combining social contexts for instruction. In L. C. Moll (ed.), *Vygotsky and education.* Cambridge, England: Cambridge University Press. 319–348.

Moll, L. 1995. Bilingual classroom studies and community analysis: Some recent trends. In O. Garcia and C. Baker (eds.), *Policy and practice in bilingual education: Extending the foundations.* Bristol, PA: Multilingual Matters.

Mundahl, J. 1994. "Help for mainstream teachers with LEP students." Demonstration given at the TESOL 1994 Conference.

National Council for the Social Studies. 1997. *Social studies standards.* Washington, DC: National Council for the Social Studies.

National Council of Teachers of Mathematics. 1996. *Standards for mathematics.* Reston, VA: National Council of Teachers of Mathematics.

National Institutes of Health. 1997. *Results of NICHD study of early childcare news alert.* Washington, DC: National Institutes of Health.

National Science Teachers Association. 1997. *Science standards.* Arlington, VA: National Science Teachers Association.

National Staff Development Council. 1994. *National Staff Development Council's Standards for Staff Development.* Oxford, Ohio: National Staff Development Council.

Nieto, S. 1995. *Affirming diversity: The sociopolitical context of multicultural education* 2nd. ed. New York: Longman.

Nunan, D. 1999. *Go for it! Level 1.* Boston: Heinle & Heinle.

Office of Education Research and Improvement. 1997. White House conference on early childhood development and learning: *What new research on the brain tells us about our youngest children.* Washington, DC: Office of Education Research and Improvement.

Ogbu, J. 1983. Minority status and schooling in plural societies. *Comparative Education Review* 27 (2): 168–190.

O'Malley, J. M., and L. Valdez Pierce. 1996. *Authentic assessment for English language learners: Practical approaches for language learners.* Reading, MA: Addison-Wesley.

Ortiz, A. A., and S. B. Garcia. 1988. A pre-referral process for preventing inappropriate referrals of Hispanic students to special education. In A. A. Ortiz and B. A. Ramirez (eds.), *Schools and the culturally diverse exceptional student: Promising practices and future directions.* Reston, VA: Council for Exceptional Children. 6–18.

Ortiz, A. A., and J. R. Yates. 1988. Characteristics of learning disabled, mentally retarded, and speech-language handicapped Hispanic students at initial evaluation and reevaluation. In A. A. Ortiz, and B. A. Ramirez (eds.), *Schools and the culturally diverse exceptional student: Promising practices and future directions.* Reston, VA: Council for Exceptional Children. 51–62.

Paulsen, G. 1996. *Brian's Winter.* New York: Delacorte Press.

Peal, E., and Lambert, W. 1962. The relation of bilingualism to intelligence. *Psychological Monograph.* 76.

Pearson, D. 1996. Reclaiming the center. In M. Graves, P. van den Broek, and B. M. Taylor, *The first R: Every child's right to read*. New York: Teacher's College Press. 259–274.

Pennington, M. 1995. The teacher change cycle. *TESOL Quarterly* 29(4): 705–731.

Pienemann, M. 1984. Psychological constraints on the teachability of language. *Studies in Second Language Acquisition*, 6 (2): 186–214.

Richard-Amato, P. A. 1988. *Making it happen*. White Plains, NY: Longman.

Richard-Amato, P. A., and M. A. Snow. 1992. Strategies for content-area teachers. In P. A. Richard-Amato, and M. A. Snow (eds.), *The multicultural classroom: Readings for content-area teachers*. White Plains, NY: Longman. 145–163.

Roseberry-McKibbin, Celeste. 1995. *Multicultural students with special language needs*. Oceanside, CA: Academic Communication Associates.

Samway, K. D. 2000. *Integrating the ESL standards into classroom practice, grades 3–5*. Alexandria, VA: Teachers of English to Speakers of Other Languages.

Saunders, W.M., and C. Goldenberg. 1999. *The effects of instructional conversations and literature logs on the story comprehension and thematic understanding of English proficient and limited English proficient students*. Washington, DC: Center for Applied Linguistics.

Scarcella, R. 1990. *Teaching language minority students in the multicultural classroom*. Englewood Cliffs, NJ: Prentice-Hall.

Short, D. 1991. *How to integrate language and content instruction: A training manual*. Washington, DC: Center for Applied Linguistics.

Short, D. 1994. Expanding middle school horizons: Integrating language, culture, and social studies. *TESOL Quarterly* 28 (3): 581–607.

Short, D. 1999. *Newcomer schools*. Washington, DC: Center for Applied Linguistics.

Short, D., E. L. Gomez, N. Cloud, A. Katz, M. Gottlieb, and M. Malone. 2000. *Training others to use the ESL standards: A professional development manual*. Alexandria, VA: Teachers of English to Speakers of Other Languages.

Showers, B. 1985. Teachers coaching teachers. *Educational Leadership* 42(7): 43–48.

Skidmore, C. 1994. *Process writing portfolio program*. Reading, MA: Addison Wesley.

Smallwood, B. A. 1991. *The literature connection: A read-aloud guide for multicultural classrooms*. Reading, MA: Addison-Wesley.

Smallwood, B. A. 2000. *Integrating the ESL standards into classroom practice, grades pre-K–2*. Alexandria, VA: Teachers of English to Speakers of Other Languages.

Snow, M.A., M. Met, and F. Genesee. 1992. A conceptual framework for the integration of language and content instruction. In Richard-Amato, P. A. and M. A. Snow (eds.), *The multi-cultural classroom: Readings for content-area teachers*. White Plains, NY: Longman. 27–38.

Snow, M. A. 1991. *Teaching language through content. In Teaching English as a second or foreign language*. 2nd ed. Boston: Heinle & Heinle. 315–328.

Speare, E. G. 1984. *The sign of the beaver*. New York: Dell.

Stern, S. L. 1991. An integrated approach to literature in ESL/EFL. In M. Celce-Murcia (ed.), *Teaching English as a second or foreign language*. 2nd ed. Boston: Heinle & Heinle. 328.

Stevick, E. W. 1976. *Memory, meaning, method*. Rowley, MA: Newbury House.

Stevick, E. W. 1998. *Working with teaching methods: What's at stake?* Boston: Heinle & Heinle.

Teachers of English to Speakers of Other Languages. 1997. *ESL standards for pre-K–12 students.* Alexandria, VA: Teachers of English to Speakers of Other Languages.

Teachers of English to Speakers of Other Languages. 1998. *Managing the assessment process.* Alexandria, VA: Teachers of English to Speakers of Other Languages.

Thomas, W., and V. Collier. 1995. *Language minority student achievement and program effectiveness.* Washington, DC: National Clearinghouse for Bilingual Education. 2.

Thompson, G.G. 1952. *Child psychology.* Boston: Houghton Mifflin.

Tinajero, J. V., and A. Schifini. 1997. *Into English!* Carmel, CA: Hampton-Brown Books.

Tizard, J., W. N. Schofield, and J. Hewison. 1982. Collaboration between teachers and parents in assisting children's reading. *British Journal of Educational Psychology* 52: 1–15.

Torres, J. M. 1994. Inclusion and the L.E.P. student. *Education Week* (26 October): 38–40.

Verplaetse, L. S. 1998. How content teachers interact with English language learners. *TESOL Journal* 7(5): 24–28.

Walker, M. 1992. *Addison-Wesley ESL: Student book* C. Reading, MA: Addison-Wesley.

Walker, M. 1996. *Amazing English.* Reading, MA: Addison-Wesley.

Whiteson, V. 1993. *Close the gap: exercises in integrating and developing language skills.* San Francisco, CA: Alta Book Center.

Willig, A. C. 1986. Special education and the culturally and linguistically different child: An overview of issues and challenges. *Reading, Writing, and Learning Disabilities.* 2 (2): 161–173.

Wong-Fillmore, L. 1991. When learning a second language means losing the first. *Early Childhood Research Quarterly.* 6: 323–347.

Young, D. J. 1989. *Affect in foreign language and second language learning: a practical guide to creating a low-anxiety classroom atmosphere.* New York: McGraw-Hill.

Zaffran, B., D. Krulik, and M. Scheraga. 1990. *Hello English.* Lincolnwood, IL: National Textbook Co.